A GOOD BAD BOY

LUKE PERRY AND HOW A GENERATION GREW UP

MARGARET WAPPLER

SIMON & SCHUSTER

New York   London   Toronto   Sydney   New Delhi

1230 Avenue of the Americas
New York, NY 10020

First Simon & Schuster hardcover edition March 2024

SIMON & SCHUSTER and colophon are registered
trademarks of Simon & Schuster, LLC

Simon & Schuster: Celebrating 100 Years of Publishing in 2024

For information about special discounts for bulk purchases, please contact Simon
& Schuster Special Sales at 1-866-506-1949 or business@simonandschuster.com.

The Simon & Schuster Speakers Bureau can bring authors to your live event. For
more information or to book an event, contact the Simon & Schuster Speakers
Bureau at 1-866-248-3049 or visit our website at www.simonspeakers.com.

Interior design by Wendy Blum

Manufactured in the United States of America

1   3   5   7   9   10   8   6   4   2

Library of Congress Cataloging-in-Publication Data is available on file.

ISBN 978-1-6680-0626-9
ISBN 978-1-6680-0628-3 (ebook)

For all the lost teenagers, yet to be found

AUTHOR'S NOTE

This book includes both original interviews and archival interviews. Original interviews are attributed in the present tense (e.g., "says"). Archival interviews are attributed in the past tense (e.g., "said"). A list of sources is included at the back of the book.

O when I die
Take my saddle from the wall
Put it on my pony
Lead him out of his stall
Tie my bones to his back
Turn our faces to the west
And we'll ride the prairies
That we love the best

—Final lyrics from
"I Ride an Old Paint," cowboy traditional

A GOOD BAD BOY

PROLOGUE

March 4, 2019

AT FIRST, THE DAY SEEMS *like all the others, made up of mother-hood's minor defeats. She cannot get him to nap on the pullout couch where they typically curl up together. Time congeals. Reading books, nursing him, only to see him remain her tiny awake overlord with a yogurt-stained shirt. Delirious, he head-butts her in the face, smashing into the bridge of her nose. She is stunned; tears prick her eyes. He gig-gles, with a note of unease at the end. She places him in the crib, a little roughly, and leaves the room.*

On her bed, she cries. She pinches her throbbing bridge. When she re-covers, she whisks him out of the house to the car, where she buckles him in. Within minutes of driving, he succumbs to sleep. Relief saturates her every cell.

She pulls over on a side street and turns on a meditative soundtrack. She reclines her seat. After an untold number of minutes, she wakes up, but he is still asleep. Out comes the phone. She reads the email her hus-band has sent her. No message, just an attached page with a highlighted paragraph from the introduction to Down Below, *by the surrealist painter and novelist Leonora Carrington:*

> The experience of motherhood led her into new depths of knowl-edge, and far from depleting her creative powers, strengthened them: "I believe that for female animals the act of love, which is followed by the great drama of the birth of a new animal, pushes us into the biological underworld, very deeply . . ."

Is this where she is, the biological underworld? She is too tired to know.

Twitter. Scrolling. And then she reads it: Luke Perry is dead. How can that be? Yes, there was the stroke on February 27 that landed him in the hospital. But she had been certain he would live. A fifty-two-year-old who stayed in good shape is not going to die from a stroke, right? At worst, it'll be a temporary setback. Instead, he is gone, leaving behind his fiancée, his ex-wife, two children, and other loved ones.

As she pores over the pictures of him online, she is taken back to her past. She is fifteen again, watching Brenda and Dylan hold each other, swaying in front of a Christmas tree. His soft brown eyes. The shine of his gravity-defying pompadour. God, she had loved him as Dylan McKay, the platonic ideal of the sensitive man hiding his wounds behind a shield of cool.

In the more recent years, when those corrugated forehead wrinkles finally made sense with his age, he joined the cast of Riverdale. *There was a generational pride that a show written for teens had picked up on one of her old favorites. She was the older sister passing down to a younger sister a favorite jean jacket, a beloved book.* Here, it's your turn to discover this now. *Though of course it wouldn't be exactly the same. Luke was now a handsome but weather-worn dad in flannel, no longer a teenager skulking the halls of West Beverly High.*

The stories of his generosity and kindness are all over Twitter. He was deeply concerned about the unhoused. He gave his money and time to raising awareness for colorectal cancer, to horse charities, Western Wishes, Soles 4 Souls, to name but a few. He loved animals, especially dogs and pigs. Why him? As if that question ever had an answer. She lingers over the two children left behind: twenty-one-year-old Jack and eighteen-year-old Sophie. His daughter is only three years older than Margaret was when she had lost her father. This math is involuntary; a hushed equation she arrives at every time she hears of a young person losing a parent.

He should've been close to the center of his life, maybe just to the right— but abruptly, it is the end. The earlier trials with her son are nothing now, not in the face of death. So much from her girlhood had been erased by time, or forever changed. Luke Perry is now part of the ever-growing list of things and people, lost or dead over the years.

She has been so involved taking screenshots, reveling in the memories of watching Beverly Hills, 90210 *alone in her room, that she didn't realize her son is waking up. His sounds fill the car's air. His lips smacking, a couple of groggy cries. For now, she is out of time.*

PART
ONE

CHAPTER
ONE

THE ACTOR HAD REQUESTED to be the last read of the day.

He needed time to cross LA traffic in his wreck of a pickup truck after a grimy day laying asphalt in some nameless Southern California tract. There would be no time for a shower. Just a white-knuckle drive to Hollywood, swooping in and out of the traffic, focusing on the character for which he'd prepared late into the night. Repeating the French words, "Est-ce que tu a un Jack McKay . . ."

His pickup, on the other hand, wouldn't cooperate. As was its miserable habit, it broke down. There he was, pulled over on the 101, trying to get his ride back in working order. The steam of the engine hissing in his face. Fetching wrenches from the back. He fantasized about leaving town. Giving up. He could go back to Ohio and join the fire department. Live a tidy life with nice people and stability. Remember stability? What a concept. He'd had a good run of it as an actor—some soaps to his name, a music video for Twisted Sister—but maybe it was time to call it. He could just go home, where anyone would lap up the story of this crazy misadventure over beers.

But then he got the old heap running again. And a cleanish shirt was scrounged from the flatbed so that he could take off the one that stunk of gasoline. He would make the audition after all, his back aching, tar on his jeans, dried grime and sweat on his face, but he'd make it. Tonight, anyway, he would not be leaving town.

———

Luke Perry focused on Dianne Young, the casting director who'd brought him in. Young was friendly and knew all the fresh talent in town: Ben Affleck, Matt Damon, Matthew Perry, guys Luke would see over and over again in waiting rooms, mumbling to themselves the same lines he had memorized. When Charles Rosin, the showrunner for *Beverly Hills, 90210*, told Young about the new character Dylan McKay, the rich boy who lived in a posh hotel alone, Luke immediately sprang to mind.

On paper, he had little in common with Dylan, but biographical details only tell a sliver of the truth. Something in him had already fused with the emotional reality behind Dylan's glamorous life. The room quieted as Perry started the scene. Dylan, from his hotel room, was calling a hotel in Paris to find his father, the distant patriarch who threw money his way, but nothing substantial like love. Dylan had every flashy toy, and his precocious independence, but what he ached for was someone to care about who he was on the inside. He was a character as ancient as dirt and gold—satiated in material, starved for connection—but retooled for mass television consumption in a new decade of American fortune.

"Est-ce que tu a un Jack McKay, s'il vous plaît?" Dylan asked with quiet turmoil. As Dylan tried in vain to track down his father, he was stripped of his ego and his playthings—the squid-ink Porsche, the trench coat, the penetrating squint—all that made him unimpeachably cool within the hallways of the fictional West Beverly High. He was re-duced to being a lost boy searching for his dad. He might get his father on the line, but he would never find him.

Rosin and Young exchanged a look. Of all the Dylans they'd seen—and they'd seen wannabes and almosts for eight to ten hours now—no one else had dared to read the lines in French, as David Stenn, the writer of the episode, had authored it. Everyone else had ad-libbed in English or skipped over it altogether.

About Luke's first audition, Rosin recalls some thirty-two years later, "Not only did I not think we were going to cast the part, I didn't think we'd make it out of the day alive. But then, hallelujah, the guy's walked in here."

CHAPTER

TWO

THERE WAS A LIFE before Los Angeles, before Dylan McKay.

On October 11, 1966, Coy Luther Perry III was born to Ann, a housewife, and Coy Luther II, a steelworker, in Mansfield, Ohio. He was delivered by the father of future Ohio senator Sherrod Brown. Luke was the middle child, between older brother, Tom, and younger sister, Ann.

One of his earliest memories was seeing a picture of fellow Ohio native Paul Newman, his supernatural blue eyes gazing into the middle distance, pinned to his mother's mirror. Luke learned that Paul Newman was an actor, and actors are who we watch when we're not watching the people in our own lives. Actors taught us how to be in the world. Luke studied them, the ones who chanced onto the family TV. On one of his favorite shows, *The Wild Wild West*, the athletic leading man Robert Conrad performed most of his own stunts, cracking his skull on one occasion when he dropped off a swinging chandelier and crashed twelve feet down onto a concrete floor. On the daytime soaps that Luke's mother favored, their titles keening with a fervor for love, for a better existence—*Search for Tomorrow, Guiding Light, Days of Our Lives*—the stories changed like the strike of a summer thunderstorm. Only the actors, Luke recognized, had the power to keep the outlandish plots afloat.

At four years old, Luke debuted in his first play in kindergarten, but his fly was malfunctioning. He kept zipping back up, and the zipper kept falling back down. His mother was terribly embarrassed. Despite his inauspicious start, his young acting career continued. Around age twelve, he and his family moved twenty miles south to Fredericktown, a place with tractors, cows, and one pizza place downtown. Population around 2,500, a number that hasn't fluctuated much. In junior high, not long after he moved, he played the lead in *Due to Lack of Interest, Tomorrow Has Been Canceled*. He told anyone who would listen that he dreamed of being a professional actor. An inventive math teacher used Luke's dream to teach the students about percentages ("agents usually take 10 percent, and if your salary is one million . . ."). Luke was also a decent left-handed baseball player who rooted for the Cincinnati Reds. There's a piece of advice Grandpa Perry gave him, "You're faster than you think, keep running," which resulted in him scoring more doubles than anyone else in Little League. He applied that advice to many other games in life. No matter what, keep going.

His parents divorced when Luke was six. According to Luke, Coy Luther II was a violent drunk who abused Luke's mother. "I always felt that I should have been able to protect her better, but I was a six-year-old kid. That's where my frustration stems from. I saw very clearly as a six-year-old kid what the problems were. Looking back at it all now, it was pretty frightening."

Imagine the burden of a six-year-old who not only clocked the issues, but who fantasized about battling his father on behalf of his mother. When a child witnesses abuse at a young age, there are two ways a person can develop: they become an abuser or they become the protector, the pattern-breaker, once capable enough to do so. Luke chose the latter, knowing that without honor and justice as personal codes, there was nothing. Coy Luther II died in 1980 at age thirty-five; although they had long been estranged, Luke did attend the funeral. Luke's true father figure was Steve Bennett, whom his mother married when Luke was twelve. Steve, a construction worker with a daughter named Emily, taught his stepson how to use drills and wrenches, the dignity of manual labor, and that a real man was kind and loving above all else.

Through Steve and the rest of his community, Luke would also be indoctrinated in the Midwest's de facto religion: humility. There's nothing more unbecoming and downright suspicious in the eye of a typical rural Midwesterner than honking your own horn. Even at the height of his fame, modesty was always Luke's default setting.

A lack of airs, however, does not mean taking a monk's vow. The guy who would be voted Biggest Flirt his senior year started young, kissing four or five girls in a row in the third grade. As a teenager, he watched wrestling and liberally quoted his favorite, Dusty Rhodes. He could barely sit still. He wanted out, the mission to head west and become an actor clawing at him to move. He frittered away some of that restless energy by pulling pranks, including sticking up the school secretary with a fake gun to get some friends out of detention, the kind of stunt a kid could play in the eighties. As the school's mascot, the Freddie bird, he unlocked legend status when he convinced Steve's construction company to drop him down onto the football field by helicopter. It was a serious leveling up from his usual fare of running around the field or popping wheelies on his dirt bike. The crowd roared for their hype man, dressed in red plumage with his gangly legs clad in yellow tights.

He made friends in Fredericktown that he kept close to him until the end of his days. He frequently dropped into town unannounced, showing up at the local tomato fest or bringing his kids to see their grandparents. To achieve his dreams, Luke had to get out of a small town like Fredericktown, but he didn't hold that against its people.

Los Angeles, indifferent to yet another actor settling into its seedy sprawl, became his home in 1984 at age seventeen. He arrived with a few Ohio friends, but also next to nothing. He worked blue-collar jobs to afford acting classes, including a stint at a doorknob factory, which almost sounds surreal in a Charlie Kaufman way, considering what he was trying to do: kick open the doors of Hollywood, one grueling audition at a time. In 1987, after 216 fruitless tries (he kept track), he finally stepped over the threshold. By this point, he was living in New

York. The gig was on *Loving*, a soap opera, his mother's favorite genre. He played a dirt-poor mechanic from Tennessee, until he was unceremoniously fired for butting heads with the producer. Then he went on to *Another World*, which in the hierarchy of soaps at the time was a step up, but then the recurring character ended. For several months, he shared an Upper West Side apartment with his girlfriend (future *Baywatch* star Yasmine Bleeth, then a fellow soaps actress), doing odd jobs for her stepdad when he wasn't appearing in music videos or commercials, like one for Mars bar where he and the other performers took turns crooning the theme song and waving the chocolate under each other's noses. In the eighties, an advertisement wasn't an advertisement without a theme song, the gooier the better.

After he and Bleeth broke up, he took his pool cue and moved back to Los Angeles in early 1990 for pilot season. The prior decade was drenched in moneyed maximalism, but not a drop of that pink froth splashed on him. He was back to manual labor, building the streets of Los Angeles. Speed bumps, cul-de-sacs, whatever the asphalt company told him to do. He squeezed in auditions when he could, his promise and potential noted and filed, but nothing was clicking. Until it did.

"It's funny, I never envisioned myself going out to Hollywood," he said. "I sort of envisioned that I would climb right into the television and just come out on the other side of it. I think, in some way, that's what happened for me. I just climbed into the box."

THE LAST RUINOUS DAYS OF swelter before the first day of high school. The basement is her air-conditioned sanctum away from her dad's sickness upstairs. It's where she plays Super Mario Brothers with the sound muted, replaced by a stream of R.E.M. The album Green is a letter written to her, with its undertow of wanting, of being misunderstood, and despite all that, still finding life astonishing even as it escapes her comprehension. The hours have whiled by like this all summer; the nights are spent sweating in front of the fan.

She runs and jumps through level one, her thumbs moving by muscle memory. Playing helps her to avoid the phone, doing something stupid like dialing his number. But then the phone shrieks. Margaret knows it's Rose because of the late-morning timing. Still, she hopes it's Nathan, but also she doesn't. She picks up the earpiece with its curly wire strained from stretching.

"Just come out," Rose pleads. Doesn't she want to go to the mall? Maybe pocket a Wet N Wild lip gloss at Walgreens just because? Get french fries at Erik's Deli? Go try on old-people glasses at the optometry showroom until they are asked to leave?

Her best friend, Rose; her lifeline in this difficult summer, transitioning from junior high to high school freshmen. No social group is the right fit. She is estranged from Nathan, whom she'd tangled with for six months, exchanging rings and meticulously planned mixtapes. They had spent hours making out in his bedroom, going from French kissing to oral sex. She is fourteen and he is sixteen, and his appetites set their course. He kept pushing to go further, and she wanted to keep up with him, despite her pleasure plummeting her into shame. He had asked her to have sex, and they tried in his cold, candlelit bedroom. She couldn't bear the pain of his condom-covered penis entering her, not even a little bit. She kept breaking into sobs, and they had to stop. He was kind about it that night but immediately after, he distanced himself. A few weeks later, he broke up with her, saying he just didn't know if he was in love with her anymore. That was a couple of months ago. Every few weeks he calls her crying, claiming he made a mistake—and she accepts his apologies, hoping they'll get back together, only to have him treat her coldly the next day. She writes about all of it in her diary, her tears smearing the ink. If this turmoil was a preview of adult existence, adulthood seemed too lashing and wild for her to ever contain or live through.

His friends, mostly older guys like him, were too painful of a reminder to be around. And as much as she adored Rose, her safe haven, being with Rose meant a strong chance of hanging out with Rose's friends, her old friends, the popular clique. At some point last year, they'd all turned against her. She could've groveled her way back in, as others had, but after the initial sting, she'd been surprised to find that she didn't want to. The weirdness in her wouldn't abide it. They didn't like her absurd jokes, her apathy toward sports and all the dumb jocks they pined for. She couldn't fake being one of them so, no thanks.

"Would it just be me and you?" she asks Rose. The sharp intake of Rose's breath answers the question.

After she hangs up, she tries to press play again on her older brother James's crappy stereo, but instead of "You Are the Everything," with its mandolin sounding like sun sparkling on river water, the tape gets snarled. She removes the cassette with a surgeon's precision, cupping the unraveled spool of tape. She grabs a pencil, perched nearby for just this situation, and carefully winds the brown shiny tape back onto the spools.

THREE

AT THE START OF the new decade, Aaron Spelling moved his office from the Warner's lot to a slick high-tech building on Wilshire Boulevard. Every aspect of the building was futuristic and shiny—except for Spelling's office. Once inside the producer's domain, Old Hollywood reigned. Jungle-thick shag carpet that swallowed a foot. Crystal ashtrays. Bowls of loose cigarettes, mints, and candy. Spelling's wife, Candy, had modeled her husband's office after Louis B. Mayer's at MGM, where everything was grand. Her version, however, was grandiose: There wasn't just a big couch, there was a twenty-three-foot-long built-in. Every piece of upholstery, couch included, was cream-colored. Candy wanted people to practically get lost on the journey to Aaron's desk, which they would know they'd reached by the mists of pipe tobacco. Spelling's butler, dressed in a starched uniform like a Chasen's maître d', fetched whiskey, wine—whatever your poison. And like all of the employees, he called his boss "Mr. Spelling."

Cartoonish though it was, the giant room made its point loud and clear. This was the kingdom of a man who, only a few years before, had a primetime show on nearly every night on ABC, known to insiders as Aaron's Broadcasting Network. He was far away from his childhood, spent in dire poverty as part of the only Jewish family in his Dallas neighborhood, bullied so intensely that he spent a year in bed at age nine. But those painful experiences taught him the power of fantasy. Spelling's "jiggle TV," as it was derisively known by critics, provided viewers with escapist melodrama and carnal beauty. *Charlie's Angels*, *Love Boat*, *Dynasty*, and others had ruled the night until a new president at ABC took over and decided to cancel all of his shows. After that humiliation, his career was ice-cold for nearly two years.

By 1990, Spelling was given another chance at a new network nipping at the heels of the big three—ABC, CBS, and NBC. Spelling, sixty-eight with two teenage children at home, had been charged with developing a teen soap for FOX, headed by founder Barry Diller, a graduate of Beverly Hills High School, who floated his longtime idea of setting a show there. Beverly Hills had the cloistered provincial sensibility of a small town but, unlike many rural American enclaves, it was moneyed. Viewers, Diller thought, would be able to see themselves in these characters, but with a heavy dose of fantasy. Spelling needed a young writer to bring the idea to life.

Darren Star was a recent UCLA grad in his late twenties who had sold a few feature films, but never a TV pilot. After meeting with Spelling at his house—Star remembers him wearing a track suit, Spelling's version of a suit and tie—he wrote his first, about a Minnesota family who moves to Beverly Hills, as a two-hour ode to John Hughes movies and ABC's authentic drama *Thirtysomething*. Star lifted elements of his life for *The Class of Beverly Hills*, as it was then called: He and his younger sister were only a year apart, so he made the main characters boy/girl twins. His good friend in high school was a bright writer type, so in Andrea went as the ambitious newspaper editor. He also loved the idea of a gang of friends supporting each other through high school. So in a nod to *The Breakfast Club*, which had an attractive face representing each social caste, he wrote in a jock, Steve; the prom queen snob, Kelly; and a nerdy freshman, David. Other characters exited or developed as the series went on, most notably Donna, Kelly's sidekick, played by Spelling's daughter Tori.

After the pilot was made, Star, Spelling, and new hire Chuck Rosin (another Beverly Hills High grad) watched *The Class of Beverly Hills* and saw that the show was missing something. The squeaky-clean Midwestern twins, Brandon and Brenda (played by Jason Priestley, a Canadian actor cast at the eleventh hour, and Shannen Doherty, a child actress who'd gone edgy with *Heathers*), needed a dark counterpoint. Enter Dylan McKay, whose antecedents included Judd Nelson, Matt Dillon, and James Dean. And before them, all the tortured poets who'd tried to catch ecstasy through adventure and verse: Rimbaud, Lord Byron, Bukowski. Dylan was a pocket version of those larger-than-life types, scaled down for high school.

After his successful audition, Dianne Young brought in Luke to meet Spelling. The super-producer had started as an actor himself, playing yokels, hucksters, and the like on *I Love Lucy* and *Gunsmoke*. Spelling loved actors, especially the ethereally gorgeous.

In Luke, Spelling saw what they all saw: untapped potential, but the difference was that Spelling was willing to stake everything on his belief in the untested actor. Here was this beautiful young man, burning with restless energy, and all he needed was a chance. He had the right kind of eyes: soulful, intelligent, and potentially all the more luminous by the lights of the camera. A compact muscular frame without an inch of flab. A smile that could slyly creep to fullness, or flash without self-consciousness. Spelling, in an unusual move, was ready to bring him to the suits at FOX as the only actor to be considered for Dylan McKay; typical practice was to bring in a few actors for consideration.

Luke was, of course, wildly inexperienced, but that was part of the appeal. During this initial meeting, much to Dianne Young's horror, Luke put his grubby sneaker up on Spelling's coffee table, a priceless antique. She longed to knock his foot down, but she kept smiling. His gesture was so gauche that it could only be naive. Uncouth and unmannered, he didn't yet know any better.

THE FIRST DAY OF HIGH school. Total student population: 2,700. Her graduating class in junior high had been only two hundred students. The mass of teenaged bodies in one place is astounding. As if she'd lifted a rock to discover a writhing pile of worms. She looks for Rose, or, against her better impulses, Nathan, but as she tunnels her way toward her first class, she doesn't recognize a single face—which is terrifying and exhilarating. What she does see: senior athletes who look like grown men; gaggles of blond girls baked from tanning beds; kids wearing black leather medallions, with a red, black, and green Africa in the center; hippie types in batik-patterned skirts and tinkling ankle bracelets, leaving wafts of patchouli in their wake. She had carefully chosen her outfit last night: a black empire-waist dress with blue-green swirly tights and canvas Mary Janes. Eyeliner heavy at the waterline. Peach blush. Silver jewelry.

As she descends the frenetic central staircase, she recognizes, on their way up, two girls from her junior high. They are both wearing New Kids on the Block T-shirts. This is how they want to be seen on their very first day? Being so openly, submissively a fan—of anything, even R.E.M.—is repugnant to Margaret. She'd seen the footage of girls screaming and fainting about the Beatles, and the tacit assumption was that as a girl herself, she too will one day lose her mind about some collection of boys who can play their instruments. She resents that it is always, always girls and not the other way around. Why doesn't she know any boys who openly worship women musicians? Nathan and all his friends have their Led Zeppelin or U2 T-shirts but never Janis Joplin or Sinead O'Connor.

Fanaticism in any context repels her. Her parents want her to cleave to Christianity like they do, yet it strikes her as hysterical, too. Or requiring a lobotomized obedience. There is no in-between. All her life, before she could even articulate it, she couldn't take to the idea of Jesus Christ. Same *with God, though at least he had the good sense not to take a physical form. Nebulous was more awe-inspiring than a blue-eyed cult leader in a robe, if she has to choose. But she refuses to choose any of it, even though that's what her parents want from her. Her father is an Episcopalian minister, the least snake-charming religion of them all, and yet, even the cool, non-hysterical, rational-for-a-church Protestant fold can't get her to believe. Not even the fact that he's sick, dying of cancer, can get her to go back to church, or to say a single word in prayer. All it does is bury her in guilt.*

CHAPTER

FOUR

"IT WAS AWFUL. IT was all over the room. It was a mess."

This is how Tony Shepherd, former vice president of talent for Aaron Spelling Productions, remembers Luke Perry's audition for the network. Shepherd worked closely with Spelling for fifteen years, and still speaks of his charming yet demanding boss in tones of reverence and exasperation. Post-Spelling, Shepherd has enjoyed a long and storied career in casting and artist relations for Disney, recently garnering an Emmy nomination for casting *Muppets Haunted Mansion*, but the experience with Luke still stands out. He remembers it vividly more than thirty years later.

More than a dozen people—nearly all white guys, the execs in suits—were settled in a room with tiered seating. In a risky move, Spelling insisted on showing the network Luke, and Luke only. Star and Rosin agreed that there was no need to bother with runners-up. Luke read with Dianne Young, the casting director who recommended him in the first place. As they built the scene, Shepherd noticed that Luke's performance was, to his mind, erratic and unmoored. His tone jumped all around—wounded in one line, flippant in the next. The inexperienced actor was rattled.

When he finished, Luke was politely asked to leave the room so the suits could discuss. In the interminable silence after the door clicked shut, a FOX executive spoke up.

"Good-looking kid, but not much of a reading."

If Spelling had been thrown by Luke's nerves, he didn't let on. "I'm stunned," he said in his Texan drawl. "How could you not love him?"

It was decided Luke should read again. Spelling leaned in close to Shepherd and murmured, "Go out there and talk to him."

Shepherd found Luke in the hallway, pacing and raking his hand through his hair. Shepherd grabbed him by the shoulders and enunciated every word: "Luke. Calm. The. Fuck. Down." That was it, that was the talk. Shepherd didn't say much else because there wasn't time. They needed to get back in there, and Luke needed to nail it.

Did Shepherd's gassing up do the trick? "If the reading was a three out of a ten before," Shepherd says, "then it rose to maybe a four or five after that."

Neither Rosin nor Star share his dire recollection of Luke's audition. "I don't remember it being a flub," Rosin says. But certainly, in Star's words, "they were never as convinced as we were." Whatever happened in that room, Luke didn't win over FOX. Diller, after seeing Luke's second try, said: "We just don't see it." FOX didn't envision the character of Dylan McKay as a series necessity. In their opinion, the bad boy could be introduced and dispensed with in maybe a two-episode arc. He'd be a fun diversion for Brenda and then he'd peel off, leaving her to fumble her way around the whims and cruelties of other boys. Spelling, Star, and Rosin had bigger ideas for Dylan.

With the meeting at an uncomfortable impasse, Spelling offered something Shepherd had never seen from his boss before.

"You know what?" Spelling said. "I am so convinced that he's the right guy, you don't have to pay for him. I will pay his salary out of my own pocket."

Less than a year later, Luke was a breakaway star. According to Shepherd, for the rest of the series, including the eight out of ten seasons that Luke appeared on, his paycheck came from Spelling, the only cast member with that particular arrangement. The first ten checks Luke got from Spelling were handwritten; he saved the stubs.

HER LOCKER. IT CONTAINS HER books, a sweatshirt on a hook, and a tiny mirror so she can check her bangs. To open the locker, she has to spin the combination dial to 0–18–0, and then thump her shoulder against the painted surface at an upward angle. It opens with a metallic clang and shiver. Her combination, 0-18-0, is the easiest in the world. Almost like the manufacturer has made a mistake. Shouldn't each number be different? Maybe it is a kind of countdown. She is starting at the beginning, the figurative zero, and when she turns eighteen, who will she be then?

CHAPTER

FIVE

JULIE RESNICK WAS DRIVING him to the airport. They'd tried, they really had. Resnick and her boss—Luke's manager, Cyd LeVin, as well as Luke's agent, Chris Nassif—had scored him as many auditions as possible for the 1990 pilot season, but no roles had materialized. All over Los Angeles, the same disappointing reality was dawning on all manner of actors, from highly trained stage thespians to local kids fresh from a strip-mall performance school. Some of them would leave. The city was in a constant groaning state of contraction and expansion, based on the capricious, fleeting ideas of casting agents and accountants. If Luke was upset, he didn't grouse about it. Julie and Cyd had focused on the positive: the number of callbacks he'd gotten, just how close. None closer than the auditions for Dylan McKay. Still, they hadn't heard back, so it was time to go.

"I just walked out of a roomful of fools. Those people have no idea," he'd tell himself after every audition. That was the only way he could personally reconcile all the rejection. He thought, "I know you're going to say no, just say it quickly so I can get to the next place." After all these years, after dying his hair black one time to appear more like an Italian car mechanic, he was too pissed off to try to force himself into a role that didn't fit. His unspoken message with each audition was, "Here's what I do. If you want this, call me, and if you don't want this, you call somebody else, and I'm out."

Resnick reached over to give his hand a squeeze. Julie and Luke were an item, but they were keeping it quiet. Not even Cyd knew, just Julie's family and her close friends, including Luke's roommate at the time, David Sheinkopf. It was frowned upon to date someone when you were an assistant to his manager, but Julie was smitten.

"He was my sweet little cowboy," she recalls. "He always had this cute shyness about him." He was romantic; every door was opened. They'd make eyes at each other over menus at a restaurant, and when the waiter came around, Luke would order for her. "He was super young to do that," she says, but they both savored the old-fashioned gesture. As for other aspects of their relationship, "I don't want to get too personal because, you know . . . but he was tender. Just tender and gentle." She never once saw him get mad. Ticked off for a minute, yes, but then his slight smile would reappear. "His shine," Julie calls it.

After a few months, the romantic aspect of their relationship eventually ran its course and they easily settled into a warm working rapport. Good thing, too, because Luke would need every ally he could get. His life was about to remake itself into a fantasy—but that was later. As they rode in Julie's car that day in June, airplanes low overhead, he was just an out-of-luck actor slumping back to New York. From there he'd gather his few belongings before returning for good to Ohio, never to act again.

Then Julie's brick-sized portable phone rang. She pulled over and immediately put the call on speaker. After all the callbacks, negotiations, and a screen test, it was Mr. Spelling's office, confirming that Luke had indeed won the part of Dylan McKay. They were five minutes away from LAX.

After they'd hung up, Julie and Luke screamed, stomped their feet on the floor mats, and then locked into a kiss as cars surged all around them, filled with passengers getting dropped off at the airport to board planes to fly home. But not Luke. He was exchanging one ticket for another. "It was like he'd won the television lottery," Resnick says.

"HI, DAD," SHE SAYS, DROPPING her heavy backpack to the floor.

Instead of an ordinary dining room table, her dad's adjustable hospital bed fills the room. He raises a hand to her. "Hello," he says. The tone makes her smile weakly. It is almost cute, how formal he is, how polite.

"Do you remember my name?"

Her mom is sitting beside him, directing a straw between his lips. She gives her daughter a warning look. "He doesn't—"

"I just want to see," Margaret says.

Her father smiles apologetically. Then he fishes for it. His face clouds with concentration and then frustration. He shakes his head, almost ashamed.

She regrets that she asked. His brain tumor, the surgeries, have wiped away his ability to say anything beyond a few simple words or phrases. His left temple still bears the scar; the rest of his hair is patchy. His perma-scruff is mottled with white. He is fifty-six, and had looked younger than his age for years, but not anymore. Now he looks a decade older.

"What are we watching?" she asks, to change the subject, not because she wants to join in. She is already planning an exit to her bedroom or, if her mother makes her stay, she will tolerate the time by thinking of anything else but here. The little TV perched on the dresser across the room from his bed shows the six o'clock news. A film of baby powder covers the dresser, which is packed with pill bottles that her mother opens and closes every few hours of the day.

Five years ago, her parents had declared that they had finally arrived at their final destination, after stints in California and Alabama, and, before she was born, North Carolina. Oak Park, an idyllic Chicago suburb, was to be the place her dad would work until retirement. A beautiful church in the center of town to call his own. It was a return to where everything *began—her dad's youth in Chicago, her parents' courtship at Northwestern, their first few years as a married couple with little boy babies crawling around. But two years after they'd arrived, he was diagnosed with a brain tumor. They tried radiation, chemo, and surgeries, but the tumor kept sprouting back. Then it leaped to his lungs and lymph nodes. He resigned. They moved out of the beautiful rectory into an awkward rental bungalow. After yet another surgery—Margaret had lost track of them all—her father took his last steps into that bungalow. Then her mother sold a property in California, their only asset, and bought a prairie-style house on the border of Oak Park and Austin, one of Chicago's poorest neighborhoods. Her father entered that home by wheelchair. The new house, next to the neighborhood she isn't supposed to walk into, has tragic turquoise carpeting everywhere, but, as her mother frequently reminds her, "you get to stay in Oak Park with all your friends."*

Just as she spun around to descend downstairs, her mom stops her. "I'm going to need your help."

"Ask Ben," she says.

"He'll help too. We need to lift him up and—"

Whatever her mother is going on about, she doesn't want to know. Change her dad's clothes? Bandage his bedsores? Bathe or feed him? Does it matter what the task is? Her hands and her smile always perform the required acts, but the rest of her is tucked away, minding her alternate reality. This, her depressing home life, is holding her back from what really matters—her friends. Boys. Booze. A life of adventure. She spends as little time here as possible.

CHAPTER

SIX

IT STARTED ON LONG Island. A little bubble of viewership, Rosin remembers, in the data, giving them hope in that first desperate season. A gaggle of teenaged girls, maybe with nicked knees from their drugstore razors, wearing dEliA and their mother's Liz Claiborne perfume, and boys too, started watching *Beverly Hills, 90210*, a show that for its first several episodes flirted with cancellation. Debuting October 4, 1990, against the heavyweight *Cheers*, the experimental slice of teen programming was made on the cheap by a fledgling network and a non-union crew. Of course, none of those cut corners mattered to these kids on Long Island. They saw their lives writ large on the television. For the first time, their voices, their concerns, were important enough to warrant an hour of TV. And they started to talk about it.

SWAPPING NOTES WITH HER NEW *friend Maddie Nichols. She has already written to Rose, but Rose has aligned herself with a new ring of popular preppy girls. She feels more kinship with Maddie, who is into theater and film. They taped themselves acting out a fake soap opera with Maddie's camcorder the other day, giggling through their scenes. Margaret has forty-two minutes before the bell rings to craft a sublimely gossipy, clever, and outrageous letter. Her biology teacher drones on. If he knows that half the class are scribbling to their peers, he has given up fighting it a long time ago. Every few minutes, she lifts her head and pantomimes engagement, even raising her hand for a question, before dipping back down to her pen. As she writes, she pictures the handoff, that moment in the hallway when, between classes, Maddie will hand her a tightly tucked triangle of paper, and Margaret will slip Maddie her own elaborately folded missive. The next period will be transportive as she drinks in the letter on lined notebook paper, its edges raggedy from being ripped off the metal coil.*

Their letters brim over with plans for after school or the weekend. They talk about clothing, tests they barely survived, and, most of all, flirting schemes. "How are we going to get Matt to notice me?" "Do you think Ethan is still into HER?" They don't talk about the purple Mad Dog 20/20 they slugged down last weekend, or the beers they shotgunned—all procured from the liquor store right over the border in Austin. Too risky to put that in print. Drinking is nothing new for Maddie, nor Margaret. That started with Nathan and his friends. One night, Nathan drank so much that he wound up in the hospital with alcohol poisoning. That slowed them down for about two weeks, while he was grounded.

They have pen names: Margaret is Leona, and Maddie is Fiona. Some-

times if Fiona is in a mood, she writes what amounts to teenaged erotica in which their crushes fall prey to their charms. Cue tons of kissing, "heavy petting," a term that sends them into peals of laughter, and then, because the bell is about to ring, Fiona abruptly ends the scene. Oh well! Fiona's customary sign-off is "Party, Peace and Penis."

CHAPTER

SEVEN

IN THE COMPUTER/TECH/ALL-THINGS-SCIENCE-Y LAB at West Beverly, freshman nerd Scott Scanlon fashions a floor plan on a lumbering desktop for "the perfect dance club."

Brandon, the new kid from Minnesota, asks him how he designed it, and Scott answers, "I used my imagination instead of my experience."

Two meathead bullies emerge out of nowhere to rough him up because they hate imagination. Brandon rushes to Scott's defense, but at this early juncture in the series, he is still too Minnesota to be effective. The bullies threaten to delete all of Scott's work.

That's when we hear him, an unbothered but authoritative voice. "Touch that board, my friend—" The camera cuts to the back of a seated figure with a supremely coiffed head, wearing a black jacket, all submerged in shadow and lit only by a Tesla lamp shooting out neon rays from a throbbing purple nucleus, a prop that will never ever show up in Dylan's orbit again. He spins around, revealing the magnificent splendor of his pompadour, the greaser's curly bang drooping down on his forehead, the crisp white tee under the black jacket, and a small gold hoop in his left ear.

"Please," he says, getting up to stalk closer to the bullies. "Touch it." Then dripping sarcasm gives way to political commentary: "You know, the tragedy of this country is that cretins like you two end up running it."

One of them starts to say, "Yeah, and losers like you end up—"

Dylan won't abide. "Let me tell you something, just so you know in advance. I'm not in a good mood today."

"I'm not in a good mood today." In the distant future, this line will be something called a GIF on something called the internet.

Dylan continues: "In fact, I'm feeling a little hostile."

"Whoa," one of the bullies mumbles, before both uneventfully shuffle off.

Threat nullified, Dylan reviews Scanlon's design. "You're doing a good job, kid. Keep up the good work." He wanders off to smoke in the bathroom, or seduce the English teacher, or whatever it is that bad boys do.

Brandon, who'd been silently observing, says to Scott: "Your friend's pretty cool."

Scott answers: "I've never seen the guy in my life."

———

In the next scene, Brandon finds Dylan, just very casually, as one does, reading a book in the most inconvenient place a person could choose to performatively read a book: in the middle of the stairway at their high school. The theme guitars sizzle as a feather-haired Brandon broaches an awkward introduction. When he asks Dylan if he wants to go get lunch, Dylan witheringly replies, "Yeah, 'let's do lunch.'" He's not into that Hollywood bullshit, see, but he's not dissing Brandon for good.

Later, Brandon and Dylan drive to the Sunset Strip, what "tourists call it," Dylan reports mockingly. Dylan may not end up running the country, but as a multimillionaire, he'll have plenty of opportunities to exercise his privilege. His sorrows are many, but it's much cuter to be sad driving around in a Porsche than in a broken-down Chevy.

Declaring the Strip dead, Brandon and Dylan jump back into Dylan's ride, where Brandon unearths a book of poetry by Lord Byron. Dylan utters one of his most iconic lines: "'Mad, bad, and dangerous to know.'

That was him, and that's me," a reference to Lady Caroline Lamb's description of her lover, the poet Lord Byron. Any teenager who's ever been called "pretentious" for liking literature, art, or music recognizes themselves with gratitude while also laughing at Dylan for being this way. It's safe to laugh at a character who embodies what you haven't yet reconciled within yourself.

By the end of the episode, when we see him calling a French operator, in some semblance of the scene Luke auditioned with all those months before, we understand that his life is undercut by misery. His extreme wealth, his exquisite beauty, his gift of swagger—they're all small and useless now. He tries to leave a message with the service for his parents, but he can't even do that. The service wasn't taking messages. He might have all the power in the halls of West Beverly, but where it matters most, he has no voice. His pleas will not be received. He hangs up, defeated.

AFTER NEW YEAR'S EVE, TWO disasters. First, her mom caught on that the peach schnapps was 90 percent water, so she had demanded Margaret spend the rest of winter break at home. That put an end to the escapades at Ethan's house, with Maddie and a few other friends. While Ethan's mom was at work, they had eaten peanut butter and jellies, and fawned over Ethan's ancient calico. Then, the main feature: wrestling, which was really a low-stakes way to straddle a boy and feel the pressure of his weight against her body. Different pairs—boy on girl—matched up and crashed from Ethan's mom's bed onto the floor, expertly contorting their feet so that they wouldn't knock over her lamp or her bedside ashtray.

But worse than the schnapps was the discovery of her diary. She had written everything that had happened between her and Nathan, more than six months ago now. Not only the botched sex but how wrecked she was after he broke up with her. On a blue-sky Saturday, she had made a plan. A few bottles of Advil, one random medication from her dad's dresser. A terse letter she wrote to her mother and left in an envelope on the floor of the entryway. She tore out of the house and walked, picking a random residential corner. After an hour or so of sitting there—and it really was such a beautiful day, the clouds racing across the blue—she didn't take the pills. For one thing, it seemed incredibly laborious to have to swallow so much. She had brought water, but probably not enough. And what if, instead of expiring in the grass quietly, something worse happened, something like her father's occasional seizures which started a couple of years ago as a result of his tumor? His first seizure was when she was in the sixth grade, home alone with him. She had called the ambulance to the house.

She abandoned the corner. When she returned home, she found the envelope exactly where she had left it. It was undisturbed, except now it bore a single tread mark from someone stepping on it. She pocketed it and ran upstairs.

The contents of the diary inspired an inquisition of sorts with James present, home from college for the break, to support her mom.

They asked her questions in a stern but frightened tone that made it clear she had been caught feeling things that were absolutely unreasonable. Didn't she realize what something like this would do to her family? She survived their questions by saying as little as possible. Mostly, she was mortified. Her mother, reading her excruciatingly detailed entries about the way Nathan's face changed during orgasm. The way pleasure shot through her. Her mother, who had once ran her hand under hot water when she caught Margaret exploring herself as a child. Margaret answered obediently: Yes, the feelings were in the past. Yes, she knew she was wrong.

So for now, and maybe forever, there is no leaving the house. Which isn't entirely bad; alone time has its allures. For the last couple of hours, she's been lurking in the finished basement, drawing in her notebook from a magazine spread, listening to Depeche Mode's Violator, waiting for the good TV to start. Secretly, Margaret thinks as she shades in her version of Christy Turlington's face, her mother resents her not for the drinking or what she had written about in her diary, but for making her pay attention at all. Her mother's two favorite phrases are "I'm tired," and "I have enough on my plate without worrying about . . ." At the inquisition, she had listed all the things Margaret is failing at. Doing her homework. Getting up on time. Showing no interest in the church, which triggered Margaret's most venomous cackle. "I'm sorry," she'd said to her mom, "but what exactly is God doing for us now?" Then she pointed in the direction of where her father lay.

Finally, it is 8:00 p.m. She turns on the TV, dials the knob two clicks over to FOX, and the garbage state of her life recedes as the opening theme plays. The guitar licks, the ending clap-clap. Beverly Hills, 90210 has been building up the chemistry between Dylan and Brenda for weeks now.

Except their first real date is off to a disastrous start. Dylan is arguing *with his dad in a closed bedroom of their palatial hotel suite. Brenda waits outside the door, listening.*

When Dylan springs out of the room, he heads straight for the liquor in crystal bottles on a credenza. "C'mon, don't," Brenda says. "You're driving me home." Dylan tears himself away from the bottle, then out of the hotel suite. Brenda follows. Out on the street, Brenda is desperate to save the date. She suggests taking a walk on the beach, but Dylan shuts her down. In his acid-washed duster, he whips around and shouts, "I've had just about enough noise for one night, okay?"

His outburst unnerves Brenda. She asks the valet for a taxi, but Dylan tells the valet to forget it. Brenda shifts into a walk-run and Dylan pursues. Then it gets ugly: he picks up a flowerpot right next to her and smashes it to the ground, dirt and flowers splaying out. Margaret, who gets easily startled, just like her dad, jumps a little, then laughs to herself. The broken pot sends Brenda into a full sprint away from Dylan, but he catches up quickly and wraps his arms around her from behind.

"I'm sorry. I'm sorry," he says.

"Just let me go." She's wriggling away from him.

"Brenda, I'm an idiot. Please don't leave."

"You're scaring me," Brenda pleads, in a tone Margaret recognizes from experience. Dylan doesn't want to scare Brenda; at last, he comes down from his adrenaline. He is about to burst into tears, but like so many guys Margaret knows, he won't allow it.

Finally, the moment happens. The two pause and lock eyes. They kiss, and it is without any self-consciousness or doubt. Brenda is so enmeshed with another human that she has forgotten herself; this is what Margaret wants, too. Forgetting was the next best option to actually being herself, which wasn't possible. Maybe in fleeting moments with Nathan, she had been herself, but for the most part, she keeps her true self out of sight.

CHAPTER

EIGHT

WHILE WATCHING A FINAL edit of an early episode, Star was struck by something: "I just remember this one scene," he recalls, "where Luke and Jason Priestley are in Luke's vintage Porsche, the two of them with those amazing haircuts, driving on some bluff over the ocean and oh my god, it was so *Rebel Without a Cause* with a nineties twist. It felt instantly iconic to me, the two of those guys together."

Luke and Priestley played on-screen best friends who didn't always get along. Their characters called each other by their first initials ("What up, D?" "Nothing, B.") and there was usually a prop around to illustrate their fraternal bond: a surfboard, Dylan's motorcycle that he was always tinkering with (a Triumph, obviously, no nineties crotch rocket for this guy), a pool stick, a pack of cards. Men. They couldn't just talk. Had to be doing something or about to go somewhere—some excuse to cut off the conversation if it got too deep. Luke and Jason liked to keep themselves occupied in real life, too. Luke always fixing or rehabbing something around the house; Priestley an admitted workaholic, always with some project or other. But they did get deep on occasion.

Sixteen-hour days, shooting the show at a studio in Van Nuys or at Torrance High School, the stand-in for West Beverly High. On those Van Nuys days, Luke and Priestley finished off with drinks, Priestley wrote in his self-titled memoir, "in craphole Valley restaurant/bars like Marix Tex Mex and Casa Vega . . . surrounded by forty-year-olds who had no idea who we were and would not have cared one bit if they had known." As the show picked up viewers, the two young men made a pact.

"We got real famous real fast, and that's why we had to talk about it," Luke said. "We just looked at each other and said, 'Let's not buy into this shit, man. We'll go into work, and they'll all scream, and we'll just go to work and not worry about any of this.' And we pretty much stuck to that."

IT HASN'T HAPPENED TO HER yet. Not really. At least, not the way she wanted her first time to have happened. But technically, for other reasons, she is a woman. The slip of blood that fell into the toilet and bloomed into the water signaled that she could get pregnant. She, this stumbling baby gazelle of a girl who longs to suck her thumb, still, at the end of her freshman year. Okay. Sure.

The setup is the spring dance. Brenda and Dylan are paired up and everyone else gets thrown into awkward but intriguing couples around them: Steve and Donna, Brandon and Kelly, who actually kiss, but none of that mattered compared to Brenda and Dylan having sex for the first time. Is it really happening? Surely they'd be interrupted before the deed. The cool-headed principal would bust in. Or furry Mr. Walsh, bug-eyed that his daughter wanted to do the same thing his son has already done, hassle-free. In the fourth episode, Brandon first had sex with his girlfriend visiting from Minnesota.

Before they escape up to room 271, Brenda tests Dylan's motives while they slow dance.

"Dylan, I'm a little nervous."

"Bren, don't be. Everything is gonna be great."

"Yeah, that's what you keep on saying. Look, it's just that we've been building it up for so long. And it's not that I'm not ready. Believe me, I am."

"What are you trying to say?"

"Somehow you'll be disappointed."

"Bren, we're not going to be judging each other up there. We're going to be enjoying each other." Margaret recognizes a sacrosanct rule: that the guy always must be more experienced. But where did that leave all the virginal guys?

"Well, I bet you've used that line before."

"Bren, you're not just another notch on my belt. If that's what this was about, I would've had you up there months ago." Another nightmare scenario for Margaret: that when she would finally be with someone, he would disappear. It didn't yet dawn on her that no one else, lover or ghost-lover, had the power to calculate her worth.

"Oh, really?"

"Yes, really."

"So what is this all about?" Brenda sets up the final hoop for him to jump through.

"Don't you know? I love you."

The moment strikes Margaret as corny, yet it also cracks open a wish. The probability of having a conversation like this—open, trusting, direct—with a boy who loves her, well, it isn't a probability at all. Nathan is the only boy who had ever said "I love you" to her, but now they are dead to each other in the hallways, and she is ashamed that she ever believed him or said it back.

She focuses on Brenda's elated face after they finish. All the knowledge it imparts from the other side of experience. Her red lipstick a leftover stain. Her hair slightly askew. Had she really managed to keep her updo intact? Had Brenda taken her hand and shielded her chignon from every thrust? Whatever, it was a waste of time to catch TV in these improbabilities. Better to surrender to the essence of what's being conveyed: a girl having sex for the first time. When Brenda rejoins her friends downstairs, still at the dance, she is so frothing over that Kelly asks, "Why are you so disgustingly happy?" Brenda doesn't say. For this brief time, soon to be spoiled, she is free from guilt or consequence, the usual traps that a woman must fall into to pay for her sexual freedom. But she doesn't fall. She skips right back into life.

CHAPTER

NINE

NOT EVERY VIEWER CELEBRATED Brenda's freedom to experience sex. Some didn't want her to get away with it. Where were the consequences? All over the country, affiliates in the South and Midwest were calling FOX to complain that the show had pushed too far.

For Star, who had written and directed the episode, and Rosin, who'd come of age during the sixties' sexual revolution, the response was a shock. The series had picked up steam, that much they knew, but they still thought they were flying under the radar. The uproar proved them wrong. Even Star's mother was disappointed in her son's choice to send these two kids astray. The episode prompted Star and his mom to have a conversation about teen sex, one that never occurred when he was an actual high school student.

Beverly Hills, 90210, in its first two seasons in particular, took a "ripped from the headlines" approach. Topics covered in an ad-chopped hour included abortion, teen pregnancy, teen parenthood, drug use, AIDS, affirmative action, homosexuality, and gun safety. The latter was delivered in season two with more finality than most: The boy who Dylan defended in his debut episode, Scott Scanlon, who, along with David Silver, stood in as the show's underclassmen nerds, shoots himself. It was an accident with his father's unsecured piece.

Most of the time, the characters who embodied the issue of the episode (such as Brandon's teen mom friend or the sex educator with AIDS who fends off Steve's flirtations) were sent packing as the credits rolled, never to be seen again. The main characters orbited close—Kelly and her addict-in-recovery mother in particular—but were rarely plunged into the turmoil of being, say, a closeted gay kid themselves. But Dylan and Brenda were main players. According to the affiliates, someone had to pay for her virginity.

Star found himself pressured by FOX to satisfy the powers who kept their show flowing to American teens.

"I never wanted the show to be moralizing," he says. "And suddenly we're forced to be. I certainly wasn't happy because I had to write the episode where Brenda regrets having sex with her boyfriend and everything felt so honest, up to that point. And this felt a little after-school special, a little moralizing." He tried to find his way to something believable—he gave Brenda a pregnancy scare, which in turn destabilized the relationship. Not because Dylan freaked out—actually, he's near-perfect in his support—but because Brenda gets scared. The relationship is now too adult for her, which rings false considering how hard she'd always fought for her independence. Shannen Doherty convincingly played it, and the affiliates cooled off—but it undermined the show's sincerity. Another kind of innocence was lost.

CHAPTER

TEN

WHEN JAMES DEAN DIED at age twenty-four in a head-on collision in rural California, just hours after the racing aficionado had received a speeding ticket, his short and volatile life exploded into stardust and became legend. In the nineties as a "deleb," those dead celebrities who make the heavenly transformation onto merchandise after death—Elvis, Marilyn Monroe, Jimi Hendrix—Dean was everywhere, on T-shirts and posters available at every mall. He symbolized teenage rage boiled down to cool rebellion.

Star and the other creators of *90210* leaned into the James Dean mythos. Dylan's hair in a pompadour. Dylan's pristine white T-shirts that would become so deliciously sullied with engine grease. Even a pivotal scene between Kelly and Dylan, in a season-three episode, titled "Rebel with a Cause," was shot at the Griffith Observatory, the site of Dean's career-defining performance.

Early on, when asked how he felt about his supposed doppelgänger, Perry got right to the point: "I'm not James Dean. And no one else is, either. . . . There was only one, and he's dead." The comparison spooked him: "In a way, if they make the association strong enough, I'll have to pay the price for the fact that he checked out early, and I don't want to, you know. I hope to still be working when I'm thirty and forty and fifty and forever. . . . When I can no longer fulfill that James Dean fantasy for them, they'll look and get it from someone else, and I'll be gone."

HER MOTHER COMES BACK FROM *the hospital, where Margaret's dad has been fighting an infection for the last week. She enters with the customary Subway sandwiches, a dinner Margaret has consumed many times. There is no more cooking; there haven't been prepared dinners since her dad, the main chef of the family, went through chemo treatments and radiation. First, he couldn't stand at a hot stove; then, he couldn't stand at all. Her mother cycles through various takeout places, or Margaret and Ben figure it out for themselves. Earlier that night, Ben had cooked himself a burger, spraying up the kitchen with grease, before disappearing back into his bedroom. Margaret didn't eat anything, not that he offered. A few months ago, Margaret, after reading about corporate farming, decided to become a vegetarian. A pescatarian, really. It is easier anyway.*

It is late, nearly ten p.m. Ben hasn't left the bedroom, where he plays Pink Floyd, the Beatles, and, to signal his dark mood, Ozzy Osbourne. There's been a lot of Ozzy lately. At the kitchen table, her mother forlornly watches her unwrap the tuna salad roll. She can't eat while her mother looks like this.

"I'm worried," *her mother says.*

There are so many conversations that start this way with her mother. Already, Margaret is summoning the strength to wish away whatever her mother had to say. To comfort her, but also to blot her words out.

"He didn't look good," *her mom says.*

"Well, he only has one lung," *Margaret says.* "And he has pneumonia."

"I know, but there was something different—"

"He's going to bounce back; he always does."

Bounce back to what? To where? The hospital bed in the dining room? She searches her mother's face. The concern pulls down her every feature.

The sturdy nose, the exhausted eyes that she rubbed whenever she took off her glasses, rubbing until it looked like her eyes would disappear. Her hair is a thin salted brown, revealing her scalp. The local Denny's, without asking, gave her a senior discount though she's technically ten years too young for it. Her mother's vanity was not wounded, because she has none.

"Mom?"

"He's not going to make it. I don't know if he'll make it through the night." Tears brim behind her glasses.

They rise from their seats and fall into a hug.

CHAPTER

ELEVEN

"Hair was very important to my dad. And if you watch, there are never sunglasses on 90210. He'd always say, 'Let them see it in your eyes before they hear it in your words.' Luke Perry's famous squint was probably because my dad wouldn't let him wear sunglasses."

—Tori Spelling, *The Hollywood Reporter*, 2015

AS IT ROUNDED OUT that first season, two American traditions helped *Beverly Hills, 90210* become a phenomenon: war and work. When Operation Desert Storm started on January 16, 1991, it was the first war to air live from the front lines. Viewers flocked to the three networks, as well as fledgling network CNN, but for some, war did not make for good television. *Beverly Hills, 90210* offered escape with its attractive twentysomethings playacting as teens, lusting after crushes, inappropriately flirting with their teachers, shoplifting, and experimenting with diet pills and all the rest.

The FOX executives wanted to capitalize on that gain in viewership on the back end of season one. Just as Chuck Rosin and his wife, Karen Rosin—who also wrote for the show—were about to go on vacation to Hawaii, Star and Rosin were ordered to churn out more episodes. It was an ingenious move to give teenagers fresh stories over the summer break, when every other show was in reruns. Star had no choice but to go with the Rosin family, their small children included, to Four Seasons in Maui. "I'll never forget sitting by the pool and drinking mimosas and then drinking some more, just writing all the time," Star says. "We had not a minute to lose."

SHE HAS RISEN TOO EARLY in her blue room. She loves this ocean-dark hue; she painted it herself. The weak dawn shines a distorted rectangle on the wall, next to where she'd copied lyrics to The Cure's "Pictures of You" on a lined piece of paper. The house is too quiet, a closed glove. Last night's dreams, or were they memories? A floorboard creak in the room. A touch on her hair. She can't sort what really happened from what she'd dreamed.

A knock on the door. She knows.

When she sees her mother's face, there is no need for either of them to say it. There is only Margaret bursting into tears in her mother's arms.

Sometime in the middle of the night. A nurse was with him. "He went peacefully," whatever that means. These are the details she hears her mother repeat all day on the phone, and then more calls, flight information. Planes coming from every corner of the country; taxis delivering them all to a nearby hotel.

A memory: Her father lifted the record out from its sleeve, his face expectant. He raised the polished wooden cover on an ancient phonograph. They were not state-of-the-art people. The house was a museum of brown furniture they'd inherited from their dead relatives. He set down the record gently, positioned the needle, and it popped into the groove. Vivaldi's The Four Seasons, "Spring in E Major." The delicate violins. The percussion created out of rushing the bows across the strings. She'd grown to love it so much, listening while they played checkers, that she'd bought it on tape, her technology.

She cleans and organizes her room while it plays. When she was little, she only put her toys back in order and made her bed to see his reaction.

He'd come in afterward and put on a big, astonished show. "Look at it in here! Fantastic work!"

Ignoring the other mourners in the house, she sweeps, scrubs, purges, and vacuums all the way through Vivaldi's spring, summer, autumn, and winter. At the end, she is sweaty and tearstained, but her room is immaculate.

CHAPTER

TWELVE

THE TWO-BEDROOM WHITE BUNGALOW on Mansfield, the same name as his birthtown, was in a dumpy part of Hollywood. "Below Sunset," the realtors sniffed. But in 1990–91, at the start of *Beverly Hills, 90210* when he couldn't afford anything better, it was home to Luke and his roommate, David Sheinkopf, another actor four years younger than Luke. They'd first met waiting on a *Young Guns* audition in New York when Luke was twenty. "Hey," Luke had said by way of introduction, his feet kicked up on a table, "I can roll a cigarette with one hand." Dave matched him with "I can roll the tightest joint you ever smoked . . . with *two*." They met again months later when both were on *Another World*, which picked up actors in a limo to bring them to set, which was "a big deal," Sheinkopf recalls. When his limo arrived, who did he find inside but Mr. Cigarette from before. And with that, they became fast friends, Luke coming down from the Upper West Side to shoot pool at Chelsea Billiards. Between shots, they'd complain about their girlfriends—Luke's relationship with Yasmine Bleeth, Sheinkopf says, was "tumultuous"— and the distasteful business end of acting. When Sheinkopf's agent severed ties right before his move to Hollywood, Luke, who would follow a few months later, gave him a stirring pep talk.

Before Mansfield, Luke lived for a few months with Alexis Arquette, an actor he met on an indie movie about wealthy, alienated teens that shot in 1989, *Terminal Bliss*. Written and directed by Jordan Alan, who was only around twenty years old, it had been shot in thirty-six days on a $500,000 budget in South Carolina. Luke wrote it off as a disaster, except for meeting Alexis. The two made a soulful connection right away. Luke told Sheinkopf that during one of the first times he'd hung out with Alexis, he'd spent hours with his friend's head in his lap, both of them stoned, picking fake dreads from the movie shoot out of their hair. Alexis, who also performed in femme drag, was assigned male at birth and announced her intention to transition to female in the mid-nineties. She later described herself as "gender suspicious."

Alexis, who died in 2016, was the fourth child in the tight-knit Arquette clan, with siblings Rosanna, Richmond, Patricia, and David. Luke stayed close with many of the Arquette siblings, particularly David and Patricia, throughout his life. In the 2020 documentary *You Cannot Kill David Arquette*, about longtime wrestling-obsessive David's re-entry into the ring, Luke helps rescue his injured friend after a match went awry.

"Luke didn't really care about sexual orientation, gender, race, or who you were. He was non-racist, non-sexist," Sheinkopf says. "He really didn't care unless you were an asshole, and then he really didn't like you. And even if you were an asshole, he respected it sometimes, but he didn't want to be your friend. He didn't bring you into his circle, and he had a very small circle of people."

While Luke confided in few people, he socialized with a wide and eclectic set. Sheinkopf woke up at two a.m. one time to someone pounding on the outside of the house. Gripping a baseball bat, Sheinkopf opened the door to find actor Sam J. Jones, best known for playing a strapping blond Flash Gordon in the 1980 movie.

"Where's Luke?" he slurred.

"Still out," Sheinkopf said.

A drunken Jones brushed past him and headed to the couch, where he promptly passed out.

"This is just what Hollywood did back then," Sheinkopf says. "Everybody knew each other." Without cell phones in everyone's pockets, it was the era of the pop-in. Sheinkopf remembers another visitor, Luke's soon-to-be wife, who came by with a present. Luke and she had recently met, as Luke would tell the press, at a dinner party; he steadfastly denied all tabloid reports that she was a fan. She smiled as she handed off the box to Sheinkopf.

"Any message?"

"He'll know what it's about."

FOR HER DAD'S FUNERAL, SHE wears a new black dress from the Gap, telling herself as she pulls on her new black tights that she shouldn't cry, that if she starts, then she won't be able to stop. She sheds very few tears at the funeral; she avoids the eyes of her friends—Rose, Maddie, Ethan—on purpose. When James starts to cry, she chokes her tears back. All she wants is to grab his hand, drape herself over his suited back, anything to make her brother stop. Or to join him. She can't, because— again—how would she stop? She takes her cues from the Mother Mary statue, a cold state of feminine grace. She is Mary's marble daughter, smiling in the receiving line. She would never wear the dress again.

IN SOME WAYS, LIFE BECOMES *easier after her dad died. While he was alive, little remained of the man with an encyclopedic mind for opera, who'd passed on his love for NOVA medical documentaries, who'd dispensed advice to the parishioners who came to him with their problems. His death is a relief, for him and her. Somewhere else, maybe, he is whole again.*

But it also means that the grief held at bay while he was alive is released. Her mother is worn out from the last few years of being her father's nurse. At night, after her mother had disappeared for hours into the newspaper, she confides to Margaret that she has been cheated. She already had a difficult childhood—alcoholic parents, her mother dying young, a verbally abusive stepmother—and now she's a fifty-five-year-old widow. The days stretch on, waiting to be filled, and without her husband, she doesn't know how to fill them.

Her mom tries to figure it out with long weekends in Wisconsin at a religious retreat center, leaving Margaret alone with Ben, her depressed older brother who exists in shadow. Sometimes James comes home from college to be there. As her fun older brother, he lets her filch a few of his Miller Lites and helps her with math, but sometimes he's testy. He's not old enough to be her parent but he acts like it sometimes, telling her what she can or can't do. She rebels in her standard manner—with cold sarcasm.

That is her mother's sorrow, and her brothers' coping mechanisms. As for her own, she is a compost bin of memories, but she keeps it tightly lidded. In her view, grief is a natural but fetid process. No one needs to see it but her. She sorts it out alone. The exact sound of his voice; she plays it in her mind at night. His exact gait: crooked, from a broken hip that didn't repair right as a child. She catalogs every single instance she can conjure with him. Age three or four, standing on the trunk in her parents' bedroom while he caught her wiggly feet in Mary Janes. Another scrap: Him wrapping her in a yellow towel after a bath. Another: "You are ti-ti" (their baby word for "tired").

The rehearsal of every scene between them didn't forestall the inevitable: decomposition. After only a few months, her memories are crumbling. Time struck a hard bargain—healing or something like it could be bestowed, but at the cost of forgetting.

CHAPTER

THIRTEEN

SOMETIME AROUND 1990, LUKE was given a Vietnamese potbellied pig by his friend, ABC casting director Alexa Fogel. Jerry Lee, which Luke named for his favorite musician at the time, became a favorite topic in interviews as man ascended, and hog waddled up, the dizzying ladder of fame. Vietnamese potbellied pigs had a real moment in the nineties—George Clooney had one too. And so did Molly Ringwald, Luke's future coparent on *Riverdale*. In her twenties and about to move to Paris, Ringwald was so overwhelmed with her pet pig Wilbur that she gave him away. Luke and Ringwald didn't know each other then, but through mutual friends, Wilbur joined Luke's collective, which included Violet and Norma Jean. One of them appeared with Luke, cradled in his arms, for the Gap's Individuals of Style ad campaign, shot by Annie Leibovitz.

Luke's fondness for mud-covered snouts was formed early. His uncle had a litter of pigs, and when the mother rolled over the runt and injured it, Luke and his family helped it get around the house. "It was beautiful," he said. "Pigs are very sweet. There is intelligence in their eyes."

Luke professed a liberated love for Jerry Lee: "I don't keep him. We sort of live together, really. It's not like I own him or anything. He hangs out with me." He spent mornings on his porch feeding apples to Jerry Lee, letting the pig wrestle the fruit from his grip.

"Oh god, yeah, I did not love the pig," Luke's former roommate, David Sheinkopf, says with a laugh. "You know, it was a *pig* living in the house." Luke, Sheinkopf says, didn't fix the pig (at least at first), and it "was marking everywhere." Everywhere? "Okay, there was a litter box on the back porch that Jerry Lee used. I do give him credit for that." Fortunately, Sheinkopf's Akita shepherd mix Sasha and Jerry Lee got along splendidly.

Jerry Lee, a charcoal-gray fellow who grew into a stately 150 or so pounds, made an impression on everyone he snorted at. Leslie Jordan, Luke and Sheinkopf's former neighbor, told a story on one of his pandemic-era videos about Luke asking if Jordan's cleaning lady Irma would come over to his place to tidy up. "Well, Irma walked over and got one look at that pig and took off running," Jordan said. "She said no, she wasn't going to clean a pigsty."

Jason Priestley generously offered: "Luke's house really has a good pig odor to it, which I appreciate."

Considering that Luke described Jerry Lee as "the Yoda force in my life," he fought like hell when the city threatened to toss his guru. In 1993, the *Los Angeles Times* reported, "The bad boy of television's *Beverly Hills, 90210* has appealed to the city of Los Angeles for permission to keep his pets, three Vietnamese potbellied pigs, at his Tarzana home." He was no longer living with Sheinkopf in Hollywood; years of primetime TV money allowed him a much bigger spread in a nearly rural part of Los Angeles.

In the city at the time, keeping pigs required a special permit. A neighbor of Luke's gave support in the article, and a city councilman said that Luke's pigs had elicited no complaints to her office. A few weeks later, Luke and a realtor friend, who attended the hearing on his behalf, were vindicated, but it was a close call. Some neighbors did show up with objections, though the tension was really over the placement of a stable on Luke's twenty-thousand-foot property. The zoning administrator punted the stable matter for another time but ruled positively for Jerry Lee and his gang.

CHAPTER

FOURTEEN

BY 1992, *BEVERLY HILLS, 90210* was watched by 69 percent of American teenaged female television viewers. The next year would see it exported to thirty countries in Asia, Western Europe, Latin America, and Australia. By the spring of 1995, reruns could be seen as often as six times a week.

THE SMALL OLD MAN WITH the bronze face is testing her.

"Ti kaneis?" Dimitri says. He smiles and waits.

"Kala ime," she answers.

He claps, satisfied. She has passed the Greek test, answering "I'm fine" to "How are you?" He has also taught her how to say fresh, so that when the Greek elders come in, she can lead them to the bread and pronounce, "Fresko." They are surprised and delighted every time.

She's a cashier at a grocery store, owned by a Greek family, near the mall. James has worked here off and on for the last couple of years of college, and he got her the job. If she wanted any spending money, this is how it has to be. The grandfather of the family, Dimitri, stands by the registers, to help shoppers and catch thieves like her and Rose, who had both seemingly aged out of their shoplifting phase.

For the first time, she glimpses lives outside her own. Ringing up their groceries and taking their money. The quiet man who always brings in his own bags, ironed. Does he live alone? There's a couple, chatty and funny, who call her a born Tetris player, for how much she enjoys packing groceries in bags, nestling each item in its perfect spot. The old man, older than Dimitri, who only buys Twinkies, who has one tooth, yellowed. The woman with a baby who uses food stamps, and then the man behind her, under his breath, "Do you really need that?" because she is buying ice cream.

One night a woman with messy hair and a long coat comes in late, right before they are closing, and asks if they have any balloons. Margaret shows her a rack, and the woman thanks her. Dimitri is on a smoke break, so Margaret hustles back to the unmanned register. Minutes later, the woman rushes out, buying nothing, screaming behind her, "Thank you!"

Dimitri and his son, also named Dimitri, figure out after closing that the woman stole the balloons.

"Why would anyone steal balloons?" Margaret asks. Could someone need decorations for a birthday party that bad? Is it for her kid?

The Dimitris don't answer her question.

CHAPTER

FIFTEEN

FRIDAY NIGHT IN HOLLYWOOD; the sinking sun sent its rose-gold rays everywhere, glinted off the parked cars. Sheinkopf and Luke were loitering on the porch at Mansfield, slugging beers and smoking Marlboros. Jerry Lee tottered around. Sheinkopf went inside, tilted the speakers closer to the window, and put on *The Eagles Live*. "Wasted Time" kicked on, with its wistful opening piano line.

"Play it, Davey Shein," Luke said. "Play! It!" Luke called his roommate "Davey" when he was in a good mood, and "David" in a put-out tone when Sheinkopf parked in his spot or let the dirty dishes pile up. Now, with the Eagles playing, every clash was forgiven. They howled along with Don Henley, soulfully tearing into the lyrics about broken relationships, crashing and nodding with the melodrama of the song. Their neighbor across the street, Leslie Jordan, watched with mock exasperation.

Their pool cues were waiting; in a little bit, they'd go to the Hollywood Athletic Club to rack 'em up. Something colorful was always going down at the Athletic Club. The upstairs VIP area was the playground of Kiefer Sutherland, Sean Penn, Madonna, Charlie Sheen, all the Young Hollywood icons. One time, Sheinkopf was there with a date, a Swedish model, and a big-time producer sent over one of his minions to request that the model take off her cutoff chambray shirt with a hood and give it to him, simply because the producer had said he liked it. Sheinkopf and his date refused, and the tension rose, until another member of the producer's entourage came over and apologized. There was truly no way of knowing what might happen at the Hollywood Athletic Club, or who would show up. And that was why they loved it.

But for now, it was *The Eagles Live*. Jordan eyed them while draining a cocktail. To this diminutive gay man with a Tennessee drawl, this was quite the show. *Oh lord, just look at these straight boys.* Were they playing air drums now?

When the song broke, they looked over to him, knowing they had captured his attention. He shook his head. "Y'all so butch," he said. All three of them laughed.

THE MOVIE ENDED EARLIER THAN expected. Maddie's dad is supposed to pick them up, but in that twenty-minute delay, an opportunity arises. They ditch the planned meeting spot and walk up the main western drag of Oak Park. They put out their thumbs, hoping to hitchhike for their first time ever, but only a few cars slow down for an eyeful, and zoom on.

Maybe the night would've ended with them heading back to the pickup spot, bored and defeated, but then they spot the house. A few flanneled guys are drinking beer from a keg on the porch and immediately size them up. Behind them, an open door gives Maddie and Margaret a full look inside. It's a party.

"Let's go in," Maddie says, voicing what Margaret already planned to say. No one is the leader between them.

Inside, Margaret scans the room for any other girls. There are none. Instead, it is about twenty or so guys, drinking, waiting for something to do, for the night to crack off in an unexpected direction, just like Maddie and Margaret are hoping. The room is sparsely furnished—a beat-up couch and a TV on low, a CD tower, and folding chairs in haphazard clusters. While some of the guys turn their eyes away from them, others seize their chance. A group of about six or seven immediately envelop Maddie and Margaret in a game of poker that, within minutes, changes to strip poker. They check in wordlessly with each other across the table. Maddie's eyes, hers. Flickers of unease, but challenge accepted.

Margaret's losses: A pair of small silver earrings. A beaded necklace. Her Keds, then her socks, all bundled by the foot of her folding chair. What she can't understand is why these guys, who seem to be at least in college, if not older, don't have any other girls there. Isn't that the point of college? Co-ed life? Maddie gets up and disappears with a tall blond guy who has been chatting her up from outside the game. Margaret had barely paid attention to him because she was too busy trying to figure out what play she held in her hands. She knows only a few basics about poker and she is getting swiftly beaten. Off goes her red-and-white-striped T-shirt. She sits in a cream-colored bra with a tiny pink rose stitched into the middle. The room is sweltering, but a chill runs over her skin, newly exposed to the air. She sips from her beer, watching a guy lose his shirt, but she is still the most unclothed in the room. She will never quit, because that would show fear and a lack of cool, but her mind is scrambling for a way out of this game before—

A hand grabs her wrist. "Can I talk to you?" a guy says, standing outside the poker ring. He raises his eyebrows so that his eyes are bulging. It is important.

"Dude," one guy grumbles. "What are you even doing?"

"Shut up," the other guy says to them. "I gotta show her something."

"Oh, I bet," another one says. The others laugh.

Margaret dips out.

He leads her over to the couch, where he and two others watch a basketball game. They seem different, quieter. The two friends look right at her with amused curiosity. He holds her wrist again and guides her to sit down next to him.

"You can put your shirt back on now," he says neutrally. Embarrassed, she slips it on. When she sinks into the cushion, the outside of her thigh is wedged close to his. She scoots away an inch or so, but he doesn't seem to notice.

"Those guys?" He leans toward her, speaking in a low voice. "Are assholes. You don't want to play strip poker with them, believe me."

"Aren't they your friends?"

"Yeah, that's exactly how I know they're assholes."

She searches the room for Maddie. Through the doorway to the kitchen, she sees her friend leaning her back against the counter, obscured by the blond guy. Maddie looks so slight in comparison. The guy is one of the most handsome there, very confident, but she doesn't like his energy. He has Maddie trapped between his two hands, gripping the counter. Over and over again he says something, and then sneaks a hand somewhere: her waist, her face, her hip. But Maddie is smiling and laughing so she decides to put her worries aside. Maybe she is just jealous. She and Maddie are in a constant competition for guys, and it is not unusual for Margaret to lose.

"Why are you here?" the guy next to her suddenly asks.

"What do you mean?"

"You and your friend, you're really young. You shouldn't be here," he says. He sounds angry. Is he actually nice, or is he just setting a different kind of trap for her? She opens her mouth to answer but can't think of what to say.

"Never mind," the guy says. "Just stay here with us."

For the next several minutes, she watches basketball with them, trying to make herself as small as possible, but they aren't even giving her dumb jokes on which to practice her best fake laugh. Certainly no one is interested in flirting with her. They don't want her here; they are troubled by her presence. She sips on her watery beer. The night is going poorly and now she's stuck, waiting for Maddie.

And then Maddie's dad swiftly walks through the front door. He is shorter than most of the guys in the room but they all shift to look at him. In that moment, he seems capable of snapping a small animal by the neck.

"Who are you?" somebody asks.

"Where is my daughter?" he loudly asks the room. None of them answer.

Mr. Nichols sees Margaret and walks right up to her.

"Where's Maddie?" he asks Margaret.

"She was just in the kitchen," Margaret says, her mouth gone dry, but when she follows Mr. Nichols in there, Maddie is gone. The blond guy, gone. Somebody tells Mr. Nichols that they took off a few minutes ago in the blond guy's car. A convertible.

She rides in the passenger seat of Mr. Nichols's sensible Honda Accord, zigzagging with him through the streets of Oak Park, looking for Maddie.

He remains enraged. He doesn't want to talk to her, and she doesn't want to talk to him. There is nothing she can say to make it better.

Eventually they discover her walking alone, in a direction away from the house. She is crying, or maybe she started crying the moment she saw them. As Maddie crawls in the back seat of the car, her terrified eyes meet Margaret's. Margaret offers the front seat but Maddie is sobbing and can't answer. Is Maddie this scared of her father? True, this is the worst stunt they have ever pulled, even worse than pool-hopping and finding a stash of beers the passed-out adults, strangers, had left behind. They stole the beers and hid them in Maddie's room, where her dad found them. Mr. Nichols is angrier now than she has ever seen him, but Maddie is fearless. Her usual mode when they are caught is to turn charming, play innocent. Something doesn't seem right.

Maddie gets grounded for several weeks. Mr. Nichols tells her mom and she doesn't get grounded but maybe, her mom says, it's time to go to an all-girls Episcopalian school in Maryland or New Hampshire or some other state she has no reference for. The pamphlets show up, of earnest, well-adjusted girls in plaid uniforms. Her mom tries to sell it to her as a fresh start. And maybe it wouldn't be so bad; she'd get to escape her life. Or maybe it would get even worse and she'd be kicked out in two months.

When Maddie can see her again, she confides in Margaret about that night. The blond guy had taken her for a ride, but he was so drunk that he slowly rolled up onto a curb and stopped. Maddie thought he might pass out then and there, but instead, he wanted to make out. Reluctantly she kissed him a little, but pushed him away when he tried to take off her underwear from underneath her skirt. He said he wanted to have sex with her. She said, No, I don't want to. *Laughing, he removed a piece of gum from his mouth. At first she thought he was just going to throw it out, but then he yanked down her underwear and wadded it into her pubic hair. She scrambled out of the car with him still laughing. At home, Maddie took a pair of scissors and snipped it out, crying all the while, knowing she couldn't tell her parents, who were so furious they weren't talking to her.*

Margaret was appalled for her friend, but this was what it meant to deal with older boys you didn't know, she assumed. Sometimes they were good, and sometimes they were not. But something lingered in her, a survivor's guilt. That it had happened to Maddie and not her. It didn't occur to her that it shouldn't have happened to either one of them at all.

CHAPTER

SIXTEEN

THE ABSOLUTELY TRUE LAUNDRY hamper escape happened in Bellevue, Washington. The date was May 9, 1991, soon after Brenda lost her virginity to Dylan. For the program's teenaged fans, the thrill of watching the two engage in a particularly lusty kiss in all their prom finery validated one of high school's most enshrined fantasies. The viewers were probably so mesmerized that they didn't notice a boom mic poking into the corner of the frame, one of the gaffes of a show working fast and furious.

At this point, the cast of *Beverly Hills, 90210* had worked enough events to realize that a certain frenzy was building. Nevertheless, no one expected what happened that day at the Bellevue Square mall. The Bon Marché, a department store with several outposts around the Northwest, had advertised on TV about Perry's appearance in the store's junior section, where he was to sign autographs for a predicted crowd of five hundred. Minutes before the four p.m. start of the event, three thousand hyped-up teenagers were lined up outside the store's entrance. Most likely many of these fans were unaccompanied by their parents, because 1991. The crowd only grew by multitudes over the next few minutes.

The *Seattle Times* article by Barbara A. Serrano doled out one delicious bit of mayhem after another. Pushing and shoving quickly turned to girls getting trampled and crushed against the store's brick wall and each other. "We got squished," said Danika Presley, twelve, of Kirkland. "People just kept pushing and cutting in line. It really makes me mad."

Girls climbed over the three-foot hedge near the doors. Others scaled trees and a nearby light pole.

The hired hands for the signing, four off-duty police officers and eight Bellevue Square security officers, were overwhelmed from the start. By four fifteen, Mayday calls were coming in on the police scanner. This was the first the police force had heard about the event; no one expected a mob for a *Teen Beat* guy.

Inside the store, Luke was stationed "near the prom dresses." Imagine Luke's expression as he looked off in the distance and saw racks of Jessica McClintock taffeta and satin knocked down by girls stalking closer to get a look.

Not everyone in the Bon that day was clued in to the store's guest of honor. A saleswoman told the *Seattle Times* that part of the unwieldiness of the event was trying to help customers "who had no interest in Perry." The article quotes two people in their forties who didn't know anything about a Dylan McKay. "Dylan? You mean Bob Dylan?" said one of them.

Very quickly, the event was shut down by the police, the junior section evacuated, and the door locked. In front of the Bon, the aforementioned hedge "looked like cattle had just grazed on it."

In some back room of the Bon, Julie Resnick brainstormed a way to remove her client. "We knew how to get him out of situations like this," she says. There was a time in Beverly Hills when he'd attended a play and word traveled while he was sitting in the theater. To smuggle him out, Resnick camouflaged Luke in a woman's jacket and scarf so he could duck out the back door. Then she sent a man dressed like Luke out the front, to disappoint the fans and paparazzi who were waiting outside.

Luke recalled his panicked calculations in the Bon's back room. "All I saw was my car's over there. There are twenty thousand people between me and it . . . [and the laundry hamper] just happened to have been there. I jumped in it, threw the stuff on, and she just started pushing."

The *Seattle Times* reported that at the end of it all, five girls were injured. "Two suffered ankle injuries, two were treated for hyperventilation, and one reported abdominal pain." Three of the five, ages fourteen to sixteen, were taken to a local hospital, where they were treated and released.

A few months after the Bon, when hopefully all injured parties had been repaired and returned to school, Luke was asked to reflect on being "the hottest thing in America right now for teenage girls."

He didn't pop one of his sly smiles. He was serious. "It's scary. It's dangerous. Hot. Things that get hot . . . burn out quick and they're gone. There's just so much ash. That's not what I want to do."

HER FRIEND PETER GETS HIS license first. His parents give him access to their old sedan, a lumbering car with plush seats and meat-locker-quality air-conditioning. Underneath the steering wheel there is a switch that sets off the world's silliest primitive car alarm. It sounds like a cat in heat.

It is the nineties, but Peter, in his Jimi Hendrix tie-dye and long hair, spiritually resides in the sixties. They cruise around listening to Simon & Garfunkel, Velvet Underground, but also the Pixies and Björk. In her hand is a bowl packed with dry ditch weed, and she hits it, finger tapping on and off the carb, as they glide down the idyllic side streets.

"Ready?" he says.

They are almost there, by the Frank Lloyd Wright houses. As they ride up to the throng of tourists, saddled with high-powered cameras to capture the architectural wonders, Peter flips the switch. The alarm cries, and the tourists turn around. The alarm still whining as they slowly drive by, cracking up at the bewildered stares. Tears roll down her cheeks. Peter coughs from laughing so hard, and pulls over at the end of the block.

"Again," they agree. It's more hilarious the second time because some of the tourists snap their photographs and play along. But Peter and Margaret refrain from a third round. Soon they have to go home. Sometimes they joke about driving to Canada, but the farthest they've ever gone is to the Mars Cheese Castle, a tourist trap an hour away over the Wisconsin state line.

CHAPTER

SEVENTEEN

AFTER THE BON MARCHÉ incident near Seattle, there was another mall visit that ended in multiple hospitalizations. This time, Luke appeared at the Fashion Mall in Plantation, Florida. The security force had been tripled, but it still couldn't contain ten thousand teens. Luke, wearing jeans and a black shirt with the words "rock 'n' roll" on it, was apparently onstage for about ninety seconds. Then, the crowd short-circuited. Kids, packed onto all three floors of the mall, were squeezed, jostled, bruised, and worse as they tried to rush the platform. One fourteen-year-old girl broke her leg. Another complained: "I got hit in the back. People just kept pushing me and pushing me, and they made me spill my Coke."

Luke wasn't hurt, but twenty-one people, ranging in age from eight to thirty-nine, were injured. "I had no idea so many people would come," Perry said afterward. "And I'm very sorry. I wish things had turned out differently. I want all those people out there to know that it wasn't my fault, for one. And two, I really did want to see them. And I'll be back." He did not come back; in fact, for obvious safety reasons, the mall events stopped altogether, but he did telephone all but one of the nine people who were treated at local emergency rooms.

———

Two days after the event, Perry was talking to *Entertainment Weekly*'s Lisa Schwarzbaum for her cover story on the show. She asked if he was upset about the Fashion Mall incident. " 'Feel my pulse,' he dared, holding out a cool, bare wrist. 'Pretty normal, huh?' "

His reaction is curious. Maybe he added, "No, seriously," and then expressed regret for his injured fans, but none of that made it to the page. What it reads like is a guy in his twenties trying to sound tougher than he feels. The verbal equivalent of blowing on your knuckles and rubbing it against your shirt. *Just another day at the office, bro.*

In order to process this runaway train of fame barreling into his life, he must've summoned every coping mechanism possible. On that day, he minimized what was happening to him. Fame was exhilarating—isn't this what he dreamed of back in Ohio?—but it also seems like it was inciting a kind of grief.

"I felt weird the first time my mother ever saw me step out of a limousine," he said around the same time. "I felt very . . . ah, I felt a little guilty, maybe. I felt a little strange. There's a little bit of uncomfortability that goes with having people who've known you all your life, certainly before any of this happened. I'm afraid they'll look at me and say, 'Why, that's not him.' And it *is* me because I don't change who I am for what I'm doing."

He was watching his old way of being disintegrate before his very eyes, but he was hanging on to himself. Still, the fans were resting all of their hopes and dreams for what a man could be on him—or was it Dylan McKay? Did they even know the difference?

"He's just a nice guy who's fine-looking and who's not afraid to show his feelings," said Madeleine Pinzon, seventeen, to a local paper. "If all the guys in the world were like him, everything would be perfect."

EIGHTEEN

FOR ALL THEIR ON-SCREEN chemistry, Luke and Shannen Doherty were mismatched in real life. They came to *90210* with different levels of experience. Doherty was an experienced child actor who'd graduated to dark comedy with *Heathers*, and Luke was a handsome but unknown soap player. As the show rose in prominence, they were equals, appearing with Jason Priestley on the cover of *Rolling Stone*, arguably the show's biggest arrival moment. But the tension remained.

Rosin points out the difference between their modes of preparation. "Shannen would come to the set and not really know what we were working on and memorize [her lines] as they were blocking." Feeding off the last-minute pressure—and perhaps rehearsing as she shot—Doherty "saved it for the last take." Rosin, despite his exasperation with Doherty's procrastination, commends her ability to always deliver an emotionally forceful performance. "She always, maybe more than any other cast member, had the goods."

Luke, on the other hand, was a "first take, best take" kind of guy who had trouble sometimes memorizing his lines—at least in the beginning of the series' tenure. As they continued to shoot, waiting for Doherty to build to her best performance, Luke wavered in consistency. "When he first started working with us," Rosin says, "he was very difficult for the editors because he never did it the same way every time, so they were hard sometimes to edit together." As the show continued, he learned to hone his performance through rehearsal.

Larry Mollin, a *Beverly Hills, 90210* writer who joined for the college years and left by season seven, describes Luke and Doherty's relationship as "frosty," but they respected what their characters shared. He remembers a kissing scene that went rogue after the director yelled cut. "They continued to kiss and kiss and kiss, and it's becoming intense, and hands are moving and it was hilarious," Mollin says. "As characters, they did love each other." They were also obeying one of the show's mantras that was scrawled on a sign in the writer's room: "Kissing is good." For one thing, Mollin said, kissing is a way of slowing a story down and savoring it. As a result of the make-out rule, bottles of mouthwash and mini-sprays were in every dressing room and jeans pocket.

Luke wasn't afraid to confront his costar when necessary. "There was a time," he said, "when I kicked her dressing-room door off and said, 'Shan, let's fix things.' And we did. I can work with her fine now. I don't have to get Shannen out of my sight so I can work, no. If she bothers me the day she comes in and she's late, I let her have it. I think that's why Shannen and I have the relationship that we do."

Distance and time helped Luke gain more perspective. In 2013, he acknowledged that "we had some problems, but those are well-documented . . . I have no hard feelings. I have nothing but love for that young lady." Soon after she made her struggles with breast cancer public, Luke's tone softened all the more, telling the crowd at a fan conference that "none of us would be here without Shannen." It was clear he missed working with her: when asked about reboot plans in 2017, Luke expressed interest in the possibility (a change from some of his lukewarm reactions in the past), citing Doherty as the person he'd love to be paired up with again. In 2018, they finally reconnected in person, after fifteen or so years of going their separate ways. "It seemed like we had only been apart for fifteen minutes," Luke said. "I love her so much."

ROSE'S MOM, SMOKING, LOOKING AT their hair—"You girls have no idea how good you have it right now." The tools: A magenta curling iron that burns foreheads without remorse. A weapon-sized can of Finesse. And next to no time. Two minutes before the homeroom bell will ring, and she hasn't even slurped a bowl of cereal yet, but it is important to take her reddish-brown bangs and clamp them into the curling iron. Lift, then with a twirl of the wrist, tuck the locks into the hot embrace of the metal. The small current of steam rising, because of course the bangs aren't quite dry from the shower twenty minutes earlier. She holds for a taunting minute, till they're close to being singed, then she lets go. They flutter onto her forehead, and she plucks the strands apart until she's gotten it to the preferred state. Out comes the can, infusing every strand with CFCs via its perfumed mist. Some final scrunches and zhuzhes, and she is ready for school. Ready for tenth grade.

CHAPTER

NINETEEN

"IF IT WASN'T FOR Luke Perry, *Buffy the Vampire Slayer* would've never happened," says Fran Rubel Kuzui, the director of the 1992 movie, speaking via Zoom from her home in Tokyo, where she's lived full-time since 2000. For a myriad of reasons, she stopped giving interviews a long time ago about *Buffy*, but today, she's breaking her silence. She wants everyone to know Luke's special connection to the beloved vampire franchise.

In 1991, Kuzui was searching for a new project. Her 1988 film, *Tokyo Pop*, starring Carrie Hamilton as a bleached-blond punk singer on a tour of 1980s Japan, garnered strong reviews, but not enough to inure her from the prejudices of Hollywood. She'd just been fired from her second picture for, in her words, being a female director. No one could blame her for already being in the mood for blood when Howard Rosenman of Sandollar Productions, founded by Dolly Parton and her former manager Sandy Gallin, passed her a script titled *Buffy the Vampire Slayer*, written by twenty-seven-year-old newcomer Joss Whedon. Secretly, she was sold on the title alone, but she dutifully blazed through it over a weekend; by Monday, she sent Rosenman a garlic pizza. She secured the option, thinking she'd make a quirky indie movie. Rewrites with Whedon commenced.

Every major studio rejected *Buffy* in its first iteration, but in its new sharpened form, Twentieth Century Fox expressed interest.

Shortly thereafter—and Kuzui admits she can't remember exactly how it happened—Luke read the script and wanted in. He had recently signed a two-movie deal with the studio. FOX was encouraged; if Luke attached himself, the movie could be a runaway success, but it would only work if the director thought the young star was appropriate for the role of Pike, a wrong-side-of-the-tracks type who, after initially bickering with Buffy, becomes her love interest. Kuzui invited Luke to a meeting at the Mondrian Hotel.

Kuzui hadn't yet seen *90210*, but she found herself intimidated by the level of fuss surrounding Luke. A few minutes before she was to meet him on the patio, she popped into the hotel's gift shop for a pack of mints, only to find his face staring her down from the cover of *People* magazine. But her nerves vanished once she sat down with him on the patio.

"It was like meeting with an old friend," she says. "We just sat and talked and talked. There was never any doubt that I wanted to work with him. He was very enthusiastic and supportive."

———

After a table read, weeks before the shooting began in spring 1992, Luke came up to Kuzui with a concern.

"Have you thought about what you're going to wear on set?"

"No, should I be thinking about this?" As a New Yorker well into her forties, she had her look figured out—artsy but classic, and lots of black.

Luke paused. "Well, there have been a few women directors on the show," he said, referring to *90210*. "And I noticed they all had stylists."

"A stylist? For me to direct a movie?"

"Oh, well, maybe you don't need it." He took in her Armani suit, seemingly for the first time. "Okay, this is going to work," he said.

Looking back, Kuzui says, "It was so cute for this twenty-four-year-old kid to be concerned about me in this way. I had been trying to be supportive of him, and he wanted to give something back, but he didn't know what else to offer me."

However naively, Luke was remarking on a very real culture at the time. Female directors, the few in existence, were under such pressure to prove their worth to a sexist industry that acquiring a stylist for in-person polish probably seemed like a small price to pay. In the early nineties, Kuzui barely had any peers. In the big studio system, there was Amy Heckerling, Penny Marshall, and Kathryn Bigelow. Many of the crew on the set of *Buffy the Vampire Slayer* had never worked with a female director. Yet here she was, making a movie about female empowerment, a statement at stark odds with Hollywood's reality.

Deep into *Buffy*'s six-week shoot at a Santa Monica warehouse, Kuzui walked off the set, frustrated by "unprofessional and unkind" behaviors within her crew. After about fifteen minutes, Luke came to where she had secluded herself.

He sat next to her. "Everybody feels really bad," he said.

"Well, they should," Kuzui answered.

"I know. And I want to apologize for it."

Kuzui looked at him. "If I were a man," she asked, "would this have happened?"

"No."

They contemplated in silence for a moment. Then he asked, "Will you come back to set with me?"

"Sure," she said. "As long as everyone understands that that's not acceptable anymore."

They stood up, and just as Kuzui was about to walk back on her own, Luke surprised her with a big gesture. He swept her off her feet and carried her, damsel-in-distress style. "He wasn't a big guy," Kuzui remembers, laughing, "but I'm pretty small, too." He walked all the way back to set, and then gently placed her right next to the camera.

Luke wasn't responsible for the bad energy that forced Kuzui to take a stand that day, but as a young star on the rise, he possessed the power to shift it. His carrying stunt might've completely rankled someone else, but Kuzui viewed it as supportive and campy, in the spirit of the film itself. And the bottom line was, they trusted each other.

Luke wasn't blind to the feminist import of *Buffy*. In interviews, Luke frequently referred to his character Pike as the "damsel in distress," for getting rescued by Buffy and for being far outpaced by her supernatural fighting skills. Of all the cast members, "Luke and Paul Reubens were the ones who got it the most," Kuzui says. She also credits David Arquette, who Luke folded into the project (he also recommended Kristy Swanson as the heroine; she and Luke were dating around that time). For camaraderie, Kuzui frequently relied on Reubens, who plays a vampire in his first big role post–Pee-wee Herman, and Arquette, who played Pike's friend-turned-vampire, but she called Luke the "great advocate for the film." He understood that playing a man in awe of a woman's strength was both the fun of the movie and its fanged bite at Hollywood's usual fare.

Luke was "always 100 percent present for me," Kuzui maintains, but it was clear "he was being torn in several directions." There was no downtime for him between takes; he was always signing stacks of photos, or being interviewed on the phone, or meeting with Cyd LeVin, his manager. LeVin believed in Luke, and wanted to capitalize on his momentum, which meant keeping him busy. Sometimes he showed up for one of *Buffy*'s many night shoots looking so drained that Kuzui had to ask, "Are you okay?" He downplayed her concerns.

His profile was so high at the time that the production was forced to hide his identity. After three hundred screaming girls showed up at one of their location shoots, an alias was created for Luke on the call sheet. He became Chet. Not to be outdone, Reubens became Beau Hunkus.

Occasionally, Luke got to cut loose in the way that Reubens and Arquette often did during their slow moments. Kuzui recalls one of those times.

"Look, I'm a doll," Luke said, wiggling his miniature replica at Kuzui and Reubens. *Beverly Hills, 90210* had just released the Mattel doll versions of several of the show characters, including Dylan McKay. Dressed in a red jacket, black T-shirt, and faded jeans (he also came equipped with "beach wear," a pair of black board shorts), his doppelgänger was ridiculously tan by human or plastic standards.

The back of the box copy read: "Dylan McKay is not only handsome but also serious and intelligent. Rebellious on the outside and troubled on the inside, he shuns his family's mega-wealthy status. He and Brenda are the hottest couple at West Beverly Hills High. Friends are Brandon Walsh, Kelly Taylor and Donna Martin."

Then, in smaller type, the words that accompanied so many toy commercials of the era: "Each sold separately. Collect them all."

Reubens, no stranger to life as a caricature, was inspired. "Ooh, I'm a doll too!" He returned with Pee-wee Herman by Matchbox, natty in his gray suit and red bow tie. Perry, Reubens, and Kuzui took to the floor and played with the dolls. Luke's stood at a diminutive 11.5 inches, compared to Pee-wee's towering 17. Mattel had gotten the forehead wrinkles right, but Dylan's lips were strangely pursed, as if he'd just bitten into a bad clam. Still, could the two dolls be friends? Could Dylan teach Pee-wee to surf? Could Pee-wee show Dylan how to dance? For that moment, a broken rich boy and a cackling man-child ruled the world.

SHE ADORES THEM; HER FRIENDS, her de facto family. A crew bound by a rousing spirit of cynicism toward high school and a ravenous pleasure in music, weed, film, books, art, humor, beer, and seeing past their current conditions to the beyond. Some of their homes are broken from divorce. Ethan called a radio station when he was eleven and told the DJ, live, that he wanted his parents back together. Margaret is the only one with a dead parent. For now, the matter is dormant. She has stowed it deep.

One night, however, it escapes with Ethan. After a weekend night where the crew polished off a case of beer bought by Ethan's much older brother, they make out a little in his bed, as they did occasionally. It is the first time in a while; he had been in a relationship that just ended. As for her, she hasn't been in a real one since Nathan a few years ago. Relationships require vulnerability, and it is too much for her to summon.

But the alcohol and the closeness wears her down, and the next thing she knows, she is crying in his arms, repeating the words "I miss him so much, I miss him so much, I miss him so much." Is that even true? Does she miss her father? He's been gone on nearly every level that counts since she was ten or eleven years old. She doesn't feel like she has the right to miss him. A version of herself watches and judges her outburst. Ah, the cascade of tears. How melodramatic. She sounds like a soap star gushing it up for the camera.

There is also something strangely reciprocal happening between her and Ethan. He counters her "I miss him so much" with his own, "It's okay, it's okay, it's okay," to the point that they seem like singers trading their parts in the chorus of an inane pop song. He has his own pains but they are not the same pains as hers. He has no wisdom to offer her. No one her age has a dead parent, no one she knows. She is desperate to unlock wis-

dom from someone, and not just her mom's psychiatrist, who turns every question back on her. Couldn't the shrink, or Ethan, or someone, anyone, tell her where to dump this off?

After another hour or so of silence and dozing between them, she gets up late in the night and drives herself home.

CHAPTER

TWENTY

WHILE JULIE RESNICK WAS on her honeymoon in Hawaii, a catastrophe was brewing. Luke was scheduled for a photoshoot with *Vanity Fair* for their July 1992 cover and he was threatening mutiny. "If you don't come for this photoshoot, I'm gonna smoke a cigarette," he informed her. He was sick and tired of playing the good little teen heartthrob.

At this point, *Beverly Hills, 90210* was a juggernaut airing in almost twenty countries, and Luke was arguably its hottest property. "Appearances were all over the place," Resnick recalls. "Photoshoots were all over the place. Movies were all over the place," meaning he had offers from big studios for big pictures with big stars. Resnick and LeVin were trying to steer him one way, while Luke was eager to tear off in another direction. "He wanted the bigger roles in the smaller pictures," Resnick says, while she and LeVin recommended the more cautious path of taking smaller roles in bigger pictures more likely to find critical and box-office success. Both parties wanted a long-term career, but there was little consensus on how to ensure it.

Resnick and LeVin had already clashed with Luke over *Buffy the Vampire Slayer*. She acknowledged that it became a cult favorite, but at the time, "it was a little edgier than what we were looking for him to do." Of course, the edginess was the point. He was "chomping at the bit to release the edginess," Resnick says. And one way was to light up a

Marlboro in front of the big-time people of *Vanity Fair*. Maybe he was only teasing about inhaling on the record, but Resnick wasn't about to take the chance. She flew back early, just to "keep him tame." Luckily, her new husband was very understanding.

Her sacrifice worked—sort of. In the article by Kevin Sessums, a cigarette didn't cross Perry's lips, but they do sneak their way into a kitschy photograph of Luke and Priestley posing together with their pants down around their ankles, wearing conical hats. Both guys clamped a ciggy between their lips, but since it passed as a prop, it wasn't so incendiary. At least for Luke—in another one of Annie Leibovitz's photographs, Priestley appeared again with a cigarette, in keeping with his mission to distance himself from the sanctimonious Brandon.

The story itself is a whole ride. Sessums, a crack interviewer, drew out all kinds of theories and thoughts from Luke, some of them disarmingly vulnerable. The interview was conducted at the Regent Beverly Wilshire on "the first full day of the recent riots in Los Angeles," so the article starts, somewhat improbably, with Luke's take on Rodney King and race relations.

He acknowledged "a lot of pent-up frustrations down there" but he saw "some beauty" in a diversity of people coming together to express their collective rage at systemic racism. "It's unfortunate that it had to [come from] something bad like that, but I think there's a little bit of good in that, too."

Sessums, a gay writer who wrote *Mississippi Sissy*, a memoir of coming out in the Deep South, pushed Luke into territory he might not have ventured into otherwise. He directly asked him the burning question on every queer's mind: Has Luke ever sexually experimented with another guy?

He says "never" but the rest of his answer shows an open mind on the question, which wasn't new to him. For the last couple of years, as the tabloids hinted that he and Alexis Arquette were sexually involved, Luke never denied the rumors. To his thinking, to deny would mean saying that homosexuality was wrong, therefore condemning his friend. "Don't recognize them as some scourge," he told Sessums. "But see them for what they have to give as people before you define them by their sexuality."

He went on to muse that in showbiz, which he called "fag-o-rama," the only gays who "offend[ed]" him are the ones who objected to being noticed as gay. "To me, it should be as open to conversation as anything else." Regardless, he understood why Sessums asked him this titillating question: "Because I'm the handsome leading man, everybody wants to get in my closet and find out I've been a fag." However playfully it was meant, it's jarring to read the word "fag" so many times. Though Luke might've let tabloid speculation on his sexuality go unchecked, he sympathized with Tom Selleck suing the *Globe* for alleging he was gay: "they just took a lot of money out of his pocket." That gripe seemed to have more to do with Luke's feelings on journalistic ethics (he didn't like that they didn't have "proof") than sexuality.

Right before this conversation on the queers, real and imagined, of Hollywood, the most salacious part of the article drops. "What I've found is that I'm very in touch with my feminine side," he said. "I ain't got no problem saying that. Any good actor is. And any good lover is. Meaning that women don't always want to be manhandled. A lot of times they want to be made love to by a man who can do it softly, like a woman." He went on to say that by their nature, women are more affectionate and physical, "more motherly." He said he could give them this side of himself, or "if they want John Wayne, I can give them John Wayne. But most women want a little more—someone who has some sensitivity, who'll take some time." He added, "There are a lot of times that people will misconceive me as being gay when they first meet me."

This quote serves up everything—an embrace of the feminine; love-making technique; the word "ain't" to remind you that this *ain't* no city boy talking; a nod to John Wayne; and mistaken sexuality.

Part of what was so tantalizing about Luke's quote is how his physical expression belied it. Like his former neighbor Leslie Jordan said, Luke was butch in presentation. To a certain kind of lesbian, his pompadour, that soft voice, his wiry frame, it was inspiration. The *Vanity Fair* cover took his rugged masculine energy and turned it up to a camp level. Sitting on a wooden bench, he wore faded jeans heavily dusted in clay-colored earth, dirt-caked black leather boots with a strap around the ankle that must be spurs, a weathered black belt with a silver buckle and some kind of Old Western black leather holster that's twisted off to the side. In his left hand, he loosely gripped an old-timey pistol, resting it on his thigh. His smoldering squint suggested that if you move any closer, why good golly, he'll be forced to put the gun down and slowly unlace your bustier. For unknown reasons, there are two strings tied around both of his thighs—to anchor the holster? Who knows, but the point of the picture is to wonder exactly how long Luke has been wandering the sun-baked vistas, shirtless, with his hair impeccably tousled, ready to seduce harlots and church marms alike.

Luke's bedroom gentility as well as his listening abilities—but with the swagger to give them John Wayne—was the pitch-perfect nineties update on the sensitive man. Hollywood delivers at least a few for every generation, as a counterpoint to the overtly burly and macho. There's Marlon Brando, or there's a sexually ambivalent James Dean. There's an aloof Steve McQueen, or there's Elliott Gould, the shaggy, approachable boyfriend (and one-time Mr. Streisand). The nineties celebrated angsty men—Johnny Depp, Jared Leto, Kurt Cobain—but in hindsight, too much leeway was given. Sensitivity can easily transmute to brooding angst. Wounded men can also be dangerous, capable of weaponizing their emotions to manipulate and gaslight. Luke didn't betray any of those dark inklings. He possessed the empathy and care-taking instincts without the self-destructive tendencies or narcissism. He might've had an ego—what actor doesn't?—but not a monstrous one. He seemed pure.

Resnick wasn't the only person concerned about how the *Vanity Fair* cover story would play. Chuck Rosin was also waiting to see what Luke would do with his biggest publicity opportunity yet. He came away disappointed.

"He made us, the writers, feel that this was a second-rate TV show, which is what a lot of people wanted to say, and did say, about *90210*," Rosin says. Sessums quoted *Vanity Fair*'s media critic James Wolcott, who mocked it as "a tribute to clear skin. . . . The show is the last outpost for American privilege. It is an ad for consumerism and status." In the nineties, in the era of the sellout, calling a show "an ad" was a body slam. Luke didn't exactly dispel the notion when he exclaimed at one point, "I am product! Hear me roar!"

Rosin had reason to be upset. Glaringly absent from the article were any enthusiastic words from Perry about the show itself, or his character. By that point, *Beverly Hills, 90210*, along with *The Simpsons*, had catapulted FOX to a major player with a unique focus on teenagers. It was the number one–rated network with teens, pulling in ratings on par with NBC and CBS for adult viewers aged eighteen through thirty-four. Not that anyone would've guessed from Luke's responses. Only once did he touch upon *90210*: "I try to reiterate to these people writing the show that these kids ain't stupid. They see. They know. Don't be afraid to talk to them about real issues on a real level, because they are way fucking ahead of you."

None of this posturing sat well with Rosin. "The brandishing of the gun?" Rosin says, rolling his eyes. "My whole thing was being against gun violence; I did six or seven shows [about that]." The problems, of course, went beyond the pistol. "The whole thing to me was really kind of distasteful, and for a lack of a better way to describe it, very Gen X. It seemed very immature to me."

Thinking about the timing of the article decades later, Rosin posits that *Vanity Fair* caught Luke at his most frustrated point. For starters, *Melrose Place* had basically taken the Dylan bad-boy mold and issued a 2.0 with actor Grant Show. Most critically, though, Luke was bored. At the end of season two, he was fomenting for major change. Every workday morning at 8:15 a.m., he called Rosin to discuss the scripts, debating over certain lines and directions for his character. "Look," he told Rosin more than once, "I'm going to be this guy forever, this Dylan McKay, so it matters to me." For a while, Rosin staved off his complaints by agreeing to shoot a scene two different ways—the version Luke wanted, and then the original version. Rosin then used his own take every time.

Once Luke got wise, he pushed hard for a shift more radical than a different line. The show had grown stale, he complained, repeating the same dynamic with Brenda, not to mention her overly protective dad, over and over again. "I want to be with the blonde," he told Rosin. This time, Rosin agreed with Luke's critique. And the love triangle that launched a million debates during lunch period was born.

ON THE PHONE, TRADING GIGGLES and commentary with Rose; their primitive version of live-tweeting a TV show. The drama heightens and they both go quiet. Rose's soft breathing in her ear.

A college guy dressed like a cowboy at a Halloween party pins Kelly to the bed, trying to have sex with her in her low-cut witch outfit. Oblivious, Brenda and Donna walk in, at first thinking they've interrupted a consensual tryst, but as Kelly runs up to them crying, saying he wouldn't let her go, they get what's happening. An outraged Brenda calls Dylan. ("It's about to get real!" Rose says.) In bound Steve and Dylan, dressed as Zorro and bank-robber Clyde, respectively, to save the day. They toss the would-be rapist outside. When the cowboy implies to the guys, "I mean, when a girl dresses like a slut," Steve socks him in the jaw for good measure.

While Dylan and Steve fix the situation, Kelly blames herself, saying she led him on. Brenda tells her clearly, twice, that she said no, but she also mumbles, "I tried to tell you that the dress was a little too much." ("I would never say that to you," Margaret promises to Rose.) Donna, sympathetic, barely utters a word, except to say the guy should've taken a cold shower.

Dylan, dapper in his pinstriped suit and fedora, returns from "showing Dale Evans the trail." He stands in the doorway, overhearing Kelly's self-incrimination. He can't stay quiet. "Can I say something? I mean, I know the last thing you need right now is another guy telling you what to do or what to think."

"Go ahead, please," says Kelly.

"You're blaming yourself for leading that guy on. But I want you to know, as a guy, it doesn't matter how much of a magnet a girl turns on, a guy always has a choice of not making her do something she doesn't want to do."

(Margaret: "Who made him the all-knowing?" Rose: "I think it's *sweet!" And maybe it is but the way he had dropped "as a guy," the self-importance, it bothers her.)*

Kelly, still in tears, counters, "I didn't make that choice very easy now, did I?"

"Yeah, you did," Dylan affirms. "You said no."

Brenda, stronger than ever in her conviction: "And what happened after that isn't your fault."

"I guess you're right," Kelly says.

A few minutes later, Donna, shaken out of her quietude, tells it like it is: "He was a rapist." When Kelly balks, Donna asks, "What would've happened if we hadn't come in here?"

———

After the episode ended, Rose and Margaret's conversation turns to guys they've heard things about, the stories and facts vague but too serious to ignore. These rumors are protective code, passed around from girl to girl, leaping over social strata and grades. Billy who had probably raped Casey. Dan slapped Liz every time they argued. Another guy who felt up a girl while she slept at a party.

They don't linger over Kelly's almost-rape. Their reality is brimming with more pressing problems: Rose's fights with her older sister; the dramas of their respective friendship groups; the crush who won't respond.

But long after she and Rose hang up, the episode still turns over in her mind. Kelly and Brenda were the ones who walked in first, curtailing the assault by surprising the guy, allowing Kelly to escape his clutches. But it was the two men who physically removed him. They possessed the ultimate authority, in brute strength and from a moral high ground. It was only after Dylan weighed in—"as a guy"—that all the women became more secure in their positions that it wasn't Kelly's fault.

What happens when the good guys don't appear? At nearly sixteen, her experience had already borne out that no one comes to the rescue. Almost never. Maddie's dad was an extreme rarity. Her knowledge wasn't gained from an encounter like Kelly's; she is fortunate, so far, that she hasn't suffered that depth of trespass, but there have been plenty of lesser invasions.

——

Michael is perched on his navy-blue bedspread, the childhood soccer trophies on his bookshelf. Band posters on the wall. A sitcom set of a high school boy's bedroom. Except for the Macintosh Classic on the desk, a sign of wealth. He had isolated her from the group hang and asked her to come over, and she was curious to see inside one of the biggest houses in Oak Park.

She had followed him down the carpeted hallway past several closed doors to his room. Their house was unnervingly quiet and palatial, though she hadn't seen much of it as he had whisked her immediately upstairs.

His hands tightly clenched in his lap, he broaches the topic.

"So, I have feelings for you, and I think there is something between us." She can hear him swallowing. "I'm wondering: Would you like to go on a date with me?"

This is the first time they've ever hung out one-on-one. From the safe vantage of the pack, she'd noticed that he was gawky and super smart, with an odd, elaborate sense of humor. She had laughed at many of his jokes—too much? He wasn't even that funny, but she appreciated the effort. His brain, she imagines, is exacting, clicking with theories and ideas, but she doesn't want him. His teeth are a batch of metal, his lips bulge. She regrets taking a seat on the bed with him.

"I don't think I feel that way about you."

He blinked away her response.

"You 'don't think'? Then how do you know?"

"I just don't . . ." she says, dwindling off.

"Well, if you don't know, that means we should try," he says, solving a theorem. "You can't know until you try."

"*Try what?*" she dares to ask.

"*A date. I'll take you out for pizza. How would you like that, hmm?*"

His parental tone throws her. She is being coaxed into a cage.

"*I don't think a date—*"

He cuts her off. "*How about this? Let's kiss. Would you want to try that and see how it feels?*"

"*Michael,*" she says, "*I don't want to.*" She is making it clear now, just as she'd seen on TV, but it had always been the theoretical stranger. Not her friend.

Rapid blinks. "*If we kiss, then you'll know for sure how you feel. It doesn't make sense to say no if you don't know for sure.*"

"*I just don't think it's going to change my mind.*"

"*Just try, okay?*"

His hand smashes over hers as he swiftly closes the gap between them. She understands now that she isn't going to get out of here without relenting. Not unless she wants to hurt him—and then what might happen? She acquiesces. The math is coldly clear. His desire is the greatest number, gobbling up her small digit, her confusion, her lack of clarity about not her feelings but how to voice them.

Lips and teeth push their way into her mouth, his tongue washing over hers, twice, and then goes in for more, but she rips herself away. He leans in again, and she springs off the bed.

"*What are you doing?*" he says in disbelief.

An appalling silence hangs between them. Somewhere, a twinge of arousal from being touched—she is a riot of hormones—but she hates herself for this. Then, him. He is putting himself back in order, ready to declare a victory. Filled with rage, she clenches her jaw, not making a sound, betraying nothing.

"*That was nice,*" he says. "*Let's get pizza soon.*"

CHAPTER

TWENTY-ONE

AT THE MANOR, THE annual Spelling Christmas Eve party was off to a merry start, swinging with friends, business associates, and the cast of *90210*. The Spellings served their traditional spread of shrimp cocktail, caviar, and sandwiches from Nate 'n Al's, an old-school Hollywood deli. Champagne was liberally refilled, never letting a drinker drain their crystal flute. The pianist kept up a stream of "O Come All Ye Faithful" and other festive songs; the carolers were due at any minute.

The centerpiece of the party was an eighteen-foot Christmas tree, decorated by a fleet of workers, because this was Aaron Spelling's way. You can take the Christmas-loving Jewish boy out of Texas, but you can't take the Texas out of the Christmas-loving Jewish boy. Go big as Houston hair on a church Sunday, or not at all.

This was Tori's favorite party, the most "normal" of social offerings from her very extra parents, but this year, she was nervous. Her scowling boyfriend Nick was in attendance, persona non grata with not only Candy and Aaron, but her castmates. Nick, as Tori described him, was an awful partner. He cheated on her, she alleges, and constantly called her ugly. She claims he leached money from her and spent it at clubs without her. He convinced her to buy a Porsche Carrera, a car she had no interest in, and then totaled it a week later. She never caught him firsthand, but she suspected him of screaming at their pet parrot and blowing cigarette smoke in its face. Even Shannen Doherty, picker of notorious flameouts, called Nick "bad news."

Yet, for a complicated host of reasons, and because she's only nineteen, she stuck with him. Wealth didn't inure Tori from an unhealthy family culture that left her feeling inadequate and lonely. Aaron and Candy loved their daughter, but they eschewed honest conversation, and often handled conflict with letters or the silent treatment. Their distaste for Nick was clear from their pained faces, but they never spoke of it to Tori.

When Jason and Luke entered the already-rollicking party, Tori beelined over to ask them, just maybe, could you say hello to Nick, too? Priestley, a diplomat, made his way over for a stiff handshake, but Luke, who initially agreed to her request, didn't cross the room for Nick. Other conversations distracted him or, more likely, he never planned to acknowledge him in the first place. Luke, eight years older than Tori, was intimidating, flirty, but inaccessible. He called her "Camel" for her long eyelashes, a compliment and a tease. Whenever they chatted, he made her feel like the only other person in the world, but she'd never had a heart-to-heart with him. And she definitely couldn't make him do anything he didn't want to do.

Stinging from the snub, Nick decided to bring their long-simmering tension to a head. He stepped up to Luke.

"What's your problem?"

"You're my problem," Luke answered. "I love her, and you should not be in her life."

Then Luke pushed him—and it zinged off from there. Luke, who longed to avenge his mother, didn't hold back. They punched and shoved each other, brawling dangerously close to the eighteen-foot Christmas tree, its weighted boughs threatening to drop pinecone-sized ornaments gleaming in gold. The pianist frantically tinkled on, distracting most of the party from the spectacle, but those nearby couldn't look away. One of them was Jennie Garth, who'd already sparred with Nick over the treatment of her good friend. Maybe she hoped Luke would finish him off.

Before the big tree went timber, Jason extracted Luke from the tangle and walked him outside. Nick stormed out of the party altogether. Tori was convinced this marked the end for her and Nick.

Outside, she told a still-inflamed Luke through sobs that she hated him. Somehow, all this drama didn't stop the party cold. Instead, the carols and champagne were brighter and bubblier than ever. Her parents didn't utter a word about the fight, but they'd soon secretly enter therapy, in hopes of learning how to pry their beloved Tori out of Nick's grip.

———

A few months later, the cast, led by Luke, staged an intervention to confront Tori about her rapidly devolving relationship. In a spare dressing room, they all took turns telling Tori how they felt about Nick, and how much they loved her. Enough was enough; they didn't want him on set anymore. Tori protested, pointing out that they were only making things harder on her, but the collective held their ground. She didn't talk to Luke, the ringleader, for weeks after that.

Tori, in her own time, snapped out of Nick's toxic thrall. During a fight with Nick that echoed so many others, something in her shifted. She recognized his language as the same slander that had hurt her in all the tabloids, ridiculing her acting, her appearance, her plastic surgeries. Finally, she was able to say for herself, enough is enough. She enlisted friends to dump all his clothes on the lawn of his sister's house and cut ties for good.

In the end, Luke's effort wasn't lost on her. He risked Tori's wrath in order to do the right thing. "I never really thanked Luke Perry properly—for hating Nick enough to throw a few punches, and for staging a bad-boyfriend intervention on the set of *90210*. So thank you, Luke, for being a real friend."

ON WEDNESDAY NIGHTS, HER FRIENDS convene at Audrey's house to watch a double-header of Beverly Hills, 90210 and Melrose Place. Audrey's older brother Mitch and his friends sometimes pile in, shifting draped limbs out of the way. Margaret and her new close friend, Audrey, are the primary viewers. Audrey is so alive, in a way Margaret can't yet access. She almost watches her like a TV show: Her red hair ("it's actually orange," Audrey always says); her laugh that rings above the noise of a room. She carries an army bag that she spray-painted the name of her favorite band on: the Smiths. She loves the things that she loves—cigarettes, acrylic paints, Morrissey at his haughtiest—with no apologies.

The dialogue to the shows is barely audible outside the chatter, the groans, and calls for more Diet Coke or cheese fries from the local hot dog place. By this time, the mid-nineties fashions have altered the 90210 cast as well as Audrey, Margaret, and the rest of their friends. Raisin-toned lipstick, tapestry vests, sunflowers everywhere, beloved by Vincent van Gogh and then a billion nineties girls.

It's easy to see when the characters of 90210 misstep, and then to reap the chaos that ensues: when David Silver swigs his speedy OJ to get through his DJ sessions; when Brenda rushes off to marry Stuart; when Steve won't drop the awful John Sears frat. The worst is when their beloved Dylan is taken by Suzanne. He, out of all of them, is always supposed to be one step ahead of the world's sleazes and scammers. If you buy the show's dubious math, he'd done all this hard-core shit by the time he was thirteen, including "running cars." He knew Stuart as a drug dealer back in the day. What happened?

Not too long after Kimberly Shaw removes her wig on Melrose Place, *revealing her patchy hair, scar, and the show's unrelenting penchant for storylines that ratchet past insanity, both shows lose their grip on Audrey and Margaret. College is looming. Brenda is gone. Dylan is a fool. Nothing is the same anymore.*

CHAPTER

TWENTY-TWO

MARK ESPINOZA HAD TWO auditions that day in 1993. The first was for *NYPD Blue* as a gang member, and he poured his all into it. He'd be the tatted-up Latino stereotype they needed him to be. Anything to advance his career, to get out from sleeping on a mattress at his friend's house.

The second, he assumed, was for a burrito salesperson, the other part he was frequently offered. It was for the show with all the beautiful people on it, that he'd seen on covers all over the grocery stores in Chicago, where he'd been acting in theater a few weeks before, and in Beaumont, Texas, where he was from. But that was not it, his agent informed him. He'd be playing a boyfriend for, hmm, probably a couple of episodes. Espinoza didn't think he stood a chance, but he went anyway, because that's what an actor does.

The audition with *90210* casting director Dianne Young went so well, she asked him to come back later that afternoon to meet the producers. In Van Nuys, he encountered a roomful of ten or so other Latinos, none of them as dark as he was from playing tennis and running outside. They were all twenty-seven-inch waistlines with full heads of hair. Espinoza, in his mid-thirties, was already thinning out a bit on top. There was no way he'd beat out these other guys. In his nicest button-down, he took a seat and discreetly fixed his hair to look thicker.

In the room, he joked with Chuck Rosin and writer Larry Mollin, keeping it light and easy. He wasn't nervous—why get tense about something that wasn't going to happen? But, improbably, it kept happening. A day or so later, he met Aaron Spelling. He came around the table to shake his hand, Texan to Texan. A FOX casting director told him later that was a no-no, getting that personal with the big boss. But Spelling reacted warmly, and Espinoza got the part.

His agent: "Are you sitting down?" The part wasn't just for two episodes, it was for two years. That's when the nerves finally hit him. What was this world-famous series, with its all-white cast, going to do with a Latino character?

———

He showed up to work a few days later and was relieved to meet the actor who would share nearly all of his scenes. "Gabrielle Carteris could not have been nicer," he says. "And we're still great friends. She couldn't have been cooler, and I thought in that moment, 'I'm okay. This is going to be okay.'"

Still, he was joining an established show in its fourth season, and fault lines were rumbling. Shannen Doherty would soon be fired; Priestley and Luke were annoyed with the scripts, wanting more as actors; and he could tell that Carteris, especially by the fifth season when she had a baby at home, was eying the door.

He didn't let any of the drama distract him. Espinoza prided himself on his work ethic, always on time, lines down cold, but by the fifth season, he was frustrated too. His character, Jesse Vasquez, introduced as a law student working through school as a bartender, gets hitched to Carteris's Andrea in a rush job, to accommodate the actress's real-life pregnancy. In the show, Andrea has unprotected sex once, and bam, it's baby time for her and Jesse, prompting their charmless courthouse wedding. The storylines were thrown at them hard and fast.

Espinoza was disenchanted with the paint-by-numbers aspects to his character. Jesse was a big baseball fan and his mother drove a bur-rito truck. Growing up as one of the few Latino families in Beaumont, Espinoza played tennis and loved—still does—Irish music. Couldn't Jesse have been more off-script too? Espinoza was acutely aware of what his representation meant; at the time, he was one of five, he estimates, Latino characters on primetime television (there were even fewer La-tinas), not to mention the first main cast member of color on *Beverly Hills, 90210.*

At a press dinner promoting the fifth season, a reporter asked him, "What are they going to do about your hair?" The table fell silent. Espi-noza says, "I wanted to pop off, but I didn't." He took a beat and recov-ered with something like, "We'll do what we need to do." Then he smiled the guy straight into hell.

In general, Espinoza felt a different obligation than his costars. "Not that I felt a *huge* responsibility, but I owed it to other Latin actors to keep my shit together. . . . This will sound terrible, but at that point, if a white actor popped off, a good-looking dude especially, he was a tem-peramental actor. But if a brown actor did it, he was a problem actor."

He credits Luke, Carteris, and Jason Priestley for keeping him grounded. "With those guys, I never felt lost. And it would have been very easy to have gotten eaten up in that environment."

He understood why Luke was pushing for more challenging mate-rial. "He deserved more . . . Luke was a completely underrated actor," Espinoza says. "Luke never made it about Luke. He knew how to hand over a scene. He was so generous that way. And not all actors are like that."

Though most of his scenes were opposite Carteris, or group scenes, the times that he acted with Luke stand out in his mind. In one episode, when stubbled Dylan is on a bender, he comes to Jesse's bar, having just discovered that Kelly and Brandon fell in love behind his back.

Jesse and Dylan are happy to see each other at first, until Jesse real-izes that the underage Dylan has been served "a Macallan, neat, don't be stingy, eh?" by another bartender. Jesse won't allow it. He takes away the drink and they face off. A blonde next to Dylan flirts her way into the conflict, handing the scotch back over to him. Not so fast. A security guard horns in.

"Jesse, do we have a problem here?"

"Yeah, I'm afraid we do," Jesse answers.

Then Dylan pipes in, "Yeah, we do. It's terrible. You see, someone's crossed a lawyer with a bartender."

Before Dylan can suffer the humiliation of being tossed out, the blonde says there are better ways to get a drink, wink-wink, and off they go. Dylan leaves a dollar, telling Jesse to give it to a "real bartender" if he sees one. Even when he's on the downslide, Dylan still tips and gets the girl.

For that scene, Luke wanted to rehearse with Espinoza several times, nailing down the movements, the timing, the shift in mood. "I could probably count on one hand how many actors I've worked with who actually liked to rehearse. He was so giving in that way."

He recalled another episode when Jesse, on the outs with Andrea, goes to live with Dylan for a couple of days. It doesn't go well; Jesse tries to pump Dylan for information about Andrea's affair with a med student, but off camera, "we had so much fun together, just joking around. It was the best time. I felt like I was one of the guys when I got to work with him, instead of just saying hi in the hallways."

Luke and Espinoza shared a working-class hustle that made them see no divisions between themselves and the people working in less glamorous positions on the show. They both loved talking with Nikki, the guard at the front gate. After *90210*, Espinoza and Luke stayed in touch through Andy Sacks, a production assistant on the show who eventually won an Oscar in 2004 as a producer for *Two Soldiers*, a short film.

On the TV show *Major Crimes*, it was Sacks, the show's producer, who knocked on Espinoza's trailer and said, "There's someone here to see you." Espinoza, a recurring character on the police procedural from 2016 to 2017, couldn't imagine who it was, but there was Luke, standing in the blazing-hot sun in crutches. He was there to visit Sacks, but he insisted on hobbling over even though he was recovering from surgery on both of his feet. "It had probably been a couple of years since I had seen him, but he wasn't going to leave the set until he saw me. That meant the world to me." Luke, as he always did when he greeted Espinoza, gave him a hug and then a big tug on his earlobe. Espinoza is the first to say he's been blessed with Dumbo wings. "He was always so affectionate and genuine. And just good. That's just who he was, and he brought that with him wherever he went."

CHAPTER

TWENTY-THREE

"I would ride every morning before I went to the studio. I learned to jump before National Velvet *because I just loved the feeling of flying. I could jump six feet bareback, and it was the closest thing to being Pegasus and flying next to God."*

—Elizabeth Taylor, *Interview*, 2011

THE SECOND TIME LUKE died on-screen was in *8 Seconds*. (The first time was in *Terminal Bliss*, a movie he hated so much, it barely warrants this parenthetical.) The 1994 biopic covers the brief but vibrant career of charismatic bull-rider Lane Frost, the youngest ever to win the world championship in 1987. Oklahoma's pride met his end at the age of twenty-five after getting horned in the back by a bull ominously named Takin' Care of Business at a 1989 competition, causing his broken ribs to puncture his heart and lungs. After his death, Frost, already beloved for his kind and friendly demeanor, ascended to legend in rodeo circles. Luke had never been cast before as a real-life person, and he was deeply moved to play Frost. The movie stands out as one of the most person-ally resonant of his career, and one with a surprising amount of staying power in American culture.

Though he discovered the script for *8 Seconds* around the same time, he made *Buffy the Vampire Slayer* first, which floundered at the box of-fice. Luke fought hard to get *8 Seconds* greenlit in his newly less-potent position. Hollywood doesn't easily grant second chances, especially for a niche topic. Bull-riding was a relic from another era, not to mention a faded genre, the Western, neither of which appealed much to people outside of rural America. But Luke pressed on for a couple of years, pitching studio after studio, motivated by his kinship with the milieu. He'd grown up around horses and cattle, and all the complicated ways they fused with country life. Animals are pets, like Jerry Lee, and domestic workers. They can also be a source of frightening power that we strap ourselves to for seconds at a time, at the risk of our lives. He understood the stoic people who thought poetry could be found on the back of seventeen hundred pounds of writhing muscle.

For all his innate comfort, he still had to undergo a transformation to convincingly inhabit the part. A dialect coach instilled in him the true Panhandle twang. Several cowboys were on set to baptize Luke in the sweat of the beast which a rider has to stay on for eight seconds, the minimum amount to be counted in competition. Luke insisted on doing the riding himself; at one point, Perry was thrown and suffered a separated shoulder. Begrudging respect was paid by the ten-gallon hats on hand.

For the film, he performed all or nearly all his own stunts, riding the bull as if he was born on the spine of one. ProRodeo Hall of Fame bull-rider Gary Leffew trained Luke for several months before the shoot with horses, simulations, visualizations, and role-playing. (Luke, for insurance reasons, wasn't allowed to train on real bulls before filming.) Leffew, known as "the bull guru," also had him watch twenty minutes of Frost's highlights every day.

Leffew recalled Luke's "incredible work ethic," which continued after the film wrapped. The day after shooting ended, Luke and Leffew went out bull-riding.

"I was hoping he'd go three or four good jumps but I didn't think he'd finish the way he did," said Leffew. "He did everything identical to Lane Frost, including riding the bull and making a beautiful ride, stepped off perfectly on his feet—which is hard for a lot of guys to do, even seasoned pros—did that little signature wave of Lane Frost's, and people went crazy! You would have thought Lane Frost came out of the grave and rode the bull for him, it was that incredible."

One of the cowboys on the set, Tuff Hedeman, Frost's real-life best friend, played with swagger by Stephen Baldwin in the movie, has sung Luke's praises ever since. In 2021, he said: "Luke Perry's the only reason that [8 Seconds] didn't turn out into a total shitshow."

During the filming, with Oscar-winning *Rocky* director John Avildsen at the helm, Hedeman liberally called bullshit. What they were showing wasn't realistic bull-riding, in his opinion. The production, according to Hedeman, asked him to exit the set, tired of his meddling ways, but Luke pulled him aside and reassured him that he would do right by Frost. And it seems that he did please the people closest to the fallen hero. After Luke died, Frost's mother Elsie praised Luke's portrayal.

"He was so conscientious of wanting to do it the way it should be done. He would come to us and ask us, 'How would Lane talk in a situation like this?' And he watched a lot of videos of Lane; so he actually had some mannerisms like Lane and actually he looked quite a bit like Lane once they got the hat on him and stuff. It was kind of eerie."

In the end, none of the actors involved—not Perry; not Cynthia Geary, who plays his wife (their early marriage tangles are some of the movie's best scenes); nor Baldwin, the most fiery of the personalities on hand—could save the movie from a lukewarm reception. Not even Renée Zellweger, in one of her first film roles, playing a groupie billed in the credits as "Buckle Bunny." *8 Seconds*, most critics complained, was too polite with Frost's legacy, though the blame was mostly put upon screenwriter Monte Merrick. The critiques were fair: there's not much on-screen to rattle or challenge anyone, and yet, at the same time, it doesn't reach the inspired heights of *Rocky* or any other movie that illuminates a physical whole body-and-spirit bewitchment like bull-riding. About the only entity riled up at the sentimental fare was PETA, which ran an advertisement in the *Hollywood Reporter* against the movie's romanticization of the rodeo scene with the headline LUKE PERRY—HEARTTHROB OR HEARTLESS?

Whatever its shortcomings, *8 Seconds* carved out a rare audience, one not often held in Hollywood's gaze. And to that audience in particular, Luke's Lane Frost made an impact more than any other character he brought to life. Writing in *Rolling Stone* after Luke's death, West Texas native Thomas Mooney attested to the movie's effect: "Before *8 Seconds*, those small rodeos felt isolated and cut off from the world. But after the spring of 1994, they somehow became important, something that, at least during the run-up to the film, everyone was talking about. It was a national spotlight illuminating the most local of pastimes, and watching Perry portray Frost (not as some hero cowboy archetype, but as a flawed, real-life everyman) felt like the world learning what a cowboy's life was really like." Seeing the movie now, in this era of the fractious urban versus rural narrative, drives home the value of reaching into those small dusty towns more than ever.

When Luke performed Frost's final moments, trying hard not to interpret the man but to actually *be* him, he channeled a death radically different from how it's usually experienced and depicted. The end of life is often an antiseptic affair, an orchestrated lowering of function through medications and machines in a hospital room or a hospice bed at home. By contrast, Frost's last moments, as tragic as they were, were also sacred and ancient. The human spirit punctured by the beastly one has the ring of a myth, a portal to one of the mysteries of existence. In *8 Seconds*, bulls are a conduit to our unconscious, the personification of our wild, unthinking side, which is essential to the rodeo mindset. Leffew says the unconscious, not the ego or analytical brain, is what's needed to ride successfully. Before Luke as Frost was struck, his unconscious mind was arriving at lightning-fast decisions on instinct. On the bull, in full communion with Frost, he was close to the twilight world. A moment later, Luke died a death that was closer to his spirit than his actual death decades later.

CHAPTER

TWENTY-FOUR

"THE CHILD IS FATHER to the Man" was an episode in season three where Luke played two versions of Dylan McKay, one at age thirteen, and the other his present-day self, a senior in high school. For several episodes prior, Dylan had reconnected with his criminal father Jack McKay, a flash smiler with sandy hair and duplicitous charm. Once the father-son relationship bore enough hints of acceptance and trust to trick viewers into being happy for Dylan, the show blew up his dad in a fiery car bomb. He is presumed dead (let's not dwell on the character's return in season ten). Dylan attended the funeral service, as well as a reception of sorts at the Walshes. "My mom made a big spread," Brandon says.

Charles Rosin said that when Luke first read the script, he didn't catch that he was playing both characters. And indeed, Young Dylan's lines, which Luke rightly identified as the script's best ones, were almost delivered by another actor. Before Chuck and Karen Rosin showed their script to Luke, they ran an outline by Spelling, telling him that Young Dylan's part would require an excellent child actor, not an easy last-minute find. Spelling suggested Luke play both parts, providing the actor with a remarkable showcase, a rare one in a show defined by its ensemble cast.

The director of the episode, James Whitmore Jr., started as an actor before directing many of the era's biggest TV shows, including *21 Jump Street*, *Dawson's Creek*, *The X-Files*, and *Buffy the Vampire Slayer*. Whitmore praised Perry's "brilliant" performance, though not everything was perfect, to his mind. Regarding a pivotal car scene toward the end, Whitmore wished he had given Luke more guidance. "Luke had a tendency to want to yell," Whitmore recalled. Over time, Luke learned to modulate one of his most distinctive tools through voice-over work. He played not only himself on *The Simpsons* and *Family Guy* but other characters, including Sub-Zero in *Mortal Kombat: Defenders of the Realm*.

Regardless, Whitmore reserved his highest accolades for Luke: "I'll say this to the day I die, but Luke was the most committed, most passionate thespian I ever worked with in my life. He wanted nothing more than to be a great actor. He wanted to explore, he wanted to go deep, he wanted to take chances, he wanted to tell the truth."

Perry's costars also recognized the depth of this particular performance. On their podcast, *9021OMG*, where Jennie Garth and Tori Spelling rewatch each episode and then convene to discuss, Garth and Spelling were floored by this one. "This is Emmy-worthy acting," Garth said, "and it's a travesty this was not recognized . . . He was already a star, but this is when people realized the depth of his ability to bring you to your knees.

"I've seen all those parts of Luke in different situations and conversations and settings and it's so fascinating how that's all in somebody. That anger and all those things he was playing with."

It also pained her as a dear friend of Luke's. "This episode, from beginning to end, is agonizing . . . and now it's even harder to watch, just having lost Luke and dealing with his death. Ugh, I can't even get into it."

But she does a little bit more: "Everyone magically left [my] house as I was watching it, and when we get to the end, you see Luke, Dylan, and, whoa, I just had a major breakdown. I went right back to that feeling of losing him."

Rosin submitted the episode for an Emmy, but it was ignored. The series never did garner much in terms of awards. The single Emmy nomination (not win) it ever received was for Milton Berle's guest turn in 1995.

IT IS HER BIRTHDAY, AND it is sad. Nineteen. Lying in her dorm bed crying so much that her roommate, a premed student who has unicorn posters and open-heart surgery photographs pinned to her wall, left the room.

She doesn't want to be here. This Midwestern super-sized university with more kids wearing ten-gallon jug hats than she's ever seen, like she is in that Luke Perry movie, 8 Seconds. On her walk to anthropology class one morning, she tried to strike up a friendly conversation with one of the cowboys. He answered monosyllabically and then speed-walked away from her. Is it because her hair is half-turquoise from Manic Panic and she has a nose ring? Maybe it's because she had no idea that "agriculture" was a major, so she laughed in surprise when he said it. She still feels bad about that.

She joined the radio station, to find her people. A better fit, but she is still mortified that she played the explicit version of "Get It Together" from the Beastie Boys and Q-Tip and not the radio edit. The FCC, if they were listening, could fine the radio station thousands of dollars for every golden nugget of profanity. The next day the station manager, always in the same Yo La Tengo shirt, said lightly but clearly annoyed: "It's not that hard to play the right one, Margaret."

A birthday card from her mother sits on her desk, with a few lines written in her distinctive tidy cursive; this is her mom's preferred way of reaching out. Her mom rarely calls. The card says her mom is proud of her, her mom misses her. It's what she wrote, anyway. There is also a check for a hundred dollars, the monthly sum her mom sends, but only when Margaret calls to remind her. Each time she asks about money, her mom always says, "Oh-kaaaay," in this tone like Margaret has fucked up. If only she could tear up the check, and all the others, and mail back the pieces. But she needs the money.

She will be leaving after the semester, transferring to college in Chi-cago. She and Audrey already planned to get an apartment together. Her boyfriend back home, Adam, is waiting to rekindle. They had gotten to-gether a few months before she left; they talk every night. She will be leav-ing this school, this dorm, the few friends she has made. She's saddest to leave Fatima, with her sweet laugh, her sardonic eyes. Fatima is tortured about lying to her strict Muslim parents about her drinking, her lack of daily prayer. Margaret wonders if she would have felt something similar if her dad had lived. Would he understand her at all? She thinks about her father watching The 700 Club, *with Pat Robertson spewing garbage about feminism and "homoseckshuals." As a child, she had cuddled up on her father's lap while he watched, having no idea what these boring people were going on about.*

It is almost four p.m., and she swings her legs out of the bed to get her-self together for her shift at the two-pound burrito place. That is its claim to fame: a tortilla wad that drunk college boys try to eat in one sitting. "Time to make the burritos," she says aloud to no one, weakly laughing. It's a twist on the old Dunkin' Donuts "Time to make the donuts" ad. Millions of commercial slogans, TV theme songs, and characters from sitcoms live in her head. "Calgon, take me away," "I can't believe it's not butter," "Baby, rain or shine, all the time, we've got each other," Dwayne Wayne's glasses.

Recently she caught an episode of Beverly Hills, 90210 *after not hav-ing seen it for months. They are in college now, most of them, but she was shocked to find Dylan down in the muck of drugs, wearing a black cutoff shirt, grizzled and hungover. She was caught between finding the lurid melodrama of his drug use funny; thinking Dylan was undeniably sexy this way; and feeling sorry for him, inside the show and outside. The writers were slowly denigrating his character to create drama. A necessity, she supposed, to keep the plot lines juicy, but she missed how flawlessly cool and in control he was in the beginning seasons. The way he was with Brenda, before the triangle. Maybe they'd let him suffer for a while and then he'd come back stronger than ever.*

Still, when he rejected Brandon's concern, instead uttering the line: "May the bridges I burn light the way," she felt fired up along with him.

———

At the burrito place, the night wanes. The first wave of party boys come in, to be felled by more rice and beans than the human body is supposed to consume in one sitting. She rings up their orders, morose, shrunken in her too-big work shirt. Her boss, Javier, comes in around eleven thirty p.m., right before the end of her shift. He is gregarious, always full of energy. She finds him to be cheering, even if he didn't give her the night off for her birthday. He did promise to come in with a surprise.

"This," he says, dangling a tiny red fruit in front of her, "is an insanely hot pepper, one of the spiciest in the world. I ordered the seeds from a catalogue. Are you ready?"

"For what?"

"To take a nibble."

"Oh no," she says. "You must have me mistaken for someone else."

"Come on!" he says. "What you have to realize about spice is that it'll burn like a motherfucker and then, the feeling will come."

"What feeling?"

"You'll see."

She looks at him. His enthusiasm is impossible to refuse. What else does she have going on tonight? Why not get rocked by a pepper?

The specimen in her hand. The oily heat of it already emanating onto the skin of her palm. He watches her pick it up by the stem. She starts to nibble off the bottom.

"More."

It is assaulting her tongue. The scalded flesh of her mouth reaches new layers of pain, and then falls numb. Tears roll down her cheeks. Then it spreads fire all the way to her chin. Javier watches every second, laughing hysterically, not with malice but with joy.

"Oh my fucking god," she says when she can talk again.

"Are you there yet?"

She pauses. Yes. An elation surges, under the fluorescents. Ecstasy, standing in the kitchen she'd never see again in a couple of weeks. Trembling from the recovery in front of Javier, soon to be a stranger, who is holding out a beer for her.

"Happy birthday," he says. "You made it."

She smiles at him through her torched lips.

CHAPTER

TWENTY-FIVE

IN 1995, AFTER THE supermarket tabloids had speculated for months that Dylan McKay was about to meet an untimely end on *Beverly Hills, 90210*, FOX president John Matoian told TV writers gathered for fall previews that Perry would be leaving after the first ten episodes of the sixth season. "He wants to make movies," Matoian said. "If there's a break in his schedule, he's open to coming back occasionally."

Aaron Spelling piped in to confirm that Dylan would, more or less, be kept in cryogenic freeze, ready to be thawed at a moment's notice. "We have come up with a dramatic way for Luke to leave the show, but it will not be anything traumatic like a death or disabling illness," Spelling said. "We want him back as much as we can get him."

For his departure, Luke chose his final love interest.

Ever since Rebecca Gayheart saw Sissy Spacek in *Coal Miner's Daughter*, set some sixty miles away from her rural Kentucky town, she wanted to be an actress. She decamped to New York City at fifteen. By the early nineties, she was studying theater at the Lee Strasberg Institute and splashing water on her face as a Noxema girl on TV when she got the call from her agent to consider a role in *Beverly Hills, 90210*. Her agent, who also represented Luke, explained that the actor, after seeing her picture and viewing her work, insisted on her and no one else to play the love of Dylan McKay's life. Maybe Luke saw a resemblance to his wife; both women have enviable manes of curly dark blond hair. Gayheart was reluctant to leave New York, but intrigued by the offer.

The two actors spoke on the phone and instantly hit it off. He struck her as genuine and grounded, which went a long way toward soothing her nerves about joining *90210*'s famously cliquey cast. On her first day at fittings, Luke popped his head in to say hi. "We just decided from the get-go," Gayheart recalls, "that we were going to become really fast friends. We had a ton of stuff in common in terms of our backgrounds."

Their rapport bolstered their work on-screen. Dylan is immediately drawn to Toni, despite the fact that she's the daughter of Anthony Marchette, a wealthy criminal responsible for the death of Dylan's father. The doomed romance escalates quickly. Like a number of characters before her—Brenda, Kelly, Valerie—Toni entered the infamous bed of Dylan McKay, plastered in the same squiggly-patterned bedsheets seen for the last six seasons. (No word on if he had more than one set but let's pray yes.) Gayheart worried that the viewers would hate her character, mainly for the tragedy of not being Brenda or Kelly, but Toni was embraced. "The show needed something like that," she says, "a real true love, as opposed to high school sweethearts."

Gayheart was not only new to series TV but to the kind of attention that came with a longtime hit. On the day they shot Toni and Dylan's outdoor wedding, paparazzi in helicopters circled overhead. The other cast members were blasé, telling Gayheart she should stand off to the side to remain unseen. But Luke, punchy from shooting his character's last episode, yelled, " 'C'mon, everybody, let's give them the finger' and we all ran out to the yard. And we looked up and flipped the bird. It was hilarious. It ended up being printed in the two raggiest of rags at the time." Gayheart pauses. "We were so lucky. There was none of the social media madness yet."

Luke gathering his coworkers to flip off the flying voyeurs was in keeping with his prankster spirit. "He was the sort of person who would bring everyone together," Gayheart says. She calls Luke "the most charming person I've ever met, and everyone will tell you that."

He was comfortable showing those sides of himself, but nothing too vulnerable. Although Gayheart found him to be honest and forthright with his opinions—"he wasn't afraid to say certain things"—she was aware that he kept his personal struggles out of view. "I think he curated his social interactions to what he wanted them to be. Or maybe a better way to say it is to what was comfortable for him." He didn't dwell on his emotions, especially the negative.

After their star-crossed lovers met their bitter ends on *90210*, Luke championed Gayheart once again to work with him in Arizona on *Invasion*, a 1997 sci-fi movie also starring Kim Cattrall, based on the book by Robin Cook. They didn't have many scenes together, but off camera, they spent plenty of time talking. One of their favorite topics was dreaming about the future. "That was our thing: 'Where do you think you'll be when you're 80?' We both really wanted to go back to that simple, small-town, back-to-nature life." A few years before Luke made *Invasion*, he had purchased a farm near Van Lear, Tennessee, where he lived part-time, a step closer to that bucolic vision.

———

In June 2001, a devastating event changed the direction of Gayheart's life. As she drove in a borrowed Jeep Grand Cherokee, the car in front of her abruptly stopped in the road, to allow nine-year-old Jorge Cruz Jr. to fetch his soccer ball. Not realizing why the car had halted, Gayheart drove around the vehicle and accidentally struck Cruz, who died in the hospital a day later from his injuries. After pleading no contest to vehicular manslaughter in November 2001, the actress was sentenced to probation, a one-year suspension of her license, a $2,800 fine, and 750 hours of community service. Gayheart paid the family $10,000 toward funeral expenses, and also settled a wrongful death lawsuit filed by the child's parents, out of court. Despite early reports to the contrary, she wasn't on her cell phone, and no drugs or alcohol were found in her system.

In the aftermath, she "didn't want to live" for several months afterward. "It just turned my world upside down and I lost faith in everything." She struggled to eat or sleep, and her career dwindled to a few small roles, all that she could manage through her depression.

She learned that some of her friends weren't emotionally equipped for the situation when they disappeared from her life. Luke, however, leaned in. He made a point to visit often. He kept his presence light, never pushing her to talk about it. His instinct told him how and when he was needed, without any hints necessary. She was especially touched when, in 2005, Luke attended her Broadway debut in *Steel Magnolias*. She tried to repay the favor when he was having a hard time during his divorce, but she says, "It was different. Luke was extremely private." He wasn't one to signal for help. She found it best to just pop by unexpectedly; he was almost always at home, busying himself with minor renovation projects that made him a regular at his local hardware store.

For the next several years, they didn't see each other as much, but they still frequently talked on the phone. Their paths crossed again on *Once Upon a Time . . . in Hollywood*. Gayheart played Brad Pitt's wife, seen in flashbacks, while Luke appeared in a small role as a cowboy on a fake episode of a real Western TV show (more on that later). As Luke had all those years ago for *90210*, he popped his head in to say hello during her fitting. Plans were made to connect at the July premiere but he died in March.

"I'm so sad that he didn't get a chance to see it and celebrate. It was such a great role for him, and Quentin loved him so much," Gayheart says.

She thought about Luke constantly that day, as well as at a recent appearance at 90s Con. Many of the participants showed her pictures of Dylan and Toni as newlyweds. On a *90210* panel, she felt his absence. "He should've been sitting next to me."

"I forget sometimes that he's gone," she says. "I'll be like, 'Oh, I want to tell Luke this,' but then I think, 'Ah, he's not here.' And it just hurts."

ADAM WANTS TO LIVE WITH HER. *They spend all day and night together, except for class, and Margaret's parade of service-industry jobs. Audrey is tired of his presence in their small, mouse-ridden apartment.*

In her women's studies class, she reads A Room of One's Own, *by Virginia Woolf, who cuts to the quick of it:* "A woman must have money and a room of her own if she is to write fiction." *Finally, a recipe for what she wants most—to be a writer. The problem, of course, is the money part, but she can scare up an extra room in Chicago's rental landscape. Adam agrees to her idea to live in a new house with Audrey and Peter, too, as buffers, leavening the intensity—and they find a place with an office for her.*

She is in love with Adam, the most creative person she's met. He writes cracked poetry in his stick handwriting. Glowing brown eyes on his abstract paintings. Let's stick duct tape on the side of our jeans. Let's write a song. *Their shared language is playful and immersive. He is patient and sweet, even if he's also easily distracted and knows how to do nothing for himself. Cooking, cleaning. Audrey and Peter complain—they all rotate doing the dishes a hundred times before he washes a single plate.*

Her mother loves Adam because of his gentle charm. Over dinner at the Italian restaurant where Margaret works some lunch shifts, her mother starts: "When you have children . . ." *and Margaret stops her,* "Don't even talk to me about this until I'm thirty." *She has things she wants to do.* "Don't tell me you want to be one of these career women," *her mom continues, worked up now,* "the shoulder pads and all that."

"That is a decades-old reference," *she snaps.* "It is different now, Mom. I don't know how I can't have a career. It would be dangerous not to." *What she doesn't mention is her memories of her mother, resentful, going back to school to get a degree after her dad died. She had always wanted to be taken care of, her mother, but in the end, she had to take care of herself.*

She watches a wistful look pass over her mother's face. "I guess you're right, it is different now," *she says.* Still, "you have a good one there, and I hope you don't let him go."

CHAPTER

TWENTY-SIX

NORMAL LIFE **MARKS ONE** of the great misfortunes of Luke's career. Not because the movie is bad, nor his performance—it's the exact opposite. Director John McNaughton's chilling suburban crime story, sandwiched between his bigger commercial hits, *Mad Dog and Glory* (1993) and *Wild Things* (1998), is a lost gem from the era. It should've signaled to audiences that Luke could tackle more challenging fare than *Beverly Hills, 90210*, but it didn't turn out that way.

The reception to *Normal Life* was so disappointing for McNaughton that for years he didn't care to remind himself of the movie's existence. The intervening years have tempered his emotions. The memories are now flush with clarity and joy, and he recounts them in his native South Side Chicago accent.

In 1995, Rich Cotovsky, a Chitown theater mainstay, offered McNaughton his funky storefront for rehearsal before the month-long shoot. For two weeks, McNaughton, Ashley Judd, Luke, and other cast members met at the Mary-Arrchie Theatre in the mornings. Afternoons were reserved for the actors to tackle scenes on their own. The Arrchie was in stark contrast to the gilded days of *Mad Dog and Glory*, when Bill Murray, Robert DeNiro, and Uma Thurman rehearsed in one of the spare ballrooms at the Drake Hotel, with coffee service wheeled in on a sterling-silver cart. But McNaughton had no complaints: "It was perfect—just down-to-earth, gritty, get the work done."

Years later, there's a moment from the shoot that sticks out to Mc-Naughton. No matter how far away *Normal Life* was from Beverly Hills, Luke was still on loan from teen soapdom.

"We're out somewhere shooting one night," he says, though he couldn't remember in which "charmless" Northwest suburb. "And Luke was in his cop uniform. And we all went to the craft services table, back when you could still do that without fear of contracting some plague. And Luke was, you know, putting a piece of ham on a piece of bread or something. He was just sort of standing there, and out on the other side of the table, on the street, were like six or seven teenage girls. Young teenage girls, like fourteen-, fifteen-year-olds, and they're just staring at Luke. And then Luke takes a bite out of his sandwich. And one of them goes, 'Look, he's *eeeating*,' like he's a zoo animal."

McNaughton stops for a moment to wheeze-laugh at the memory. That was reality for Luke on the *Normal Life* shoot. On the one hand, they were immersed in this bleak critique of capitalist America, and then on the other, there were teen girls, with all their hope and affection for one of their favorite stars, hoping to catch a glimpse. "He was used to it," McNaughton said. Luke gave them a wave and finished his sandwich.

———

Loosely based on Jeffrey and Jill Erickson's real-life bank-robbing spree in 1991, *Normal Life* is a Bonnie and Clyde story steeped in nihilism. Set in the faceless, nameless outer suburbs of Chicago, *Normal Life* could be anywhere where people are struggling to pay their bills, never mind create any sustainable meaning out of existence. Similar to *8 Seconds*, it illuminated an often-ignored aspect of American existence. It feels all the more relevant now, with the middle class disappearing in a haze of debt and inflation.

Luke's police officer Chris meets Pam (Judd), a chaotic blonde bent on self-destruction. A moment from their fast and furious courtship:

the astronomy-obsessed Pam, while straddling a bewildered but en-thralled Chris, looks up at the night sky and says, "I wish I could fall into a black hole . . . I'd like to die that way. I'd disappear into the super-dense nothing, but my image would linger forever on the event horizon, and in a billion years an alien starship would pass by and see me still falling." When Chris responds with, "Oh god, you're so crazy," she rolls off him and races toward her car, about to peel off, but he convinces her to stay. "I've never felt anything like you," he pleads.

In McNaughton's hands, there's no way out of this American life, not romance, not wealth, but not knowing what else to do, Chris and Pam try on the suburban dream. Pretending, at first, comes easier to Chris. He's the one with a family, a brother he can talk to, and par-ents who seem nice enough. After he marries Pam, he tucks her into a dumpy apartment and hopes she'll be inspired to cook, clean, and housewife it up, but Pam goes even more feral than before. When the in-laws visit, she pounds Budweiser and locks herself in the bathroom while wearing headphones blasting hard rock. Later, when her father-in-law dies, she's so uncomfortable with the occasion's demand for sympathy that she shows up to his funeral in Rollerblades (surely that particular nineties skating fad has never been delivered with more fuck-you energy). She greets conflict in the marriage with aggressive sex, self-mutilation, or suicidal ideation, which makes John Gottman's four horsemen (the predictors of divorce) look like show ponies.

There's a turning point in the movie when Chris, finding Pam with a gun to her temple, picks up one of his pieces and does the same. The pact is made: Pam and Chris will follow each other into hell, no matter who descends first.

The debts pile up. When Chris loses his job because he's not willing to go along with the force's casual corruption—another way in which this movie still feels timely—the tension he's been carrying all along spills into action. Perry's eyes, usually so warm, are flat and expression-less as he robs one bank after another. For him, the violence is temporary and a means to an end. He wants to quit after they've bought a nice house in the suburbs, and he's opened a used-book store—one of his recommendations to a cop buddy is Jim Thompson's cult noir *The Killer Inside Me*. But Pam wants more. It was not enough to join him on a few of the heists. She wants to exist only in the blistering world of high-stakes crime—or nothing at all. Tearfully, she tells Chris, "I can't hang in there anymore. I can't do it. I'm not a normal person."

In the reviews for *Normal Life*, many critics focused on Judd's searing performance in a flashier role than Luke's, but his didn't go unnoticed. Michael Wilmington at the *Chicago Tribune* wrote, "Not only does Judd do exceptional work, she's backed with passion, skill and authority by co-star Luke Perry." The problem was, as Wilmington notes earlier in his review, that *Normal Life*, like the couple at its center, had already been doomed by forces greater than it. The film's distributors, New Line Cinemas and Fine Line Pictures, had lost confidence because the movie was screen-tested at a suburban San Francisco mall and the audience responded poorly to Luke as a cold-eyed bank robber. The imaginary leap required to picture Luke Perry as anyone else but Dylan McKay, whose worst offense was being a very sad rich boy who struggled with addiction, was just too great.

It didn't help that *Normal Life* was as bleak and unsentimental as a mainstream movie could be in 1996. Unlike *Pulp Fiction*, released a couple of years before, there wasn't a fun soundtrack to counterbalance the violence. Shot by cinematographer Jean De Segonzac (who would become one of the visual architects for the HBO prison series *Oz* a year later) in a disaffected documentary style, and directed with a pitiless eye by McNaughton, the movie is absent of disapproval or moral judgment. New Line and Fine Line wouldn't risk it. They allowed it a meager opening in New York, Los Angeles, and Chicago, where local critics Gene Siskel and Roger Ebert championed it. McNaughton was crushed by the limited release, and it changed his point of view on making movies. The man who had once made *Henry: Portrait of a Serial Killer* dodged darker fare afterward, saying, "If you want to see how horrid the world is, just walk out the door."

"JUST MAKE THE CALL," ADAM says. The phone is between them on the floor of their bedroom in the house they share with Audrey and Peter. It is a terrible bedroom—the sole window faces a brick wall. About once a day, a measly shaft of light illuminates part of the brick. The light mottles back to darkness within forty-five minutes; she has watched the process several times.

"I don't know who to call," Margaret says. Her red eyes are exhausted from their daily chore. She has not been able to stop crying for a long time now. Every time she dries up, she attempts to jump back into herself, to write, to do yoga with a book she picked up on her own, to run a sponge over his dishes, to sit uncomfortably with her friends, anything. No matter what, it is only a matter of time until her face seizes, her chest locks, and the tears soak out of her eyes, glazing her neck and darkening the front of her shirt. Running away from everyone when this happens is her usual recourse, but Adam, her love, always follows. He calms her until her body is a desert with no tears left.

The phone is waiting. He is nearly begging her. For him, she will call. She picks up the hulking yellow pages and rifles through till she gets to psychiatrists. Her finger traces down the page and stops cold at a name. Why her finger stopped there, she will consider for years to come, but for now, she reads the name: Dr. F. She reaches his answering machine.

"Hi, my name is Margaret"—the saline is already pricking the back of her eyes—"and I'm wondering if I can . . ." How does she say it? ". . . come into your office soon. I'm not feeling well." Not feeling well. Ugh, does she have the sniffles? She makes a face at Adam, to indicate that she's already bungled this call, but he gestures for her to go on. "Also, what your fees are. I mean, how much? I'm in college and . . ." She scrambles to politely say *she's broke, and has no health insurance. "... and I'm on a budget." She is proud of using a sensible, neutral phrase.*

Dr. F. calls back an hour later. In a comforting tone, he asks her a series of questions. She pictures him taking a straitjacket out of his closet with one answer, and then putting it back with the next, and then out again, and so forth. When she tells him that she entered a store the other day and thought all the people were dead, and maybe she was a walking ghost too, he pauses. "Can you come in at two p.m. tomorrow?"

CHAPTER

TWENTY-SEVEN

FOR SEVERAL DAYS NOW, Luke had donned the taupe vest, pants, and airy shirt designed by Jean Paul Gaultier, only to sit and not film anything. He was a beautiful unused vessel, but that was life for a TV upstart who wanted to endear himself to the country club of movies. Dylan McKay could pay his way into any club in existence but not Luke. He was playing a small role as Billy Masterson in the opening scene of *The Fifth Element*, from French director Luc Besson. Set in 1914 Egypt, the look of Luke's scene was desert chic plus vintage silent-era movies. It was a departure from the rest of the futuristic $90 million spectacular. In his review, Roger Ebert wrote, "It offers such extraordinary visions that you put your criticisms on hold and are simply grateful to see them." But the gratitude only went so far; he also argued for "a fierce trimming. . . . [T]he movie should get out of its own way." In the end, none of its considerable flaws would stop the 1997 movie from becoming a staple of cable replays. Bruce Willis's roguish charm. Milla Jovovich's bandage dress. Gary Oldman looking like a skater overlord. It was next-level eye candy.

What was supposed to be an eight-day shoot for Luke turned into thirty-two, most of which he spent on call with his wife in London. He ultimately appeared in only a few minutes of screen time out of 126 minutes. No matter.

SUNDAY MORNING. 5:45 A.M., ADAM *drops her off and drives back to fall asleep again. She's the first one in, after the line cooks, with her mascara slapped on in the predawn, last night's beer sour in her mouth, despite brushing her teeth. She brews coffee, sets bowls of creamer on the tables, ties her black apron around her waist, where she will pocket her tips from the diner's customers. By the end of the shift, she'll have a wad of syrup-stained cash. It is her life five days a week, around her college classes.*

By 8:45 a.m., all the other waiters have shown up. They buzz and slide by each other, cracking jokes about Table 34's frat boys or the couple breaking up at the two-top by the door. For the rush, the manager, as always, plays No Doubt's album Tragic Kingdom. *The bouncy pop-ska of "Sunday Morning" propelling them, Gwen Stefani's high vibrato and controlled shrieks rising above the din. Forks scrape, plates clatter, laughter and lighters strike in the smoking section. She's beyond sick of the album, wants to rip the silver disc out of the six-CD stereo, but there's no denying the Pavlovian response. She moves faster; the orders piling up in her pad; stacking plate after plate up her arm, trying not to burn herself.*

In her section, the hostess has sat Divorced Dad with his two kids. They come in every single weekend. She always greets him warmly, and every time he turns to her with an utter lack of recognition. He orders too much, but she never dissuades him. Instead, she brings every item at once, as he always directs her to do, so that each child is ringed by a fortress of breakfast treats—pancakes, bacon, sausage, juice, milk.

This morning she approaches, and the little boy is drawing in a notebook, while the older sister, maybe eight, stares at her with wide eyes. Margaret throws her a smile, and a shy one is returned.

"What can I get for you this morning?"

Divorced Dad has a new toy. He holds it up to his cheek, talking. It is black and slim; it almost looks like he's speaking into his wallet.

"I can't pick it up till Tuesday," he's saying. He holds up a "one minute" finger to her.

She stands awkwardly; she can feel one of her tables, waiting to order.

None of the waiters know what to do about these new toys. More and more of them are showing up, whipped out at the most inopportune times. The customers who use them fall into a profile: men, most of them young, moneyed, or, more typically, desperately trying to appear moneyed. There are some women, too; Gold Coast fancy ladies calling various hired hands while they pick over their egg-white omelets in their Nike workout clothes.

"No, that's not the—"

"I'll come back," she tells the children, the only ones listening to her.

When she returns a few minutes later, after taking the other table's order, he is angry.

"My children are starving," he says. "We were supposed to order ten minutes ago."

It hasn't been nearly that long, but there is no point arguing with him.

"I understand," she answers.

She vows to never get one of those stupid things.

SHE TAKES THE L FROM work, or Adam drives her in his car with a butter knife permanently jammed in the tape player, the only way it'll work. The back door is unlocked; she lets herself in. Climbs the carpeted stairs, the whirring of the white-noise machines enveloping her. When she's in the second-floor hall, nearly every square inch of the walls are covered in framed paintings, colorful, roughshod. He has explained: these were made by untrained artists, some of them from mental institutions. Outsider art.

In his waiting room, issues of the New Yorker, Harper's, Metropolitan Home *with his wife's name on the sticker. When his door opens, the other patient slinks down the hall and the stairs, out of sight. It's her turn.*

———

Dr. F., portly and white-haired, asks her to read what she has written, the words of the condemning voice in her head.

"Who do you think that is, Margaret?"

The snark and the blistering attitude can only be herself at thirteen, the age when her father took some of his last steps in their rental, the house they had downsized to after he had to resign.

It is not the only thing he uncovers. Another time, from across the room as always, he is beaming at her. Proud. She's confused.

"This process, it has its hooks in you."

"What do you mean?"

"This is beginning to affect you. You're trusting me more now."

Two times a week, she climbs those carpeted stairs. He has waived his fee. He thinks, given her state, the note she wrote in high school to be read after her death, it is no longer safe for her to soldier this alone. She doesn't disagree. Besides Adam—and that is wobbling—this is the other real thing she has. Or is it? It is an arrangement: she confesses, he listens.

He doubles down and describes her as "attached" to not only the process but him.

"I don't like that word," she says.

"Why not?"

"It makes me sound desperate. Clingy."

He nods. "This is what it feels like to trust that someone will be there for you," he says. "And that might feel strange because you haven't had enough of that in your life."

CHAPTER
TWENTY-EIGHT

THERE ARE AN UNTOLD number of social media accounts, bots, and collectives of people quenching their obsessive thirst for all things *Beverly Hills, 90210*. Some of the Facebook groups contain more than one hundred thousand people. These municipalities of mega-fans hash over the merits of certain characters, their multiplicity of hairstyles, and questionable life choices. There is something for everyone: Andrea stans, champions of Steve's mullet, the David Silver rap groupies, and critics of the Walsh parenting style. There are threads, hundreds-deep, about the show's worst boyfriends and girlfriends (anti-shoutout to Brandon's racist beach babe, Brooke). There are even diehardss who say the nihilistically bad tenth season is the best one of the whole series (shiver).

By far, the controversy that rears up the most is the Dylan-Kelly-Brenda love triangle. On a daily basis, a portion of the world's internet power is sapped toward who Dylan should've chosen—Kelly or Brenda—and if they should've given him the choice in the first place. Fans break it down: Brenda was done dirty. She left for Paris and voila, her boyfriend and best friend cheat together. But wait, wasn't Brenda straying herself with "Reek," played by Dean Cain, who she also duped by exposing him to her intolerable fake French accent? But wait again, Kelly told Brenda she had a long-standing crush on Dylan the first time he ever came up between them. By girl code, didn't Kelly rightfully claim Dylan? They'd known each other since kindergarten; they were marked by the same brand of dysfunctional absentee parents. But Brenda, a product of an intact home, was the one who had the stability (despite her flair for melodrama) to be there for Dylan in key moments. She was the one who, when he's fumbling with his tie before his father's funeral, so lovingly helps him to steady himself. For the *90210* historians, this was also the episode where the writers planned for Brenda and Dylan to get back together, but the working relationship with Doherty was too fraught to follow through.

The essence of the debate is which woman was the soul mate and which one was the savior. But it's a false binary. Why is it either/or? Occasionally, a wise soul comments that no good can ever come from trying to "save" a man, but everyone tramples right over that point. The fire-and-brimstone vehemence with which people attempt to mathematically prove who was right and who was wrong for Dylan is astounding.

Why all this rancor for a bunch of pretend people? It is easier to argue and feasibly win about Dylan, Kelly, and Brenda than it is to score a victory in real life. For most of life's raw deals, there is no restitution, restorative justice, or recourse at all, but it's easy to rifle through Dylan's romantic foibles and pronounce from on high, "He should've picked her."

The actors of *90210* have been asked the same questions time and again on the romantic choices of their characters. Sometimes they dole out clear answers that are then cited by the communities like scripture. For instance, Jason Priestley and Jennie Garth have often said that their characters should've ended up together. Fans love the end-game dependency of this answer; even if the "right" outcome was thwarted, there is comfort in knowing what should've happened. The writers may have birthed the characters and steered their destinies, but in the eyes of the fans, the actors are the true custodians of the story.

As for Luke, his answers varied. In 2012, he paid respect to chance: "They always want to know: Brenda or Kelly? It is a question that has stood the test of time. I always take out a coin and flip it and say, 'Oh, today, it would be this one. Tomorrow, it would be that one.' I'm a big coin flipper."

In 2016, he made a rare declaration, possibly to honor his former costar who had recently shared her breast cancer diagnosis with the public. He named Dylan and Brenda as his favorite couple, adding that "none of us would be here without Shannen . . . she gets thrown under a bus, I've been accused of driving that bus. The reality is, she's a very big part of the success of that program." He acknowledged that he directly benefited from her presence: "I'm just really glad she was there for me as a scene partner." His answer revealed a truth about the relationship and why it still matters to fans. Brenda and Dylan represent the sanctity of first love before any mistakes—or any change at all, including growth—can mar it. For a spell, they existed in a snow globe, perfect and pristine. Their relationship was the kind of delusion TV does best—damaging if we chase it too far in our own lives, but when we can catch a glimpse of it, it is sublime.

AT THE BAR, THE OLD lady sweeps through with a basket of "spiced" brownies, and then the tamale man comes, to assuage the effects of the weed brownie with grease and cheese. She is wrong to say what is already tumbling out.

"Did you notice that I didn't flirt with you at all this week?"

The longest pull of beer she's seen. And Jeff likes his drink. When the bottle is moved away, his lips betray a small slip of thrill.

"Did you miss it?" She lights an American Spirit, something to do. She's still only a half-hearted smoker; her father's cancer that spread to his lungs.

"Let's not talk about this here," he said, raking his hand through his wavy hair. Their coworker, another editor at the paper, was winding his way back from the bathroom.

She is editing the books and dining section at a Chicago alt-weekly, her first real job. The salary is low, but the perks are high. Free books, free meals, and access to all kinds of cultural events she couldn't afford otherwise. A few months after she started, Jeff joined the paper, too.

At first, she didn't take much notice of the curly blond guy who leaned over the proofs, catching errors, but it was a tight-knit staff. They hung out more and more. He was fiery in a way Adam was absolutely not. Caustic, with an edge of self-loathing. He could be insufferable sometimes—she'd lost count of how many indie rock bands he claimed as "seminal"—but at least he had a sense of humor. "You can punch me the next time I say it."

They had talked about their feelings for each other, but no one was supposed to act on them.

The idea that a person could love two people, she thought, was a fallacy created by men. Dylan McKay kissing Brenda and Kelly, one after the *other, in the halls of West Beverly. Jeff, her best friend, fellow adventurer, though she might just mean drinking partner. Going-out partner. They are biting into Chicago's dusky throat together while Adam is at home, building websites, teaching himself code. It is admirable, and she is bored. What is wrong with her?*

CHAPTER

TWENTY-NINE

LUKE RETURNING TO *BEVERLY HILLS, 90210* in 1998 lifted the spirits of the die-hard fans and the FOX executives who wanted to revive a withered show, but it wasn't exactly a victory lap for the actor.

At first, Luke played his return for laughs to the press. "Elephants come home to die," he said. "I guess that's what I'm doing." He instructed an *Atlanta Constitution* writer to start her article with "Not unlike a young Orson Welles . . ." to which she obliged. He compared returning as Dylan McKay to "driving your very first car again. Sometimes it's uncomfortable. Most of the time it's very familiar. But I know how the damn thing works, you know?" When asked if he was surprised that *90210* was still around, he answered that the "show's constructed mostly of silicone and hairspray, both of which have a life expectancy of at least one hundred years. So God only knows how long this thing can be on."

To a young fan who asked about the return on MTV, he was more reflective. "I like knowing where I'm going to work every day. When you do movies, you're always living in a hotel, some place different. I have a family now, and I don't like dragging them around. I did that a bit last year and I didn't like it . . . I like to go home."

The fan confessed that she had recently returned home from college in California, despite professing to all her friends beforehand that she expected to love it and presumably never come back. She was inspired to admit she was wrong, she said, by Perry returning to *90210*. After he acknowledged the similarities of their situations, he said, "For me, I was very clear when I left the show. I didn't say, 'I'm leaving and I'm going to be the greatest thing ever.' I said, 'I'm leaving because this doesn't feel right for me right now.' I didn't say, 'I'm leaving and I'm never coming back, I hate you people.' I said, 'I gotta go away from this right now.'" As for his return, "I knew I was going back to a place where people loved me. They loved me when I left, and they loved me when I came back. And that makes it okay."

One of those beloved people was executive producer Paul Waigner, whose central duty, Rosin says, was "taking care of the actors." If they were unhappy, Waigner would try to resolve the issue on their behalf. Waigner, Rosin says, "was very close to Luke, very protective," and vice versa. Perry told friends in later years that he returned to *90210* to be with Waigner, who had been diagnosed with cancer. He died in January 2001.

Surely, all of these reasons fed into his return, but in some circles, another narrative emerged: Luke had returned, hat in hand, with his dreams of being a box-office juggernaut turned to ash. In other words, he couldn't hack it. Or so the story went. TV actors who dared to leave the nest met two possible fates: They either soared, like George Clooney post-*ER*, or they became carrion for the late-night comedians and snarky columnists of the time.

Whatever goodwill Luke had drummed up in himself for his return, by 2000, it had vanished. For the last two seasons, his character had been reduced to a pastiche of Dylan mannerisms and recycled foibles. An unsentimental *Los Angeles Times* piece about the show's final days pulled this thin gruel from the show's prodigal son:

> "Apathy coupled with whatever is a nasty cocktail," he says, asked about doing the show now versus then. "Nobody is walking through anything on camera, that much I am sure of. But you know, it used to be a lot of fun and now it's not as much fun and it still could be. I'm just a little disappointed about that."

In 2001, when asked whether he'd entertain a *90210* reunion, Luke responded with some of the strongest words he ever gave publicly about his best-known role. "Never say never," he said. "But it would have to be damn interesting, and they would have to buy me a small island somewhere." Then he kicked the casket shut: "Dylan is history, and *90210* is over. We are on to a different party now."

PART
TWO

CHAPTER

THIRTY

IN THE LANDSCAPE OF late-nineties TV, HBO's *Oz* was not only set across the country from *Beverly Hills, 90210*, it was its tonal opposite. *Oz* was prestige before prestige had been named. It was prestige when prestige was still contained to the living rooms of those with enough money for cable. On the other side of the dial, FOX's long-running teen drama had devolved into a druggy nadir with statutory rape and domestic abuse storylines, but none of them had the electricity of *Oz*. *90210* was a dead show walking, while *Oz* was an obscene, shiv-happy Shakespeare.

Set in an experimental prison ward inside the fictional Oswald State Penitentiary in New York, *Oz* debuted in July 1997, the first show to be released under Chris Albrecht, a longtime HBO executive who became president of original programming in 1995 (and eventually chairman of the network from 2002 to 2007). Albrecht ushered in a new focus on original scripted television, previously a disorganized, haphazard endeavor for the network. Under Albrecht, HBO's original programming became a refuge for writers stifled by the limitations imposed by the broadcast networks.

Tom Fontana, who was running *Homicide: Life on the Street* for NBC in 1995, was under pressure to keep *Homicide* action-packed, the cast handsome, and the philosophical chitchat to a minimum. But in the era of the "super-predator" and the "three strikes and you're out" laws, there was much more to say about law and order. For one, Fontana noticed that every TV police procedural ended with a criminal being put behind bars, and then said criminal is never seen again. What if the viewer could peek into the life of a prisoner, too?

In retrospect, it's amazing that it took until July 1997 for anyone to have this idea for a TV series and successfully follow through. The U.S. had been in the middle of a prison explosion for years; state and federal incarceration rates grew by more than 200 percent between 1980 and 1996, with the "war on drugs" acting as a powerful vacuum sucking many young lives into its machinery. Fontana tried pitching light versions of *Oz* to the broadcast networks, but it wasn't until he met Albrecht that he and his *Homicide* partner, Barry Levinson, received the green light, and more freedom than he expected. Fontana was given a million dollars to shoot a seventeen-minute pilot presentation. When he told Albrecht his idea to kill off the leading man by the end of the episode, Albrecht cried, "I love it!" That set the tone for their creative partnership; Fontana was not only given permission to break many of the most sacrosanct rules of television, he was cheered on.

One of the scant common elements *Oz* shared with *Beverly Hills, 90210* was its reliance on guest actors. Survival was far from guaranteed in *Oz*'s Em City, so new faces were regularly trucked into the prison population to eventually clash with the long-timers. Rap legend Method Man, NBA veteran Rick Fox, KISS drummer Peter Criss, Joel Grey, and *Love Boat*'s Gavin MacLeod all had their turns. In 2001, Luke appeared as the Rev. Jeremiah Cloutier starting in season three for ten episodes.

In an interview with Oliver Jones for *Us Weekly*, Luke took care to show the distance between who he was when *90210* started and the date of the article, February 2001. For starters, he was now a family man. At the time of the article, Luke's youngest—his daughter, Sophie—was less than a year old, and Jack was only three. He also looked different. He wore a rumpled shirt and his tooth was chipped, which the producers at *90210*, he said, would've treated as "a national emergency." The pompadour was gone, replaced by a shaggy Christ-like mane.

THE STATION AGENT PATIENTLY EXPLAINS in accented English: "No, sorry, that train doesn't exist."

Margaret: "Pardon me?"

Station agent, again: "There is no train."

The agent spills out timetables and maps, all to prove that there is no train, zero trains, not at all a single train, from Málaga, Spain, to Lisbon, Portugal. Their travel agent back in Chicago messed up, or lied. She wanders back to report the news to Adam, waiting on a bench in his leather coat and messenger bag, inhaling a cigarette with quick drags, his way. Because they can in Europe, they obnoxiously light up everywhere.

Adam and Margaret need to get to Lisbon by nightfall for a hotel reservation. Defeated but determined, they wheel their luggage to a rental car desk in the station.

Some options are presented at the counter, sensible economy vehicles. The most expensive upgrade: a sexy black Mercedes convertible. Adam, lover of cars, of slick technology, wants this one, Margaret can tell. They whisper to each other at the counter, the clerk pretending not to listen.

"Let's get it," she says. "Let's just do it."

"Are you sure?" This is purely ceremonial.

"Let's just put it on the credit card. Fuck it."

He slides the card over. They can't really afford it—their entry-level jobs are good though not lucrative—but they are adults in their early twenties, free to make the call. They can splurge on their honeymoon.

This minor disaster on their honeymoon, at least this can be easily repaired. She wants to encourage his pure pleasure, she owes him that. She has hurt him these last few months, betrayed him, and she is desperate to push away her constant guilt.

The highway is not that different from an American one, but each for-

eign symbol and sign thrills her. Traveling punctures the stasis of her daily life. Every single experience becomes a novelty. The biggest hit of newness came on that first day, a week ago, when they landed in Paris, direct from Chicago. Waylaid in a café while the hotel prepared their room, she successfully ordered them omelets in her basic French. As they were eating, another couple approached, also speaking in French. After a few exchanges, she realized that the couple was mistaking them for natives. These two actual French people, who were unfamiliar with Paris, were asking her for directions!

———

Six hours in the car. She wears a scarf on her head, like Tippi Hedren in the beginning of The Birds. *They don't stop anywhere to linger. There isn't time. The ripping wind silences them both for hours, a relief. A chance for both to internally make plans for a fresh start. Despite their best efforts, Margaret knows what will be heading for them at night. Tension had stolen into Paris, into Spain.*

After checking into their Lisbon hotel, they ignore their exhaustion and walk into town. They dodge motor scooters zipping down narrow cobblestone streets, headlights piercing the dusk. They snap photos of graffiti, exotic because it's here: "Sexista, apalpa a tua consciencio." A plate of giant shrimp. The animals intact with beady eyes, antennas, and translucent tails. Biting into a shrimp head? Now, that is something she's never done before. The earthen, tangy juices of the sea explode on her tongue, almost making her retch. She washes it down with Vinho Verde, then some more Vinho Verde in a twinkling courtyard nightclub. They are together, and she rides the rushes of their old love. The night almost permits them escape from the inevitable. Almost.

The arguing, the processing, the sadness commences in their new room. In a new country. The sheets starched and untouched. The problem is that her indecision has destabilized everything. He is robbed of his confidence.

She tries to illuminate why this (mostly) emotional affair happened, but her honesty isn't helping. He shuts down, grows quiet. But she is determined to get the relationship back to when they had shared every thought and idea with each other, back to when an hour before seeing him again after a day apart, she didn't try to distract herself from the excitement; she reveled in it. Adam is a good person, and she refuses to see how choosing a good person could be a bad idea.

CHAPTER

THIRTY-ONE

TOM FONTANA, WHO MET Luke through their mutual friend and *Oz* star Dean Winters, wasn't sure at first what role would suit an actor who'd aged out of his bedroom poster era. It was imperative to utilize Luke's fame—it was too glaring to ignore. Despite never having watched a lick of *Beverly Hills, 90210*, Fontana cast Luke in *Oz* because he liked him and trusted Winters's recommendation. A rodeo cowboy, a too-obvious pick because of *8 Seconds*, was ruled out. He also considered a controversial soccer player or baseball legend, but soon enough, the evangelical minister character emerged.

"I always said that *Oz* was an equal opportunity offender," Fontana says from his New York office, "and I had really underserved the Christian evangelical community."

So he created Reverend Jeremiah Cloutier, a zealot that honed in on one of Luke's most appealing qualities—his "incredibly genuine essence." Fontana took that sincerity and charisma and injected it with a dark, manipulative force. Cloutier is serving time for embezzlement, but Luke embodies him as someone who might be grifting himself as much as anyone else.

Whether he's a sham or not, Cloutier does possess some otherworldly gift or influence that makes certain prisoners at Em City flock to him. Fontana told Luke: "I think this man was a fraud who convinced himself that he wasn't a fraud, and so there are times when he is actually in touch with something greater than himself." Luke's performance hinged on maximizing that nebulous, shifty quality. The role comments on acting itself. Two things are true about acting: playing another person is inherently a con game, a trick, a lie. It can also offer the most honest, searing insight into the human condition.

Oz afforded Luke an incredible opportunity to change what audiences had grown to expect from him. He was ready to radically rebel against the typecasting that threatened to limit his career.

"As much as he appreciated his stardom," Winters said, "it was also like an albatross. He couldn't go anywhere." Soon enough, his vastly different appearance as Cloutier allowed him to melt into the city like anyone else. Perfect for the early aughts when a good proportion of New York's male residents looked like George Harrison in his *All Things Must Pass* era. His long beard and Jesus locks allowed him to slink in and out of their mutual friend Chris Barish's nightclub hassle-free.

Luke's rebirth was nearly complete—except for one important rite of passage.

In the whole history of television, there was and still is no showcase for male nudity on par with *Oz*. Any given week, viewers were treated to a bacchanalia of male genitalia in an array of sizes and flaccidity. Seen in flashes or long looks, the camera shied away from nothing, so long as the actor was willing to go there—and most of them were, sometimes in the heat of the performance. *Oz* actor Sean Dugan remembers nudity waivers being generated on the spot.

Winters admitted the whole parade started with him. In the third episode of season one, an expert on prison life told him that when anyone goes into solitary, they get tossed in naked. So that's what Winters did. "And everyone on the show hated me for that," he says.

When Fontana told Luke that he'd written in a nude scene for him, he approached the subject with delicacy, as he always did with his actors, male or female, ready to plead his case.

Luke's reaction was immediate. "He loved it. He totally understood why it was right for the character," Fontana said. "He had a great sense of humor and a great love for the whole process of acting and telling stories."

Winters joked that Luke's internal monologue went something like this, as they set up the shower scene: *All right, these guys are gonna do it. Then I'm gonna fuckin' do it.* Even when he wasn't required to be there, Winters often biked through Manhattan to the set at Chelsea Market at Fifteenth and Ninth Avenue, to watch Luke perform. Was it because he felt responsible, as the one who backed him to Fontana? "It wasn't about watching to see someone fail; it was about watching someone succeed . . . I had no doubt that he could bring it. Zero doubt."

Pre-*Oz*, Winters estimated that he had stumbled on an episode or two of *90210*, tops. He could tell Luke was "doing the best with what they gave him," but otherwise, he hadn't seen him act before introducing him to Fontana. He went on instinct. "There was never a question and it wasn't because he was a star. It was the way he composed himself, and the way that he spoke. He thought before he spoke, and he listened. Any good actor knows that the key to acting is listening. And Luke was a really good listener. And that's something that I picked up on with him. Like on all our crazy nights out in New York and the East Village, at nightclubs and blah, blah, blah, you know, through all of that, he always listened no matter what was going on around him. And that's a sign of a really good actor."

The day of the scene, Winters watched Luke in action. A post-shower Cloutier, his towel stolen by inmates, snaps up his Bible to cover himself. He's hunched over, humiliated, but also trying to stand tall at first, to cast off his evident fear. His muscles tensed for a further attack as he skulks back to his bunk. The inmates cackle and catcall; by the scene's end, he's almost curled around the good book.

About the use of Cloutier's bible as a loincloth, Fontana says: "Yeah, I'll roast in hell for that one."

Whatever Luke needed to do to blend in and be part of the show, he did it without question. He appeared in the background for many scenes, in the way an extra would, something that another actor might've deemed a waste of time. There was "never a diva move" from Luke, Fontana says. "I don't think he was capable of it."

Luke's reaction to his character's walk of shame was understated. He said, "Oh, yeah, I got to do a scene where Jeremiah is walking butt naked down the hallway. They're spitting on him, he's wearing nothing but the Bible, and I thought, 'This is not Beverly Hills!'"

FOR THE LAST FIVE YEARS, she has come here to Dr. F.'s office. He has shown her how to build a timeline, a map, and a system for making sense of her late childhood. The simple exhuming power of talking about it. She is still a long way from hearing that thirteen-year-old's sour voice and befriending it, thanking it, but she is better than she was.

On her last day with him, she cries without shame, scared to let go, naming her every fear. She is moving to Los Angeles with Adam. They have survived their young marriage so far, but the city where it all happened, and almost didn't, must be left behind. Too many haunted bars, dank and dim apartments, rats of memory in every gangway. She applied to graduate writing programs, most in New York, where she knows more people, but somehow it is the one program in LA that manifests. California has its draws too. Her two oldest brothers live out there; it was where she was born and had left at age five. The purple sage mountains in the distance were some of her first memories.

Her mother, who doesn't have much money to spare from her part-time job as a librarian, helps them before the move by paying for their car repair. She is excited for them, though she knows nothing about their challenges. It will take Margaret years to realize that leaving her mother was more permanent than she thought; they will never live in the same city again. Their regular dinners, by turns combative and tender, ceased.

At the close of her final session with Dr. F., she asks: "Can I hug you?"

He has always occupied the farthest corner of the office from the tweed couch. Perched in an Eames chair, sometimes puffing on a pipe. "Wow, you're really milking the psychoanalyst cliché," she'd tease him. Since a tumor had appeared on his lip, he'd quit smoking. From her position on the tweed couch, she read his expressions—mirthful, sympathetic, bemused—but has never been near enough to know the details of his face.

Up close, she sees his brown eyes filled with tears from behind his glasses. The sunspots on his cheekbones near his beard. Where his white hair thinned near the temples. She sees that he is almost nervous, or shy. Tentatively, she steps closer and tucks herself into his arms.

"Take good care of yourself," he says, his voice tremulous.

A hug between patient and therapist; she is acutely aware of not making it weird, but she wants to stay there. To know him the way his two adult sons do. She hopes they understand their luck, the curious split in the atom of time that allowed their father to live, and hers to die.

"Thank you," she says, "for everything," and forces herself to pull away.

THIRTY-TWO

SEAN DUGAN WORRIED HE'D never see the inside of Em City again, not after season two. A year had passed with no word from *Oz*. Anxiety mounted. *Did I bomb? Did I piss someone off?* He pushed the thoughts away. Then, busy in Massachusetts with the American Repertory Theater, he got a call that he had been written into season four and they would need him next week, or they'd have to recast. Not so fast! He finagled an exit from the play.

Here he was on set, as inmate Timmy Kirk, meeting his scene partner. "The first day we met, it was literally an AD saying 'Luke, this is Sean; Sean, this is Luke.' Then, bells ring, camera rolls, and action: 'Would you like a blow job?'"

Dugan and Luke chatted easily after that icebreaker of a scene. "He was incredibly sweet. I've never met anyone like him," Dugan said. "I've never met anyone as famous as Luke who was as disinterested in their level of fame. It takes a real level of groundedness that I don't think was common, though it was certainly more common then than it is now." In the era of Tik-Tok, Dugan noted, Andy Warhol's fifteen minutes of fame is an irony-free aspiration instead of a condemnation on how vapid and shallow we are as a culture.

There were a lot of legends in the *Oz* universe: There was Rita Moreno, one of the most famous performers in the world from *West Side Story,* playing a nun and psychologist working with the prison population. Broadway luminaries such as Austin Pendleton and Joel Grey were guest stars, while Kathy Bates, Steve Buscemi, Matt Dillon, and Brian Cox all came through as directors. But Luke was one of the most broadly recognizable the show had ever seen. None of that mattered to the actor who simply wanted to throw himself into a new role. Luke left whatever ego he might've had back at home. Good thing, too. Anyone who came to *Oz* with a holier-than-thou attitude risked meeting a swift end. Dugan recalled a guest star who graced the production with his presence three hours late on his first day. The script was changed on-site to immediately kill off the character.

When the cameras weren't rolling, Luke wanted nothing more than to talk about his farm in Tennessee and his young family. "He just beamed talking about these little people who he loved so much." It set Dugan at ease: "It's hard to be starstruck with someone who's so completely relaxed and unassuming."

As a longtime working actor, Dugan has had plenty of opportunity to think about fame, at its most corrosive and exhilarating. For a while, when he was first recognized around New York by *Oz* fans, he drank up the attention. "Wow, this is why I moved to New York," he thought. "I've arrived." But then another reaction sank in: hesitation, caution. "You delegate a level of ownership of your life over to other people," he said. Fame requires maintenance. Family or a certain creative risk-taking is often compromised. He could tell that Luke wasn't interested in sacrificing those ideals either.

Dugan remembers Luke's vast knowledge about the technical aspects of filmmaking. "He knew everything about lighting lenses, he knew how to use his voice incredibly well. I remember him talking about the idea of putting a camera way far away from the actors and grabbing a really long lens so that the actors can just do their thing. And I was nodding, like, 'I really only know a little bit about what he's talking about' . . . And of course, he was exactly right. I admired that he had clearly spent his time on *90210* just being a sponge and absorbing all of the information."

ON THE LONG FLIGHT TO *Los Angeles, she drifts down the aisle, lightly bouncing against the seats, until she makes it to the tiny bathroom. After she pees, she checks herself in the mirror. Holds for a good lengthy stare. She spots something. In her dark brown hair, across her sideswept bangs, there is an interloper. A single spy sent from the future. It is one gray hair. The first one she has ever seen. She extracts it from the mass and holds it at an angle toward the mirror, twisting it, lifting it. It behaves a little differently than the others. It is wavier, thinner. She considers letting it live. Showing mercy. Will it summon others? Has it already sent out its panicked signal? An exacting pinch and a yank, and it is gone. Somewhere over Colorado, she drops it to the floor.*

THIRTY-THREE

DEAN WINTERS BROUGHT LUKE to a Fourth of July party in the Archive building on Greenwich Street near Christopher Street. He didn't tell anyone ahead of time about his special guest; he was planning on surprising his sister, who was ten years younger than Winters and a rabid *90210* fan.

The moment they walked in, "it was like when the gunslinger walks into the saloon." Soon enough, everyone regained their composure and chatter resumed. Nobody wanted to be the fangirl or -boy who sent Luke backing out the door. Winters's sister kept her delight hidden behind nonchalance. Luke folded right into the scene, striking up conversations, passing the weed along.

After a while, the party roaring with life, Winters, his then-girlfriend Fannie, and Luke sat on the couch, near the front door. Anyone who was heading out into the night, Luke stopped that person with a command: "You cannot leave this party unless you Riverdance out that front door," he said, referencing the popular theatrical show filled with Irish folk music and rigorous, floor-tapping dancing. He wouldn't take no for an answer.

Women in espadrilles, men in Diesel shoes, everyone jigged their way over the threshold. One guy, Winters remembered, went so hard on the County Cork spirit that he actually broke his toe. "The guy had to go to the hospital and get it set," Winters said. "Luke felt so horrible."

EVERY SUNDAY NIGHT SHE WATCHES Six Feet Under. *She is living Claire's life—or is Claire living hers? The commonalities: Both are the youngest with older brothers. A dead dad. Sarcastic wit covering for their deep-feeling sensitive natures. She is studying writing at the same school in LA as Claire, though the name is spelled backward on the show. The dream is that she, like Claire, will transform her pain into art.*

She's meeting new people, reading new books, doing new drugs or more of the old ones. Chopping up lines, lines of text, and sniffing them in, all of them. At the end of the continent, she is free to be another. To start again. And yet, she keeps seeing people that she recognizes, mistakenly, from her old life, maybe high school or a prior job. When she walks into the bar in Hollywood, a dark, carpeted setup in a strip mall—the strip mall being where most mystical things in Los Angeles are stored—she spies the back of a man in a suit with dark oiled hair. She thinks nothing of him as she takes a seat at the almost empty bar, waiting for a friend. From her stool, she can see his face, both directly and reflected in a mirror.

He's familiar. She stares at his mirror reflection, thinking it will come to her any second now. And because she's staring, he feels it and looks back, at the mirror, and then directly at her. He gives a slight, knowing smile, and looks away. Then he shifts and overly involves himself in considering the glass that holds his drink.

She realizes he's Chris Noth from Sex and the City, *the other show she watches on Sunday nights. Was that slight smile a flirtation, an acknowledgment that "Why yes, I am"? A minute later, her friend enters and in her distraction, Noth slips away, and it becomes a story. She thinks about LA becoming a slow succession of famous boyfriends, past and present. Will all the crushes of her girlhood reveal themselves? She wonders if she'll ever see Luke Perry.*

THIRTY-FOUR

MARGARET: "DID YOU EVER think about bringing Luke into *Sex and the City*? Like as a date or boyfriend for any of those ladies?"

Darren Star: "In hindsight, I wish I had. He would have been great on the show. You know, Kristin Davis was on *Melrose Place*. God, Luke would have been great, and he would've been the right age. So that was a missed opportunity!"

CHAPTER

THIRTY-FIVE

WHEN HIS OLD FRIEND Luke called, looking for a place to stay in New York while he filmed *Oz*, Chris Barish offered the second bedroom in his downtown apartment. The spare was sitting empty. What Barish didn't think to mention was that the second bedroom had no actual bed. Just a ratty couch. "But Luke didn't care about stuff like that," Barish says. They bought an inflatable twin and Luke was happy.

Luke wasn't so pleased, however, when Barish's all-purpose assistant, Mr. Alex, insisted on cleaning his room. He'd been pressuring Luke to let him in for a tidying, but Luke resisted, saying he'd do it himself. But Mr. Alex disobeyed his wishes and snuck into Luke's chamber. Somehow, in his frenzy to freshen up before he was caught, he popped the air mattress. "It was the only time I really saw Luke get mad," Barish says. Mr. Alex apologized profusely, and all was forgiven.

Barish and Luke went back to the Planet Hollywood days. His father, Keith Barish, a film producer whose credits include *The Fugitive* and *Sophie's Choice*, had cofounded the restaurant chain with Robert Earl in 1991. During the early and mid-nineties heyday, Luke was a mainstay at the Midtown and Beverly Hills locations, frequently photographed in a PH bomber jacket or a company cap. Showing up to events and openings together, Luke and Chris became tight. They were closer in age than a lot of the other investors like Sly Stallone, Bruce Willis, and Arnold Schwarzenegger. Luke had been an investor when the restaurants

were thriving, but by the late nineties, Keith and Luke both had abandoned Planet Hollywood. Soon after, the company filed for bankruptcy.

In 1994, Barish remembered flying to Maui together to open a new
location. Somewhere over the Pacific, they really became friends, helped
along by the great lubricator: alcohol. "I must've had a few cocktails on
the flight and I passed out on [his wife] Minnie's shoulder," Barish admits. "According to Luke, I was drooling, but I don't remember that."
For years afterward, Luke ribbed him. "Hey, Chris, remember that time
you drooled on my wife?"

A few times, Luke came out to visit the Barish family at their summer house in Southampton. They played football on the beach and in-
stalled themselves at the bar at Barrister's for beers. Whenever they ate
out, Chris, who founded a chain of craft burger and beer restaurants,
Black Tap, noticed that Luke never ate much. Luke continued to endear himself to the whole family. Keith Barish was already a fan, but
Chris's mother Ann became smitten when Luke, hearing her grouse on
the phone about a broken fence, pulled out some tools and fixed it on
the spot.

Luke, Chris felt, knew his world better than Chris knew his. "He
seemed to have a lot of different friend groups," Barish says, and he only
casually knew a few isolated key members.

There was a way in which Luke enjoyed being there for people but
didn't necessarily expect or seem to need it in return. His ability to show
up just when needed was almost uncanny. When Barish opened his first
Black Tap in Soho in 2015, Luke, unbidden, showed up only a couple of
days after it opened. When Barish and his first wife, Michelle, amicably
divorced, Luke called to check on both parties, taking no sides, listening without judgment. He understood their ultimate shared concern:
"It was really about our daughter Bee," Barish says. "He wanted to make
sure she was okay."

Luke was something like a godfather to Barish's firstborn. While visiting New York in 2008, staying at the Rhiga Royal on Fifty-Fourth,

Luke was one of the first friends to meet the newborn. "The right friend was there at the right time," Barish says.

As Bee was inconsolably crying, Luke picked her up and calmed her by singing "I Ride an Old Paint," which was playing from a children's music CD. The cowboy traditional has an evocative, mysterious provenance. The narrator rides his paint, a spotted horse, and tells stories to himself. About Old Bill Jones and his tragic life, about the horses with matted tails and raw backs, and how, after he dies, he wants his bones tied to the back of his favorite paint. Plaintive and soulful, it captures a long night alone with one's thoughts, the immediate and the profound, while circling the cattle so they don't run off.

The poet Carl Sandburg published the song lyrics in 1927 in his *American Songbag*, an early catalog of American music. He heard about the tune from two poets, Margaret Larkin and Linn Riggs, who told him all that they knew about it: "The song came to them at Santa Fe from a buckaroo who was last heard of as heading for the border with friends in both Tucson and El Paso." Many musicians have covered it, including Woody Guthrie, Johnny Cash, and Loudon Wainwright III, but Linda Ronstadt's version from 1977 is the most gorgeous.

When Michelle asked Luke how he knew the song—she'd only heard it as a children's lullaby—he said, "It's an old cowboy song . . . and I'm a cowboy."

SHE IS ALWAYS LOOKING TO meet more writers, and she has never attended a literary awards ceremony, so she takes the volunteer job arranged by a well-connected friend. The assignment is to help the photographer, Angie, a stocky figure in red glasses with a fade cut, document the ceremony and the afterparty. During the ceremony, at Angie's insistence, she mostly sits and listens to the speeches. The writers often acknowledge years of work and struggle. She is fumbling her way through a novel; their stories renew her hope.

Now that it's the afterparty, Angie gives her a task.

"What I need you to do is just go around and talk to people, see who's interesting or who would make a good photograph. I'm an extreme introvert and would rather cut off my thumbs than talk to a bunch of strangers."

Floating around the party, Margaret chats people up and gathers them for Angie's photos. Afterward, as they are packing up, Angie turns to her: "You're a Sagittarius, right?"

Ever since she moved to Los Angeles a few years ago, she's had more conversations with people about astrology than her entire time in Chicago. She admires how every follower of astrology, meditation, or witchcraft she knows treats it as deep-probing philosophical work, skeptics be damned.

Still, when Angie correctly named her sun sign, she prepared for a superficial conversation. Angie will hit the typical Sagittarius traits, and she'll affirm or deny. For a minute, it does go that way: "I could tell. You like a party." Margaret concurs. They talk of her love for travel, that she's honest to a fault, but then:

"Did you lose a parent young in life?"

Her scalp tingles. Far away, she heard a kind of ringing bell in the undertow of the hotel staff vacuuming that must've been there all along, but she hadn't noticed it before. Margaret stops packing Angie's photo bag.

"It was your dad," they say softly.

"When I was fifteen. How did you know that?"

"I just see it. I can always tell when someone has crawled through the sludge."

They hand Margaret a card. "Call me for a full reading sometime. I just do it for friends and people I get a strong feeling about."

A few days later, Margaret calls Angie. Besides a palm reader's neon storefront she had dodged into a couple of times after her breakfast shifts in Chicago, her mind hungering for some knowledge she couldn't access from her current position, she's mostly stayed out of the purview of psychics. She doesn't want to get ripped off or freaked out. But Angie doesn't go by that term anyway. Just a dabbler, and therefore no fee. In their flat, near-affectless tone, Angie gives a mix of information, not so much predictions for the future as truisms about Margaret. Some don't resonate, but others, when she hears them from someone else's voice, settle as facts. Most important, Angie talked about ways she can use her father's death, the grief of it, to her advantage. "It is a gift, if you want it to be. You've already started to use it. Just keep going."

THIRTY-SIX

THE *OZ* EXTRAS, MANY of them former or current members of the Latin Kings, the Crips, or the Bloods, had muscled up to Luke, outfitted in his Reverend Jeremiah Cloutier spectacles and shaggy hair, but still recognizable. They wanted autographs, or a little impromptu Dylan. In the era of the flip phone, there was little to no documentation of him playing the whole bit: Dylan's salty squint, the low and hushed tone. *It's not like that, Bren.* Sometimes the prisoner stand-ins asked for gossip: he diplomatically declined to trash-talk any of the leading ladies of *90210*.

A few minutes after wrapping, with the spring evening still ahead of them, Winters went looking for Luke. Maybe they'd go to Pastis again, one of the first restaurants to fancy up the Meatpacking District. The last time they were there, the burgers had taken an eternity to come. When Luke asked the waiter, nicely, if anything could be done to speed up the order, the beleaguered guy said, "Yeah, you wanna go make them?" Cut to Winters and Luke, standing on the line in Pastis's kitchen, shaping raw meat into patties.

Winters was still searching for Luke. A PA said he had gone to the roof. *What roof?* Winters thought. He'd been filming on *Oz* for three years now and he'd never known there was a rooftop to access. He found his way up there through a warren of concrete stairs and heavy doors. His eyes were wired from working all day, his body on the verge of collapse. But he still thrummed with an alchemy of his character's shady energy and his own exhaustion.

Near the edge of the flat, expansive roof stood Perry with his back to Winters, facing west toward New Jersey. Luke didn't turn around; he just lifted a hand in greeting. His eyes were on the sky, beginning its transformation from day to night. The pink-orange sunset crisped the edges of the low buildings, turning windows into fiery mirrors. Winters approached cautiously, worried about his friend. Luke was going through a rough patch in his marriage. He was away from his wife and little children in Los Angeles. They didn't talk about it too much, they didn't need to, but Winters knew.

"Hey, are you okay?"

As he stepped closer, Winters spied the tears streaking down his friend's cheeks, into his beard. Then Luke took a mellow drag from the hand-rolled joint in his fingers. A smile crept in.

"Brother, there is nothing wrong," he said in his whispery way. "This might be one of the happiest moments of my life."

Behind the bars of the fictional prison of *Oz*, Luke was free. They stayed up there for the entire sunset, smoking the rest of the joint, until the night settled in.

AFTER MUCH LURCHING ABOUT, IT *finally happened. She left Adam. At age thirty, she is living alone for the first time in her adult life. She adores everything about the one-bedroom apartment in semi-sketchy Koreatown: The vanity in the hallway draped with her jewelry. The classic Saltillo tiles in the kitchen. The clawfoot tub, and, most of all, the babbling of the fountain floating through the bank of French windows overlooking the front garden. She keeps the windows open all day, only reluctantly locking them at night for security, which she has to take more seriously now.*

When she told her mother, a long conversation ensued. Her mother listened intently and offered understanding: "You're both good people; you'll land on your feet." From her mother, she needed to know that she was still good, despite hurting someone she loved. Relief poured into her, hearing those simple words.

At the end, her mother's habit of summarizing a phone call into one line: "All right, so you're getting a divorce . . ." A pause. "But don't do it again." Then she emitted a nervous titter, a clue, perhaps, that she knew these words were beneath her, beneath their conversation.

She isn't following her mother's commandments for adulthood: marriage, advanced degrees, a career that could be—should be—sidelined at once for children. She feels more like an adult now than she ever has. For breaking the marriage and choosing long-desired independence, despite the fear.

A quiet resilience is building. She will find a way to get the things she wants—love, children, writing as lifeblood. Adulthood is all striving; she didn't imagine it that way at age fifteen. She thought the totems simply accumulated, unstoppable as aging itself. But if striving is what life demands, then so be it. Already, her job writing for a newspaper has enabled her to afford this apartment on her own. The stability she has upended in her life, she'll figure out how to regain. What other choice is there but to figure it out? This is her life. Her life. Maybe it sounds dumb to say, but she honestly isn't sure she understood that until now.

CHAPTER

THIRTY-SEVEN

IN THE LAST FIVE minutes of the 2004 stage adaptation of *When Harry Met Sally*, chunks of plaster rained down on the shoulders and coiffures of the startled audience at the historic Theatre Royal Haymarket in London. A chandelier was falling from the ceiling. The West End production starred Luke and Alyson Hannigan as the titular will-they-or-won't-they couple. It wasn't Luke's first stage rendezvous. He debuted on Broadway in 2001 as Brad Majors in the Tony-nominated revival of *The Rocky Horror Show*. The grand dame, boasting two thousand lead crystals and dancing nymphs, took a sudden dive four feet down from its original position, left to dangle precariously on a safety rope. Needless to say, this was not the romantic denouement anyone had in mind.

The packed house, with tickets going for up to forty pounds, found itself guided to safety by none other than Harry himself. Once he caught wind of the offstage drama, Luke broke character, jumped down to the floor, and ushered patrons away from the pandemonium. One theatergoer said, "He was obviously quite concerned to get members of the audience out, as were the rest of the cast. He was very gallant and the rest of them conducted themselves brilliantly. It was a great performance and it's a shame it had to end this way."

After the upheaval, fifteen people required treatment for minor cuts, bruises, and shock—injuries reminiscent of those nineties mall stampedes—and the theater closed for a few days for safety checks.

Luke's rescue mission might've been the most positive development to come out of the run. By and large, the reviews were less than impressive, sometimes downright eviscerating. When he died, none of that mattered anymore. His heroics on a random Saturday in London were remembered fondly by the theater world, a moment when the man cut through and made more of an impression than the character he played. And luckily, everyone already knew every moan of the faked orgasm scene.

THIRTY-EIGHT

THE MACHINES CROWDING THE hospital bed were keeping Jason Priestley alive. Intermittent beeps and zigzagging lines, following his blood pressure, his weak pulse. An oxygen mask fogging over his bruised face, injuries sustained from slamming into a wall at 180 miles per hour during warmups for a race at the Kentucky Speedway. Both of his feet were broken as well as his back. For forty-five seconds after the accident, which included him caroming into the concrete again after the initial impact, the paramedics could not find a pulse. For that liminal moment on August 11, 2002, Jason Priestley was officially dead.

Luke, in Tennessee at the time, came to his friend's side. Walking into the room, he was terrified at the sight. The bloodied gauze, the swollen skin disfiguring a face that had so often been compared to his own. After two days in the hospital, Priestley still had not verbally responded to anyone who came in the room. The doctors questioned his cognitive function.

The nurses told Luke that he needed to speak loudly, if he had any hopes of breaking through to his friend. Over the tubes and blanket, Luke crawled into Priestley's bed, and put his face right near his.

"Jay, Jay, it's Luke. Wake up. Jay, I'm here for you. Wake up."

Through their purple pouches, Priestley's eyes cracked open, but he didn't respond.

Encouraged, Luke continued: "Who am I? What's my name?" No answer. He repeated the questions.

Priestley, his throat sore from being intubated, whispered: "Coy L. Perry."

The doctors and nurses were confused. Until Luke informed them that Coy was his given name. People close to him knew he hated to be called Coy because of the association with his biological father. In Priestley's fragile condition, was he still razzing his buddy? Whatever the impetus, dredging Coy out from the depths of his mind was a great sign. Two days since he had entered the hospital, and finally there was some hope that he might possess the mental fortitude to climb back to good health.

———

More than twenty years later, Priestley spoke with CBC reporter Ian Hanomansing to promote his documentary on the former Toronto Maple Leafs owner, Harold Ballard. Priestley looked older than his fifty-three years; the accident and its surgeries took their toll.

Hanomansing asked him to respond to some *90210* trivia questions, a light and easy gauntlet. He was asked to recall his favorite directing moment on the show. Priestley was at the helm for several episodes, including Luke's exit in season six, when Dylan finds Toni (Rebecca Gayheart) shot with a bullet that was meant for him. For a while, Priestley was simply lost in the pleasure of the memory:

"So we had rain towers everywhere, and Luke was falling to his knees and, you know, looking up into the heavens and crying, 'Nooooo,' you know. I had a big camera on a crane, pulling away from him in the rain, and you know, Luke and I were just having the best time shooting all that stuff and"—his eyes changed, his voice slowed—". . . I think back to those kind of moments now that he's gone."

Hanomansing: "You must miss him a lot." Speechless, Priestley nodded a few times, glanced to the window nearby, then back again.

CLOTHES HAVE DROPPED. FROM THE couch, he pulls her on top of him. Hands over her skin. His breath on her ear, murmuring, asking, but she can barely respond.

They had met at her friend's engagement party. The celluloid of her last few hours was missing several frames. Champagne. Cinders. Catering. The former house of Ava Gardner or Marlene Dietrich or some other Hollywood ghost with notable eyebrows. God, they all had such fabulous eyebrows back then.

The body that is hers is unoccupied. Moving but with the commands fading across a droop of cables. Isn't she supposed to be turned on? At some point she was, but now it's just acting. She's been phoning it in for the last several minutes, waiting for desire to come back. Something is not right.

She climbs off him to the other end of the couch.

"Is everything okay?"

"No," she says after a moment. Embarrassed, she's suddenly way too naked for her taste. His erection, awkwardly, hasn't had time to deflate to the new moment.

"It just went really fast," she says, "and I don't think I'm feeling it anymore."

"Oh," he answers. Suddenly she is aware of being in his small but polished mid-century home—that she had driven to, through the hills, going fifteen miles per hour so she wouldn't smash some B-list actor's parked car on a hairpin. What exactly is she supposed to do here now? She puts on her underwear and approaches the calico cat curled up on a chair; she pets it, to immediate purrs.

"That's Annie," he says. "She doesn't really leave that chair."

"I have two of these at home," she says.

"Did I do something wrong?"

She shook her head. "I'm not ready, I guess." She gets on the rest of her clothes as rapidly as possible without actually speed-dressing. "I just got out of a big relationship a little while ago."

"I get it."

In her car, with a twenty-minute drive home. It's nearly two a.m. She took Sunset, the neon of the hotels and the pawnshops and the 99 Cents store lighting the pavement.

CHAPTER

THIRTY-NINE

THE YEAR IS 2021, and all the children who survived "The Big Death," a hormonal plague that wiped out all of the grown-ups fifteen years ago, are now adults. Jeremiah, played by a brooding and meditative Luke, is on a mission to find Valhalla Sector, a mysterious place his viral researcher father told him to seek out shortly before he disappeared. Navigating his way through a roughshod society teetering on anarchy, he picks up Kurdy, a cynical and wounded wanderer played by Malcolm Jamal Warner. At first, the two men can't quite trust each other, but circumstances keep throwing them together. An uneasy alliance is formed.

Luke starred in and executive produced *Jeremiah*, a Showtime fiction series that aired from 2002 to 2004. On one of their very first days of filming, the Twin Towers fell from a terrorist attack in New York. Luke and Warner, who had just met for the first time, were the sole Americans on set. There was also Warner's mother, his manager, who had come out to Canada to help him get settled. Needless to say, her flight home to Los Angeles that day was canceled.

"It felt like, *What's going on? Where is this leading?*" Warner remembers. He and Luke were "blown away and fucked up. We were concerned for all our friends in New York. Fortunately, everyone we knew was okay."

That rough start exacerbated an already difficult shoot. Warner estimated that 85 percent of the shooting involved being outside in thick, gloomy Canadian forest. Both actors left their Yaletown, Vancouver, apartments in the dark of the morning and would return late at night, five days a week. If it poured rain while they shot, so be it.

"I'm too old for this [stuff]," Luke said. His family had decamped with him to the area, but he hardly had time to see them. "I can honestly say that I don't know if I would have done this series had I known it would be this much work." Then he adds more diplomatically: "I'm not complaining. All actors are lucky to have the work. So if I get tired, I try to pump myself up all that much more."

The sun-deprived grind prompted Warner, for the first time in his life, to ponder if he had seasonal affective disorder. Yet, despite the physical toll, he felt a freedom that had eluded him for years. He was away from *Malcolm & Eddie*, a UPN sitcom that had challenged him for four seasons. Warner had received his acting education on *The Cosby Show*, led by star and cocreator Bill Cosby, who's since been accused of rape, sexual assault, and sexual harassment by more than sixty women. Out of habit, Warner still calls his former mentor Mr. Cosby, but now in a bitter tone. Cosby had emphasized their collective responsibility to provide positive images of Black people. *Malcolm & Eddie*, on the other hand, was the complete opposite, according to Warner. "I was the only one who cared about the images," Warner said. "I was fighting writers, producers, the studio, the network, fellow actors. I spent four years on that show feeling like Don Quixote."

Jeremiah wasn't without its troubling optics as well. Warner, before he screen-tested, insisted that they change certain things about Kurdy, namely that he was illiterate and, in the pilot, that he's found hanging upside down from a tree. "Not in the year 2000, no, you can't do that," Warner says. Fortunately, creator and showrunner J. Michael Straczynski (best known for *Babylon 5*) listened to Warner and changed the script.

The person who most established the tone on set was Luke, the number one on the call sheet. After Warner's Don Quixote years, it was a relief to follow Luke's lead. "He made coming to work a joy. Even with the grind and the SAD and all that, he still managed to find the joy in the longest day.

"Luke would always say he was a fool with a capital L," Warner says. "He was a nut who enjoyed life. He didn't take himself too seriously and he didn't take the ride so seriously. The whole thing was a roller coaster. You take the bumps with the thrills. His whole thing was always, 'We're so lucky to be doing this, to get paid to do what we're doing.'"

Both had come of age as actors in the firestorm of immediate fame (Warner was only fourteen when *The Cosby Show* debuted to instant high ratings). Both understood that early success was a gift, not to be taken for granted. Warner's mother sat her son down early on in *The Cosby Show* phenomenon and asked him what he planned to do when the show inevitably ended. She pointed out that every actor has their hot and their not-so-hot periods, and that in order to protect themselves, they needed to have a plan for the downtimes. To this day, Warner is a multi-hyphenate, a musician and a poet. Her wise advice never left him.

Luke and Warner "always talked about the peaks and valleys, because that's something that we shared. By *Jeremiah*, our valleys weren't that low, but we shared longer stretches of unemployment than we would've liked."

———

By the making of season two, the grind had intensified. Luke, as an executive producer, witnessed the increasing tension between producing studio MGM Home Entertainment and Straczynski, who were at odds over the creative direction of the show. As for Warner, he had always been told that Jeremiah and Kurdy were "a bromance," but he found himself having to fight the showrunners for equal screen time. He didn't tell much of this to Luke. "There were things I would probably have shared just as actors, but because I saw this weight on his shoulders, I didn't want to compound that."

Luke's burdens went beyond *Jeremiah*'s growing pains; after ten years, his marriage was ending. Here he was in Vancouver, away from his home and his friends, and no longer with his family. Luke confided in Warner.

"The divorce hit him hard," Warner says. "He was really concerned about the relationship with his kids." Though Warner was in a long-term relationship at the time, he had experienced his own heartbreak when his former girlfriend and fellow *Cosby* alum, Michelle Thomas, died of cancer in 1998. Luke's pain brought him back to his own experiences. "When you're a guy and you're watching another guy's heart breaking, it's really hard."

Luke's troubles, Warner says, didn't affect his performance or energy on set. But Showtime canceled the series before the debut of season two, stating they no longer wanted to make science fiction. The reviews had never been particularly strong: MORE SIGH-FI THAN SCI-FI, read a *Seattle Post-Intelligencer* headline, but *Jeremiah* had a loyal following. All fifteen episodes of season two had been shot and edited, but Showtime tried to wrap up the series by showing only the first seven. The fans kicked off an extensive fax, email, and phone campaign, demanding "The Missing Eight." Ten months later, the network aired the last eight episodes. It was a sign of how deeply the show had resonated with its audience.

In Luke's view, the cancellation was premature. "I would've loved to continue on *Jeremiah*," he said. "I was pretty angry about it . . . I said to the channel, 'I think you're making a big mistake.'" He talked about one day finishing the story as a series on SYFY or as a feature-length movie, but the chance never did arrive.

Jeremiah, Luke said, was a show about the collective consciousness. He believed the collective always moves toward doing the right thing. The end of the world allows people to be stripped of their prior identities, a rebirth that he found creatively exciting: "You start to see the value of someone in a completely different way, when you take away their job title or whatever. 'Oh, so you're an accountant, big deal.' When the world goes to shit, it doesn't mean anything... that was always much more interesting to me... when people start to see each other as something other than face value, or whatever role society had assigned them."

SHE'S AT HER DESK AT *the newspaper, where she's worked for a few years now. Fighting distraction.*

Clicks over to Facebook: She posts a picture of a rotary phone, in turquoise and white. Maybe she's been watching too much Mad Men *lately. It's impeccable. She wants to be Betty calling Don in her sea-green nightgown.*

She goes back to writing her article, but she has to hunt through the transcript for usable nuggets. The New York musician had spoken to her from a van with his band crowded all around him, in a tone that seesawed between shy and passive-aggressive. At one point, when the van pulled over for a break, he admitted to being uncomfortable because everyone was listening. He apologizes, but the interview continued, dry and stilted. Too bad, she's a huge fan, not that she told him. In general, she doesn't.

She primarily writes celebrity profiles of musicians and actors. There are some celebrities (an imperfect word; some are celebrities only to a niche audience) who really only want to talk to a fan. The journalist is a snake in the grass, but a fan is a friend willing to grant latitude and then some. Sometimes she can feel the celebrity wondering which one they are talking to: fan or foe, as if those are the only two categories that exist. They needle for how much of their catalog she knows, inserting pauses that are meant to be filled with compliments. And sometimes she obliges, but only when it's authentic. Or so she tries. Sometimes, relenting to her people-pleasing side, she ends up saying something fake.

They don't know what they're getting out of her, and likewise, she doesn't know what she's getting out of them. What's really genuine between them, in such a transactional situation? Case in point: One musician cried over his father's death to her, in a candlelit hotel room. She felt honored to share this experience with him until she heard through the grapevine that this was his "thing," crying in front of women journalists. Now she doesn't really know what happened between them. A performance?

One of her editors pops out of his office and stands at her cubicle, his arm slung over the wall.

"Don't be one of those people," he said.

"What people?"

"That phone you just posted?" He rolls his eyes. "Oh yes, the beautiful past. When boys were boys and girls were girls and all that shit."

"That is not what I was pining for."

This editor is one of the digital proponents. He thinks the act of printing news on paper is Jurassic and futile.

"What is it, then?" he continues. "What is the point of that?"

"It conjures up an atmosphere. Bygone objects," she struggles to explain, "they feel unreal and yet someone used them every day. Then they go into a museum."

"It's not even your nostalgia. It's the sixties. Did you ever use a rotary phone?"

She did. She asked her parents to put a phone in her bedroom in the third grade. They complied with a rotary, maybe to slow her down.

She squints at him. "Aren't you wearing a Madras plaid suit right now?"

"Get back to work," he says jokingly.

———

"Nostalgia is to memory as kitsch is to art," the historian Charles Maier wrote in 1995 while, presumably, crushing a pair of rose-tinted glasses into the concrete. When she stumbled on that quote years later, she thought about the conversation with her editor, and so many others like it. Nostalgia causes suspicion; too much of it, and people suspect they are being manipulated. For good reason: Nostalgia can be the sugarcoating on the past. Embedded in some of our most precious bits of nostalgia are the mistakes and prejudices of our prior selves. There is a balance between eying it critically and forgiving ourselves for who we were.

Regardless, nostalgia has its merits, not to be taken lightly. For centuries after the term was coined in 1688, nostalgia was considered a malady. Lately, it's received just dues. According to Social Cognitive and Affective Neuroscience in 2022, it's actually good: "In particular, nostalgia boosts self-esteem or self-positivity, increases meaning in life, fosters social connectedness and social support, encourages help seeking, enhances psychological health and well-being, and attenuates dysphoric states such as loneliness, boredom, stress or death anxiety."

The attenuation of loneliness, boredom, stress. Death itself. Yes, the suffering recedes and the joy flows in when she dives into the scents, music, and images of the past: Anais Anais. Marilyn Monroe posters. Oversized Bart Simpson T-shirts. Black velvet chokers. Herbal Essences shampoo. Boyz II Men. Sassy magazine. Venus Zine. The sound of a VW Karmen Ghia starting. Gregorian chants. Clinique's Black Honey lip stain. "Joe lies." Chinatown velvet flats. Tracy Chapman's "Fast Car." The smell of clove cigarettes. The smell of Noxzema. The sound of a dial-up modem. Luke Perry's eyes.

CHAPTER

FORTY

DAVID MILCH'S EXISTENTIALIST SERIES *John from Cincinnati* will go down as one of the most befuddling chapters in all of prestige TV.

In his 2022 memoir, *Life's Work*, Milch, a protégé of Robert Penn Warren and a graduate of the Iowa Writers' Workshop, explains his influences for the 2007 HBO show that ostensibly follows the Yost family's three generations of surfers. Like a lot of things Milch, including his gritty and poetic series *Deadwood*, the chapter on *John* resists clarity in favor of fascinating digressions and tangled koans. He writes about the ocean wave as a symbol of time. "It comes again and again. It keeps saying, 'Will you know me now?'"

Luke played Linc Stark, a predatory surfing agent. To the Yost family, Linc represents the crass commercialization of surfing. Linc is not about the wave as a metaphor for time; he's about the wave as a delivery system for money. Luke's presence here has layers: Here's this actor, so well-known from the commercial world of network TV, playing a surfer who could almost pass for a fallen Dylan McKay but on prestige TV. The show is messing with our sense of terra firma, for TV and in terms of reality. By the time we get to Mitch Yost levitating a few inches off the ground after a surf, it's clear the usual laws are only around for subversion.

The clearest reason for *John from Cincinnati*'s ambitious but ultimately dissatisfying first and only season is that, plain and simple, it didn't get enough stewing time. After the abrupt cancellation of *Deadwood*, the wounded creator sallied forth with *John from Cincinnati* in a matter of months, in order to give the few hundred production people laid off from *Deadwood* another job, and to avoid becoming "suicidally depressed" himself. Honorable reasons but it wasn't ready: in the ten episodes *JfC* lasted, before it was canceled by HBO, Milch often appeared on set with partial scripts or no scripts written for the actors. Due to all the last-minute scrambles, he also frequently ran well over budget.

John McNaughton, who directed one of the episodes, puts it this way: "There's only one person I've worked with who I would call a genius and that's David." As for his unorthodox working methods, "you either roll with it and admire his insanity and brilliance, or you don't and then you're going to be so unhappy."

Luke approached his role with a philosophy similar to McNaughton's: let the genius cut his mad path. He called Milch "the greatest writer on television, hands down. You won't hear me qualify that in any way." The two met in the nineties when Luke had to drop a role on *NYPD Blue*, where Milch was a writer, for contractual reasons. When Milch first told him about the role, it was over breakfast. Luke recalled Milch pulling some wrinkled script pages out of his back pocket to show him, pressing them down on the table. Then in his gravelly voice, Milch launched into a loose pitch of the show. Luke was in awe already: "He's the greatest teller of his own stories . . . he owes no loyalty to anything but his creative vision."

Casting Luke as Stark was in keeping with the skewed logic of the show. Everything in *John from Cincinnati* is familiar to the viewer, but off-kilter. Familiar faces abound from much more traditional TV—including character actors Ed O'Neill, Luis Guzmán, and Willie Garson—but they're part of such a strange world that seeing them incites an unsettling déjà vu. The pilot of *John from Cincinnati* aired right after the series finale of *The Sopranos*, with its infamous closing frame. When a scruffy Luke appears as the first face in the pilot, an eeriness is immediately foregrounded. We *know* this guy.

McNaughton fondly remembers filming scenes with Luke, Rebecca De Mornay, and Garret Dillahunt. "Those three actors were so wonderful to work with, and there was no time pressure because David just didn't care," McNaughton says. During one afternoon, Milch disappeared, bringing everything to a halt for two and a half hours, as he wrote a scene on the spot for an elder Latina he had befriended on the block. Milch had already bought a lot of the Amway she was selling, and compensated her for filming in her house. Now he wanted her in the show, perhaps to capture a real-life resident of their setting, the depressed border town of Imperial City, California.

The woman appeared for a few minutes, serving up an endearingly stilted performance, but no discernible plot value. Either way, McNaughton didn't mind. "Milch has amazing instincts. You're just happy to be in his insane orbit."

Like McNaughton, Luke didn't question Milch's impromptu and sometimes inscrutable filmmaking decisions. At one point, Milch insisted they reshoot one of Luke's scenes over and over again, long after the rest of the episode was shot, for no particular reason that McNaughton could parse.

"I don't know how many times I came in to reshoot that one scene, maybe five times," McNaughton said. "It was a pretty nice paycheck in the end."

Luke, as McNaughton remembered it, didn't get fatigued with all the reshoots or express any impatience. "He understood the game," McNaughton said. "Again and again, he came in and did his job. Luke came from the working class, like me. You go to work and you do your job."

Luke recalled if not the same scene McNaughton referred to, then another one that demanded reshooting. The actor was "having trouble getting to where I'd need to get in that scene." Milch took him aside, Luke remembered, for a pep talk: "'Listen, asshole, you're a great actor. I need you to be great *right now*.' That's all it took . . . I thought, 'Great, cool. I'll kill and die for this guy.'" He said Milch was the only director he ever worked with who called him a great actor.

CHAPTER

FORTY-ONE

IN 2006, LUKE SUPPORTED Sherrod Brown's Ohio Senate run with frequent stops around his home state. At one rally, he said, "I don't do politics. It ain't my thing. And I don't play parties, but I do play the man, and I've known this man my entire life." Sherrod's father, Charles Guiley Brown, delivered Luke in Mansfield and remained his doctor "for the first twelve years of my life," Luke said at a rally. "He taught me about patience and compassion. He taught me how to sew myself up." Dr. Brown was likely the man who stitched Luke's eyebrow after he ran into a soda machine at a bowling alley, giving him that trademark bad-boy scar that Dylan McKay milked with each squint.

Sherrod returned Luke's praises on the trail. "About a week and a half before [my father] died, he got a call from Luke Perry . . . he just called to see how my dad was doing, and to thank him for his taking care of him as a child." Luke's down-home characteristics played well for Sherrod, who won the seat and has remained in office since. Luke wasn't just the long-time patient of a small-town doctor who he stayed in touch with, but also a former trailer-park resident and a high school graduate who never made it to college, all of which he mentioned to the Ohio voters. Often while wearing a trucker hat, in style at the time, but he wore it before, and he didn't ditch it after the look became a cliché of the hipster aughts.

A political operative named Michael O'Neil tweeted about meeting Luke on the road for Sherrod. "Luke did events across Ohio. We offered a driver, but his high school buddy drove him in a beat-up car. Zero ego." Luke carpooling with his buddy in a clunker was a point of pride for him, no doubt. "I'm not here because I'm from Hollywood, I'm here because I'm from Ohio," he said on the trail.

Two years later, when the 2008 presidential election was less than two months away, Luke appeared on Chicago's WGN. The anchors intended to discuss *90210*, a reboot for a younger generation. Entertainment reporter Dean Richards introduced the interview, recorded the day before the newscast. Luke sat in a director's chair at a bustling urban square and was brought on camera with a chyron reading, LUKE PERRY, ACTOR-ISH. Wow, rude, but certainly a clue to the tenor of the ensuing conversation. Richards dove in: "The number one question with [the] new show *90210* that everyone is asking: Is Luke going to be joining the cast, as Shannen and Jenny [have]?"

Luke, his smooth expression betraying not a hint of mischief, said: "Well, you know, it's interesting that you would ask me that, because I think I *am* going to support Barack Obama. I think he's absolutely the best choice that we can make right now."

Richards, after some fake guffawing at Luke's answer, informs the viewers that Luke continued to pitch for Obama for the next thirty seconds, "because, you know, we only have a certain amount of time to talk to these guys on the satellite. And he's thinking he's burning up the time." Richards interrupted Luke and dive-bombed again: "Have the producers of that show approached you? Have they talked to you at all? Do you have any interest, if they have?"

"Well, I don't have a lot of experience in political campaigning, but I don't think that's what it's about. I think you just really got to believe what you're talking about and—"

Luke's response was muted. Just as Richards forged ahead for the third time, the producers decided to end the runaway chat, to everyone's relief. We don't see Luke again on camera—but the WGN news desk was not finished with him.

"Why didn't he just say, 'I don't know'?" asked anchor Robin Baumgarten, wildly blind to the point. Richards, Baumgarten, and one other reporter proceeded to slam the actor in absentia, bleating more than once, "You're Luke Perry!" One of them dares to call him a "loser." In their eyes, he was a one-trick pony who should remain in his stultifying lane for life. From the perspective of fifteen years later, Luke comes off the better player, who doesn't stoop to petty condescension. Unsurprisingly, nearly all of the YouTube commenters, where the video is preserved as "Luke Perry Bizarre Interview," agree.

His working-class ideals made him a natural ally to all underdogs, which, in Hollywood, translates to the WGA. Before the 2023 strike fused the WGA and SAG unions to fight the encroaching decimation of their livelihood against AI and other technological game-changers, the WGA held a strike from November 5, 2007, to February 12, 2008, negotiating for residuals rates for new media. Luke joined the picket line, and at one point, according to novelist and TV writer David Iserson on Twitter, "He got infuriated by someone talking shit to the writers, and so he beat the guy's car with a picket sign . . . his was not an attainable cool."

THE FRONT DOOR SHUT, AND the dog's entire posture electrifies. Whimpers escape out of his tan-and-white-furred throat. He watches the door for the next twenty minutes, waiting for his foster mom to return.

"It's okay," she tells him, petting his bristled back fur, but he ignores her. She doesn't really believe herself either. Why on earth did she think adopting a dog would solve all her problems, namely the breakup that's eating her alive?

She had seen the chihuahua after crying on her mat in yoga class. Tears leaked past her temples as her yoga teacher read the Rumi poem with the line "Love is a black lion, thirsty and blood-drinking, it pastures only on the blood of lovers." She didn't want to be the person crying in yoga class, but it couldn't be helped. The poem mentioned Mount Qaf, which caught her ear. She read about it later: in Persian mythology, it is a distant ideal mountain that can never be reached. Mount Qaf, she thinks, is the mystical healed place where she has everything she wants.

After her boyfriend admitted to months of secretive cheating, she discovered that there had been flings all along. And to think she had once sat at a Nick Cave concert next to him, sobbing to "Into My Arms," wondering if she might be with him forever. To be so wrong about someone shocked her; she had always believed herself to be an acute judge of character.

The breakup has woken up all the other losses she foolishly thought too dormant to cause trouble: the sharp loneliness of her childhood, especially those long years as her father dwindled into death. She kept it all silent for years, which was its own pain. Until Dr. F.

She wasted two good years on bullshit. Unlike when she divorced Adam, time isn't on her side, or so the pernicious fiction went. According to the conceptually musty but undeniably powerful biological clock, she is running out of chances. Where is the dedicated partner, the adorable children, the meaningful, satisfying career?

A few months later, she sits on her couch with a guy on their second date, the dog now named Flynn napping at their side. Her date is sensitive, smart, and attractive, but she already knows he isn't the one. Still, she never misses an opportunity to probe another person's psychology. They talk about former relationships, insecurities, success, and what they wish for.

He says, "I should tell you something: I lied about my age."

She waits for him to continue. She doesn't remember what age he wrote on his profile, only that it was in the parameters of her generous search terms.

"I said I was thirty-one, but I'm actually thirty-two."

She blinks. "But that's only a year."

He draws in a breath. "I thought it sounded better for my career. Like what I've accomplished for a thirty-one-year-old is good, but it's not so good for thirty-two."

She understands.

FORTY-TWO

"IF I'M BEING HONEST, my first impression of Luke was not great," says former child actress Ari Bagley. She unfolds their first working day together on the Utah set of *Scoot and Kassie's Christmas Adventure*, a wholesome affair directed by former Mormon missionary Benjamin Gourley. Released in 2013, the movie is representative of a roughly ten-year period starting around 2008 that sees Luke doing a spate of corny, barely seen movies.

Bagley, then eleven years old, was exhausted from being repeatedly thunked in the head with a dodgeball in a prior scene, and in comes this nineties legend, the one everyone gushed about, especially her mother's friends. Instead of warmth and charm emanating from her on-screen single father, she encountered an impatient working actor eager to get on with the show.

"I think he had a bad experience working with kids on set in the past," Bagley recalls, "because kids, well, they make everything harder to do. And here he was doing this movie with a bunch of kids and a dog saving Christmas." Bagley pauses. "He was a little short with me, at first. He was trying to teach me things, trying to speed up the process, but just the way it was coming across was more condescending than anything in the beginning." She says that it "took him a while to warm up," but once he did, Bagley, who's been acting since age six, was grateful to learn from him, some of it practical.

Don't take too many bites of anything you have to eat on camera, because you'll have to swallow those bites eight more times. Don't look down for your mark on the floor, just wait until your toe bumps against a little sandbag and you'll know you're in the right place. (He was the one who brought in the sandbags, when he noticed the kids couldn't stop looking down in the middle of their lines.) *And for God's sake, don't peel a banana from the stem.* When Ari and her sister Camrey Bagley Fox, who also appeared in the film (plus two of their younger siblings), prepped breakfast in one scene, Luke caught them denuding the fruit in this most upsetting manner. Do as the monkeys do, he told them, and start from the other end with a small pinch. A decade later, Bagley says, "every time I eat a banana, I think, 'Luke Perry,' and I can't open one by the stem anymore."

He also taught Bagley and the other young performers to advocate for themselves. When they were clearly fatigued from shooting too long, he wrangled breaks for them. As a child actor especially, "you never want to speak up and make anything harder, but he taught me that it's important to do that when you need to," Bagley says. He made certain Camrey attended her prom by switching the order of scenes shot that day, insisting on doing his after hers.

In his glory days, Bagley says, "he probably never thought he would end up shooting a movie with a bunch of kids and a dog. But it was a good example, because he still had a positive energy on set, and he still put his best foot forward. He wasn't throwing it away."

Bagley wasn't the only key cast member who clashed with Luke in the beginning. The dog playing Scoot, a female German shepherd barely a year old at the time, bristled with energy. Between takes, they all played with the canine thespian so she could focus when the camera was on. In one of their first scenes together, Luke was nicked on the chin when the overzealous pup jumped up to kiss him. Everyone on set, Bagley recalled, worried that Luke would insist on replacing Scoot. But over the next few days, he became smitten with his costar, feeding her treats and running her around for exercise.

CHAPTER

FORTY-THREE

SOME OF LUKE'S MOST successful ventures reunited him with his *90210* costars. In 2002, Jennie Garth landed a leading role as the fussy, uptight Val in the WB sitcom *What I Like About You*, with Amanda Bynes as her younger sister who crashes into her life in New York City. Val's dating adventures figure into several plot lines; in season three, Luke appears as Todd, a plumber who Val had a fling with back in high school. Naturally, their history leads to a flashback that sends up *90210*, five years after it went off the air.

As actors, even when their characters were sparring, what existed between Garth and Luke always seemed more playful and affectionate than Doherty and Luke's fire-and-ice extremes. The satire of *What I Like About You* gave them a chance to revel in that fun-loving energy. Garth, wearing a facsimile of the black-and-white prom dress that Kelly and Brenda bickered over, is crying into her locker about a breakup when Todd manifests as a low-rent Dylan with a pleather jacket and obvious sideburn pasties. Todd moans that Brenda has dumped him from Paris and just like in Beverly Hills, he starts making a move on Val. They kiss, but then Val shuts him down. "My loss," he says, and then looks mock forlornly to the side, waiting for her to follow the feminine script of assuaging a man's fragile ego. She takes the bait:

"Did I hurt your feelings? I'm sorry."

"It's okay, everyone does," Todd says, before moodily adding, "I'm gonna go."

"No! No, don't go."

He looks at her quizzically.

"I mean, you're so tormented," Val said. "No one understands you. You're empty inside. Your heart hurts you, doesn't it?"

"Well, uh—"

"Shut up, Todd."

Val grabs him for a steamy lip lock, her strength undone by his wounded soul. The scene is a comic wink to what viewers naively accepted as a nonnegotiable part of the contract in the nineties. Love, we were taught by the Dylan McKays of the world, meant taking care of his emotions first. It meant mistaking the man's neglect and ego trips as a reason to try even harder to center him and disappear yourself. Be his perfect girl who always responds, and never leads. It had been only five years since *90210* went off the air, but the viewers had grown up. The right one shouldn't require dismantling your internal security system.

———

In his down period, certain projects popped out from the clutter, including another reunion with one of his *90210* costars. In 2008, Luke developed and brought to life a character named John Goodnight for the Hallmark channel, for the first of three movies. Jason Priestley directed the 2011 debut, *Goodnight for Justice*, because, as Luke told the press, he knew he could scream at his old friend (and be screamed at in return) without worrying about it—all in a day's work to get the best shot.

Luke didn't miss the opportunity to create a character that played to his assets. In fact, he brought those qualities to new campy heights. John Goodnight is a nineteenth-century circuit judge, touring the Wyoming territory with a gun slung lasciviously in front of his pelvis, to the point that a viewer wonders how he can comfortably walk. He's smooth with the ladies, overly familiar with the bottle, and yet, for all his louche ways, he's studious with the law and applies it for good. Luke inhabits Goodnight with a low, steady pulse, an old hunting dog asleep on the porch, snapping to life when honor and chivalry require it.

Luke told *USA Today* that he dreamed up Goodnight after reading about President Andrew Jackson's time as a circuit judge with the Tennessee Superior Court, but unlike America's racist forebearer, Goodnight challenges the white, male status quo with his rulings. He treats a prostitute with dignity, protects a Black child from in-court harassment, and decides in favor of Native Americans. In other words, the modern enlightened man but in dust-coated, sweat-starched Western garb—old-school swagger meets new-school empathy.

The first movie went on to become the channel's most-watched film of the year, and was followed by two sequels, helmed by other directors. After *8 Seconds*, it was Luke's most rewarding experience in the imaginary Western territories.

The two paired up for several interviews promoting the film, showcasing their easy rapport. They also frequently attended fan conferences to reminisce about the old heady days of fame. An *ET Canada* reporter compared Luke getting mobbed at the mall and smuggled out in a laundry bin to something that happened to Justin Bieber.

Jason turned to Luke and asked how it felt to be "the Justin Bieber of 1991."

"Real good," Luke said dryly.

A LAST-MINUTE ASSIGNMENT: GO INTERVIEW Justin Bieber for a behind-the-scenes chat while he's being photographed for the cover of Rolling Stone. *She knows the drill: all biding and waiting, for maybe fifteen minutes of the celebrity's sustained attention.*

The occasion is Justin Bieber's eighteenth birthday—official emancipation from childhood, at least in principle. The location is down a dizzying driveway from the Pacific Coast Highway, planted feet from the shore in Malibu. The Sandcastle is the architect Harry Gesner's family home, hand-built in 1974 from sustainable materials he salvaged from a silent movie theater and a schoolhouse; the fire department had called him to come pick up huge telephone poles about to be trashed. Curved glass windows look out on the ocean, crashing mere feet away in azure and foam. Across from the view, a brick fireplace with a stone hearth designed as a stage for his wife, the actress Nan Martin. Today, the hearth holds discarded pieces of clothing, a makeup Caboodle, clamps, and lights.

Bieber is getting ready. A masculine weight has crept into his speaking voice, but it still largely carries the lightness of a child. His frame is slight, his cheeks still padded with baby fat. None of it matters; his orchestrated leap into adulthood is already underway. Soon, the darkening profile; the sexy lyrics; the rumors that he had allegedly, long ago, been relieved of his virginity.

Margaret sits on the hearth, taking notes. Bieber's publicist keeps pushing off Margaret's request for time.

Bieber's crew rests on the carpet by the windows. They are a loose assortment of young people mostly buried in their phones, unless their services are required.

"Is this dope?" Bieber asks them, wearing a cut-off flannel shirt and jeans he selected from the racks.

They snap to attention. "Ooh, I like it," followed by more encouraging words, then someone piping in, "Roll up the jeans just a bit, though." He tries it and receives a series of exploding fist bumps. Then hair and eyes fall back into the blue light. He shimmies into more looks: slouchy denim, baggy T-shirts, hoodies, jean jackets. All the while, his crew reads him bits of news or gossip, sometimes pertaining to himself. He reacts with studied nonchalance, or occasionally, a slight smirk.

At one point, Bieber suddenly breaks into a song, "End of the Road" by Boyz II Men. Some members of his crew supply harmony. As his mellifluous voice pours into the lyrics, his whole being takes on an exalted, spiritual purpose. His eyes close, his face uplifts. Everything quotidian, mundane—honestly, silly—disappears about him. His outsized talent is staggering. Margaret wipes away tears.

———

The interview never happens. The publicist, at the end of the day, tells her Bieber is simply "unprepared" for a quick chat.

The only way back up the crazy, winding driveway is by golf cart. Somehow she ends up in Bieber's golf cart with one of his entourage driving. She sits across from Bieber in the tight space, gripping the side bar. Throughout the afternoon, he had given her a friendly smile a time or two, but she has no idea if he realizes that she's the reporter he had declined to speak to. He is palpably relaxed now that he's done with all his commitments.

As they zip up the hill, the driver is taking it way too fast. They hit a sudden dip in the road with too much speed, and the golf cart sails into the air. They are utterly aloft for way too long, multiple seconds, to the point that none of them can speak. She and Bieber share a look of stunned panic. The wheels are still not on the ground and the vehicle is tilting. Finally, the wheels crash down at an angle and somehow, impossibly, the cart rights itself.

"Holy sheeeeeee-iit!" he says. Then he laughs, punk-confidence style, a teenager scoffing at a roller coaster, and sticks his tongue out of the side of his mouth. She has to laugh with him. It is all so ridiculous.

FORTY-FOUR

ON OCTOBER 28, 2011, Luke Perry died, according to a joke media outlet calling itself Global Associated News:

> The actor and novice snowboarder was vacationing . . . in Zermatt, Switzerland, with family and friends. Witnesses indicate that [he] lost control of his snowboard and struck a tree at a high rate of speed . . . The actor was wearing a helmet at the time of the accident and drugs and alcohol do not appear to have played any part in his death.

The story continued, stating Perry had been air-lifted to a local hospital but had likely expired upon impact. The news spread on Twitter and Facebook but was quickly straightened out by Perry's representatives: "He's very much alive. The last thing he'd be doing is snowboarding in Zermatt." (Really? The *last* thing? There's a picture of him online from 2008, skiing at Sunshine Village near Banff, Alberta, Canada.)

Turned out that cooking up celebrity demises was Global Associated News's kink. Brad Pitt, Jeff Goldblum, Hilary Duff, Eddie Murphy, and Adam Sandler had all met their tragic ends at the hands of Global Associated News, which wasn't so global at all. It was the lone work of one American prankster, Rich Hoover, who told *E! News* in 2012 that his faux obits were always accompanied by a disclaimer at the bottom of the page stating that everything was "100% fabricated." However, since no one has ever, not once, scrolled down to the bottom of a web page, it always went unread, allowing the story to proliferate. Hoover insisted that it was "dark comedy, done in poor taste, I'm guilty of that, but the intent is not to be hurtful to one's character." Global Associated News has long since vanished, save for an abandoned Facebook page.

———

"I'm feeling pretty old tonight," Stephen Colbert said on his show, in October 2016. The occasion, he revealed, was Luke gracing the cover of AARP's magazine for his fiftieth birthday. He held up a copy of it. For the millennials, he started to define AARP, then Luke Perry—then, actually, "Let me start by defining 'magazine.'" Part of the joke seemed to ride on Luke's faded influence, but it was bigger than that. Putting the magazine down, Colbert dug in: "It seems like only yesterday I was watching *90210*, shopping for flannel shirts on my way to a Ross Perot rally, drinking a Zima while legally purchasing entire albums of music." He added, "If you're old enough to be a Luke Perry fan, you won't have long to wait." Wait for the Grim Reaper, that is. The bit concludes with "Jason Priestley" coming onstage in the form of a white-haired elder walking with a cane.

THE RAIN SLUICES DOWN THE room's windows, slaps on the porch's tin roof, and spills out from a gutter onto a patch of mint. Inside the room painted yellow, she reads a book under a single crisp sheet, waiting for him to come back. The feeling of waiting is ripe, expectant. She cradles it as she turns the pages, the thunder punctuating every few scenes.

Sand everywhere. The floorboards are dusted from the beach. The bottom of the bed, where their feet rest, is gritty. In their bathroom, the tub bears their damp bathing suits, which they'll return to tomorrow.

Here it is, glowing, so she will inspect it closely. She is old enough now to understand how happiness works for her. A dawning that spreads warm through her being, suffusing it amber. A clock in the kitchen ticks off time, but it doesn't matter. Returning to her desk in a couple of weeks is an eternity away; the various work passwords already scrubbed clean from her memory.

Her boyfriend's sister and her husband enter the kitchen, just outside her door. They set about making dinner, murmuring to each other instructions and bits of info from their day, sometimes soft laughter. No words can be made out from her bed, only the comforting tones of domestic duty.

Then the man who she is falling in love with enters the room, his dark hair salted from the ocean, his twinkling eyes searching hers, asking if she wants to walk in the rain with him. He produces an aqua rain slicker for her that he found somewhere in the old house. She says yes.

PART
THREE

CHAPTER

FORTY-FIVE

CASTING DIRECTOR DAVID RAPAPORT first met Luke when he auditioned for DC's *Legends of Tomorrow*. He was excellent, Rapaport says, but ultimately didn't win the part.

Rapaport watched *Beverly Hills, 90210* while he was in high school, and Luke, flush in his heartthrob years, made an impression. "I was enamored by him, in a way. He felt like such a star to me. He had the looks, the talent, the whole kind of package." Rapaport brought him in again, this time for a role on *Riverdale*, the CW's neo-noir adaptation of the Archie comics. He wasn't sure if Luke would have the earthy, comforting qualities needed to play Fred Andrews, Archie's dad. The range wasn't a question—Rapaport was aware of *Oz* and *8 Seconds* and other showcases for Luke as a multifaceted actor—but would he have the humble warmth to act as *Riverdale*'s moral ballast?

When Luke read the first time—with Rapaport and his assistants clamoring to meet one of their teen idols in real life—there was none of Dylan McKay's broody sex appeal. Instead, Luke was low-key. In the scene, Archie, torn between his love for making music and his commitment to the football team, has been caught by his dad in a lie. To buy more time for making a decision to quit football or not, Archie told the football coach he was working for Fred, but he told his dad he couldn't work due to varsity football.

"My first question is, who are you lying to? Me or your coach?"

"Neither," Archie said. Then, after a beat, "Both."

Fred suppresses a knowing smile. The conversation shifts to Archie's future. Football, Fred points out, will lead to college, then business school, preparing Archie to work with Fred on his construction business. But Archie admits that he doesn't want to work with his father in construction. He wants to make music, or at least to have his possibilities open.

"I would never force you to play football," Fred said. "I don't care if you play football. And you don't have to work with me or for me, ever again. But some advice, man-to-man? These decisions that you're making now, son, they have consequences. They go on to form who you are and who you'll become. Whatever you decide, be confident enough in it that you don't have to lie."

The scene introduced Fred's personality, as a dad and a man: he's honest and understanding, loving but firm. "It was the first time someone had come in who really connected to it in a way that felt undeniably real," Rapaport says. "In that moment, I discovered a newfound affection for him, a new understanding for his talent." There was a certain quality that stood out to Rapaport: "It was *casual*, so casual in the way that Luke was also casual . . . He was always about making other people comfortable, always being kind. It was never about ego with him which is incredibly rare." Though Rapaport could've requested more reads or screen tests from Luke, he didn't think it necessary. Fred Andrews had arrived, cast from one audition.

Despite the similarities between man and character, Luke was initially skeptical. "I didn't really want to read the script when they first sent it to me," he admitted in January 2017. "I just didn't know what the take of it was going to be." He was ultimately sold by showrunner Roberto Aguirre-Sacasa's clever retooling of the characters and their milieu. Aguirre-Sacasa has been adapting Archie and his pals to a modern world ever since he wrote a play in 2003 in which Archie comes out as gay and moves to New York. Back then, Archie Comics sent the student at Yale's School of Drama a cease-and-desist letter, but after penning the successful series *Afterlife with Archie*, wherein our hero battles his way out of a zombie apocalypse, Aguirre-Sacasa had proved himself. Archie Comics entrusted him as chief creative officer in 2014.

Luke had once warred with Jim Walsh and now he was playing a variation of Jim Walsh. On *Riverdale*, the parents play second fiddle to the young upstarts. Rapaport had already selected Cole Sprouse and Lili Reinhart as Jughead and Betty, respectively, so he took his casting cues from Reinhart's depth and Sprouse's intellectualism, as well as *Riverdale's* grim take on the original comic. Luke was the first of the parents hired. Then, soon after finding Marisol Nichols as Veronica's mom, a versatile actress known from the *Vacation* and *Scream* franchises, Rapaport arrived at an idea: What if all the parents were familiar from eighties or nineties vehicles?

Betty's mom, played by Mädchen Amick from *Twin Peaks*, fit into that concept beautifully, but as the series advanced past its pilot, requiring more casting of other key parent figures, Rapaport wobbled. "I kept questioning it, like, is this still cool? Do we want to continue this or is it going to get cheesy?" He plunged ahead and landed Skeet Ulrich, another *Scream* veteran, as Jughead's dad, and Molly Ringwald as Archie's lawyer mom, from *The Breakfast Club* and *Pretty in Pink*.

The concentration of these actors deepened the sense that *Riverdale's* world was built on the burial grounds of pop culture of yore: the Archie comics, obviously, but also postwar noir cinema and atmospheric teen classics like *The Last Picture Show* and *River's Edge*, David Lynch's surreal small-town nightmares, and the darkest undercurrents present in *Beverly Hills, 90210*. Sun-saturated Beverly Hills, as depicted by natives like Chuck Rosin, had an underbelly not unlike Riverdale. Both were sweet-on-the-surface hamlets, replete with a fifties diner where all the kids flirt over milkshakes, but underneath lay teenaged lives riven by dark forces: acrimonious divorce; parents with secrets; forbidden love; drugs.

Fred's bio feels closer to who Luke might've been had he stayed in

Ohio. As owner of his own contracting company, Fred was a working-middle-class guy who lived in flannels and faded jeans, ready to tackle an on-site problem at a moment's notice.

"I like playing the dad because I like *being* a dad," Luke said. As Fred, "I'm the grounded one, and I'm the guy who really cares about [Archie], who cares about doing a good job and being a good construction worker." At this stage in his life, Luke was far away from his history as a teen sex symbol or a Hallmark dreamboat.

He wasn't relying on his one-time stock and trade, but some viewers—and some *Riverdale* characters, for that matter—lusted after him anyway. Teen vixen Cheryl Blossom tells Fred at one point, "You're looking extremely DILFy." *Slate*'s Rebecca Onion, in a piece titled "Luke Perry's *Riverdale* Role Made Him a Sex Symbol All Over Again," explained his updated appeal: "Luke Perry's forehead looked a bit preposterous on *90210*'s Dylan McKay, but on Fred Andrews, Perry's famous furrows and receding hairline were perfect. . . . [H]e's a grown person, with grown-person problems—and he's beloved." Contrasting him with Ulrich's character F. P. Jones, she argued that it's Fred's dependability and lack of flash that elevated him to DILF status: "Where FP, who's a formerly incarcerated gang member, is dangerous and sometimes unreliable, Fred is comfortable. FP is wild and charismatic; Fred does things right. It's a testament to Luke Perry that his straight arrow was as much fun to watch as Ulrich's live wire."

In other words, he's still got it—but for a generation now too saddled with mortgages and school drop-offs to bother with bad-boy dramatics. Bring on the man who will fall asleep next to you while binge-watching Netflix.

ABOUT FIFTEEN MONTHS LATER, SHE would find herself at the Sandcastle again, standing in front of the windows at high tide, grasping David's hands in hers.

She begins her vows: "I take you, David, to be no other than yourself, loving what I know of you, trusting what I do not yet know . . ."

The tide outside crashes every few moments in a roar that nearly overtakes their voices. His eyes, impossibly warm, are held in hers. Somewhere between the sea and his gaze, it is inscribed.

———

The night before had been a different story. At one a.m. in their hotel, she ransacks their bags for the pieces of pottery and shells she'd bought from an Etsy lady in Scotland. She had fallen in love with them. They were meant to be inked with the names of all the wedding guests, something she planned to do two weeks ago, then a week ago . . . but now it is hours before their wedding, and they aren't anywhere to be found.

She bursts into tears.

"I can't find the fucking pieces," she says.

"You've looked in all this?" He gestures to their overstuffed luggage.

"Of course," she snaps.

"Okay," he says. "We can always just write everyone's name on a piece of paper and just let them—"

"Oh my god, no!"

He freezes, unsure how to react.

"Oh my god," she says, "why am I like this?"

"You want it to be great, and it will be. It already is!"

A few minutes later, he returns from the car, victorious, with the stones.

He pitches in for a while, and then wanders over to the bed for a break, and passes out in his new, for the occasion, clothes. She could rouse him, but instead she finishes the job alone, enjoying the focused solitude. At an unknown hour, she collapses next to him.

———

When she married Adam, she could barely utter the word wife. *Sure, their love was faltering, but there was more to it. She preferred to describe herself as* partner. *The term implied what she actually wanted: an egalitarian relationship that wouldn't consign her to all the gender roles that a wife connoted. She actively feared losing herself in wifedom, drowning in the washing machine before she'd had a chance to claim herself out of the grief and ashes of her imploded family. As a young woman, she simply wasn't ready for a new, complicated identity. How could she be when she'd struggled to occupy the most basic vestige of herself?*

But now, at age thirty-seven, she is equipped to pluck what she wants from the idea of marriage, and discard the rest. She savors the power of standing in front of her friends and family and promising to love someone with integrity, grace, and openness.

———

Her mother wears a cobalt-blue silk dress with a strand of pearls. There are so many faces to check in with, to delight over, but she keeps going back to her mother. At the first ceremony to Adam, Joanna had been late, nervous, tugging at an awkward hairpiece she decided to try for the first time that day, to cover her thinning hair. Margaret felt ashamed of her, and then guilty.

This time, Joanna appears calm and content. The years have softened things between them; the anger Margaret used to burn with has cooled into acceptance. She has learned to take what her mother could offer, could be—sweet, caring, a sender of endless newspaper clippings about cats or books. A person of gentle grace, but she hasn't entirely let go of the fantasy mother. The mother she could confide everything to without fear of rejection. The mother who would allow her daughter in. Out of necessity or temperament, her mother is a partially inhabited presence. Private, some would call it, but it feels more like absence. A part of her always away, ruminating on old trauma. More than she used to, Margaret understands. She ruminates sometimes, too.

There is a moment she wrote into the ceremony, in part for her mom. The officiant, their good friend Jade, reads: "Margaret's father, Edwin Wappler, passed away in 1991 when she was fifteen years old. She would like to honor his memory today with a line from T. S. Eliot, her father's favorite poet: 'To do the useful thing, to say the courageous thing, to contemplate the beautiful thing: that is enough for one man's life.'"

CHAPTER

FORTY-SIX

AT DINNER ONE NIGHT at Sutton Place, a hotel in downtown Vancouver where they were shooting *Riverdale*'s pilot in March 2016, Luke told the younger members of the cast that life was about to change. David Rapaport listened with rapt attention. "He saw the bigger picture of it," Rapaport recalls. "He was like, 'This is going to series. This is going to be something special.'" Rapaport nursed the same feeling—"It was undeniable, the magic that can happen with a show's cast."

As Luke held court about Hollywood and protecting yourself from the corrosive effects of fame, Rapaport noticed a less-than-attentive response. "With all due respect to the kids, they could not give a shit. They had no context, really, of who Luke was. They didn't grow up watching him, so it didn't mean the same thing."

If Luke's advice went unheeded that night, it didn't take long for the inexperienced cast to realize their folly—and to know him well enough to listen.

One of his most impactful relationships was with K. J. Apa, his on-screen son. The New Zealand native was nineteen, and new to the country and American television when he was cast as Archie after a six-month international search.

Luke, identifying as parent, on-screen and off, became friendly with Apa's Kiwi mom and native Samoan dad, calling them with weekly updates on how their son was doing. The young actor told *The Tonight*

Show with Jimmy Fallon that "if I had a cold or something, he'd be like, 'I got him, I brought some Gatorade to his apartment the other day.'"

The influence extended to his professional life as well. When they appeared together in October 2018 on the *Today* show, Hoda Kotb asked Luke if he had given any advice to Apa. "'Concentrate on the work, and play different parts, and treat everybody well.' He's doing great," Luke said. Apa had also visited Luke's farm in Tennessee, his inner sanctum reserved for those closest to him.

On *The View*, Apa was asked to reflect on his loss. "He's one of the best people I've ever known in my life . . . I hope I can be half the man he was."

That sentiment was echoed by Madelaine Petsch, another cast member Luke bonded with and personally mentored. Petsch credited Luke with teaching her how to conduct herself on a big set, in interviews, how to save her money. "He was somebody who I could look to as an oracle . . . navigating this really strange time . . . of skyrocketing into being known in the world, something he knew so well. And he taught me how to do it with grace and with humility."

Luke was never on social media but he helped her gain perspective when she experienced some "weird drama." Feeling like the world hated her, she called him for advice. "He was like, 'Just breathe. Where are you? We're going to dinner.'" At a steakhouse down the street, "he just spent the entire night talking to me about how none of that shit matters. It's about who you are on the inside."

FINALLY, SHE HAS FOUND IT. Her look. What she has tried over the years: Too dark. Too blond. About the latter, her mother said, "I wish you'd change your hair back," which made her keep it for at least three more months. Too asymmetrical. Too razored. Too long. Too short. Too somebody else.

Now it is shoulder-length, give or take an inch or two, her natural brown with blond highlights but not stripes. And bangs. Bangs are a must. She'd love to call them Birkin curtains, but that ideal only visits haphazardly. Mostly, the bangs are not so much French chanteuse as California neglect.

The hair, it is always yearning for something now, something it has lost: moisture, when she used to be an oil derrick. Thickeners, where she was once a fortress of follicles. Where is the weight, the heft, the pile she once possessed? The thickening products are made with sea salt. Biotin. Procapil. Some borrow the language of Silicon Valley; let's "reboot hair density." There are theories. Whole schools of thought. The problem is shampoo. The problem is an unhealthy scalp. The problem is your gut biome.

She spends some of her evenings scrolling reviews generated by bots or twenty-two-year-olds with horse manes. Every few months, she orders a new one, while wearing her glasses, recommended by Oprah, that are supposed to block the iPhone's light. Every time, she is excited for the package to come.

CHAPTER

FORTY-SEVEN

CHICAGO NATIVE MARISOL NICHOLS and Luke briefly met when Nichols appeared on *Beverly Hills, 90210*, playing Wendy Stevens, Ray Pruit's single-episode fiancée. Nichols was thrilled with her luck; she nabbed the part a few months after moving to Los Angeles to pursue acting full-time.

That was 1996, the last time they saw each other. Now it's 2016 and Luke and Nichols are playing old flames drawn together again. In *Riverdale's* first season, Veronica's mother, Hermione Lodge, is tempted by her history. She still feels something for her former high school sweetheart Fred Andrews, but she hopes no one will notice. Hermione, waiting on the release of her incarcerated husband, Hiram, is supposed to be a taken woman. Struggling to make ends meet, she takes a job at Fred's construction company, helping to clean up his finances. The two become close, again.

After a few episodes of buildup, Hermione and Fred finally kiss. She felt lucky to be sharing the scene with an actor who wasn't angling for his close-up or star turn. "He was extremely generous," she says, "and all about the work." In the episode, the kiss is witnessed through the window by Hermione and Hiram's daughter, Veronica, who immediately considers the act a betrayal of her father. But Luke and Nichols thought the story of their characters' reconnecting shouldn't just be played as a cheap way to stir up conflict between mother and daughter.

Nichols says that when they got the script, "Luke was like, 'Come on!' We called the writers and talked to the director. . . . We were both so upset because we had been building up the storyline between me and him and we thought it should've been more of a moment on its own." In the end, Nichols and Luke lost the battle but it was a signal to the *Riverdale* writers that they were on notice. Luke wasn't the type of actor who never questions the direction of his character. "He was all about protecting the integrity of the work," Nichols says.

Upon Hiram's release from jail, Hermione confesses to Fred that it was she and Hiram who were behind buying out his business. Nichols internalized the deception so intensely that she couldn't get through the scene without crying. "It's a horrible betrayal to a person who doesn't deserve it. And I always maintained that Hermione wasn't like Hiram—she has a conscience." The director asked her to do one last take with dry eyes, which she just barely managed. "And of course, that's the one they used."

She's still not convinced it fairly represents her character, but all these years later, what stands out to her now is how much Luke supported her through the tears. "You really want someone there who will catch you when you fall, and Luke was one hundred percent that person."

———

Nichols has been toting along her daughter on sets since Rain was only a few weeks old, nursing between takes on *24*. When Rain was almost eight years old, Nichols brought her up from Los Angeles for *Riverdale*'s pilot (eventually, they fully relocated to the area). On a day off, Luke suggested that Nichols ride the ferry to Granville Island with Rain, but Nichols, who didn't know Vancouver at all at that point, was intimidated by figuring out the ferry alone. Luke, who knew the city well from *Jeremiah* and other shoots, volunteered to come with them. They spent the day rowing a little boat, weaving in and out of artisanal shops, and hitting the Public Market.

"You could tell he was a great father," Nichols says. "He would tell me the tricks he used to do for Santa coming for Christmas, and I'd tell him the little tricks I was doing." They frequently discussed the sacrifices and logistics it took to keep up as a working parent, especially on a hit show.

By season two, *Riverdale* was on a new level. "When people started camping out at our set in Vancouver, waiting by the gates to catch a glimpse of us, I knew it was something," Nichols says. *Riverdale* jumped from thirteen episodes in season one to twenty-two for the second and third. In TV, it's common knowledge that the hardest schedule is a one-hour drama. The work days ballooned to fifteen, eighteen, or, in one case Nichols remembered, twenty-one hours, leaving her to drive home at seven in the morning. Depending on where they were shooting, sometimes the drive back to the city was as much as an hour and twenty minutes. (After working one fourteen-hour shift in 2017, K. J. Apa fell asleep at the wheel and crashed into a light pole. His injuries were minor, but the accident kicked off a SAG-AFTRA investigation into set conditions. The show was presumably cleared of all issues, since it continued for several more seasons.)

"We were exhausted," she says, "but you're trying to be grateful for everything you have." She knew that "one minute you're the hottest thing in the world, and the next no one knows your name."

Luke reminded them all to have fun. "He was tickled by the whole thing," Nichols says. "That was the only way to describe it. He was such a young boy at heart, and he just really enjoyed it. And he was so used to it." His laugh was infectious, she said, and can be glimpsed in a post on Molly Ringwald's Instagram from October 11, 2019, Luke's first post-humous birthday. In the video, Luke is on the floor, taking a selfie with Sprouse. His laugh starts as a little sputter and then rises up into glee.

SHE IS DIGGING INTO A vat of lentil curry in the humble kitchen of the hermitage when she senses another person behind her.

A man, close to her age, in a ragged T-shirt, Birkenstocks, and soccer shorts.

"Hello." His loud whisper sears the room. He looks giddy to see her, anyone.

They are not supposed to be talking; it's a silent retreat. Since they are in the kitchen, they are allowed to whisper but her stats are tainted now. She had wanted to see how long she could last without opening her mouth.

"Where are you from?" he asks. He shares that he's from Switzerland. They exchange a few more whispers about how gorgeous it is here in Big Sur, as they take turns microwaving their meals, and then the conversation is done. It is time to return to their respective bedrooms, stark, simple spaces with no more than a bed and a desk.

"Good night," he says, and slips out the door into the black air. She doesn't see him again.

———

The next day. It appears to be lasting a thousand hours. She has napped, she has walked, she has meditated at a bench near the mist-shrouded ocean, hoping to last an hour, but after twenty minutes, the bugs drive her out. She walks to a new bench in a better spot. A break in the fog, to the south, allows her to see pools of light turquoise in the water, a horizon of gray ripple. Highway 1 ribbons through the green passages of land, then a tunnel, where cars gracefully slide in and out. It is staggering to take in.

On the bench, she sinks into an unwieldy meditation, bombarded

*by memories from the last few weeks. She has done it; she has pub-
lished a novel. Her mother read the book and left her a voicemail. "It
was just"—pause—"charming." Her five-city book tour. In Washington, DC, the kind man who listened to Pop Rocket, the pop culture
podcast she regularly appeared on, arrived with a gift—an on-the-
road cocktail kit. The older couple in Minneapolis who looked uncomfortable the whole time—did they mean to attend her reading?
A bunch of her high-school girlfriends came together to the Chicago
reading, including Audrey and Rose. All these lost and reforged connections. All these readers taking in the novel she'd spent years writing,
crying into. She had basked in the reception and grappled with the
attendant disappointments for weeks. But now she needed silence. To
get back to herself.*

———

*So here she is, with the Roman Catholic monks living in the Benedictine
monastic tradition. On the third day, she slept so long that she missed
lunch, the one hot meal of the day.*

*The friendly oblate at the bookstore (another place for quiet talking)
gives her permission to go to the monk's large kitchen, where the food is
still out.*

A monk greets her.

"I slept through lunch," she says.

*"Well, you should go to confession, then," he says playfully. He has
giant blue eyes and is shockingly muscular. Where's the gym? She hasn't
noticed one on the premises. Who are these men? They bustle all around
while she feeds herself another delicious vegetarian meal. Two of them
toss a football. One young guy in dreads and tie-dye says he's going to
walk down the road to listen to the music drifting up from a wedding
somewhere below.*

———

The next day, Sunday, she sees them all at service in the austere chapel.

A dozen or so monks in white robes singing a psalm, facing one another in two rows. Their bowed heads, their hushed reverence. Behind each row is a section of pews where she and others sit, thumbing through hymnals. At the end of the service, the monks lead everyone into a dimly lit rotunda with an altar in the center. Everyone shuts their eyes for meditation.

Silence with a group of people has a different pulse than lone silence. Each person reinforces the next person's efforts. She feels like she's holding hands with all of them.

She hasn't been to church in more than a decade. It has always been too much. Anger, alienation, and trauma would rise at the sight of pews, the tall waxy candles, the hanging vestments, the men wearing them. And for a moment, here, the tears come to the back of her eyes, thinking of her father, walking in his white robe with his distinctive limp from a childhood injury, scenting the air with a silver orb of frankincense. But they are not angry tears, and they soften back into her, unshed.

FORTY-EIGHT

EARLY IN THE FRENZY of season two, Luke had a message for assistant director Gabriel Correa.

Away from the ears of a director who was floundering, Luke put his hand on Correa's shoulder and murmured, "Hey, *you* should be directing one of these episodes."

"Luke, nothing would make me happier," Correa said. He had joined *Riverdale* in season two from the WB's established hit *Supernatural*, where the Brazilian native had risen from third assistant director, second assistant director, and then first. Despite the gig being comfortable for him, he left for *Riverdale*, a new show that he wagered would allow opportunities for him to direct. He was only trying to figure out how it would come to be.

"You'll be great at it," Luke continued.

"I really want that to happen," Correa said.

Luke shifted into strategizing. "Don't worry about this season. You just started. Just push it through to next season and it'll be your time."

Then, he gave Correa a look that said: *I've got your back.*

The support meant everything to Correa. "This is coming from somebody who's a pro, who's an iconic TV actor," Correa says. "And he's not a bullshitter. He had no reason to say that to me." Correa was aware of his own strides—coming up from São Paulo, Brazil; getting through film school in Vancouver; learning a different language—but receiving affirmation from someone else confirmed he was approaching this latest hurdle in the right way.

The winning tactic, as far as Correa was concerned, was to keep the plates spinning on season two's insanely challenging episodes. For each script, Correa was the guy breaking it down and organizing it into data for filmmaking—how many sets, how many actors, what days they'd shoot what and so forth. The work in and of itself was familiar, but "from a production standpoint," Correa remembers, "it was like nothing I'd ever seen in my life." The ambitious scripts were long and crammed with storylines that called for as many as ninety scenes in one episode.

The trick was always, as Correa saw it, to spend time where it was deserved. "My style isn't to look at my watch and yell at people to go," Correa says. He was all for efficiency, but when a moment needed it, he advocated for slowing down and protecting the actors working to deliver it. Luke, Correa recalled, was particularly sensitive to when a moment required delicacy and not speed.

But the network didn't see the issue the same way. The CW insisted on keeping each episode's shoot to eight days, but it was never enough, Correa said. They'd push a day onto the next episode's schedule, thinking they'd get a chance to make up for it, but by the end of the season, there was a huge backlog. To catch up, there were multiple units shooting scenes from three or four different episodes at the same time. Each set with its own director, bustling in and out.

At times, even when he wasn't called for on set, Luke became something of a train conductor, noting when the timetables were off. "He'd come stand behind the chairs and say, 'Guys, that's take eight,'" and add a little warning whistle.

Thanks in part to Correa's astute leadership, *Riverdale* survived its second season—and he was rewarded with directing his first episode: episode fifteen in season three, "American Dreams," which features F. P.'s fiftieth birthday party.

The birthday party was a big scene with many key cast members, but Luke almost got cut. Aguirre-Sacasa was going to give him a day off, Correa says, but in the end, the moment between Ulrich and Luke stayed. "It was a lovely little scene," Correa says, between two characters who'd "been on a roller coaster and were meeting for this simple tender moment at his birthday." After Luke wrapped, he stuck around and observed Correa finally having his time in the director's chair.

In a quiet moment, Luke approached him.

"I see what you're doing," he said. "Just keep doing your thing. You're doing great. You're not wasting any time, and you're getting your moments. Keep going."

———

Four years later, Correa can't retell that encouraging moment with Luke without crying.

"This is hard," Correa says, catching his breath.

Soon after shooting his episode, Correa flew to LA to edit it in person. He could've worked remotely, but for his first, he wasn't about to chance it. He paid for his flight out of pocket, but once Ulrich heard that Correa was paying, he offered for him to stay at his house in Studio City. "That's the kind of environment the show was," Correa says, "that's the type of support these guys gave to me." Correa took him up on it and drove to Hollywood daily to edit.

He was in LA for four days, including a weekend. His wife flew out to keep him company. Correa had already received news of Luke's stroke. There weren't any updates coming from Luke's family. The last he had heard was that it was a big stroke, potentially bad.

"I was worried," he recalled, but he remained optimistic.

On a sunny Monday morning, Correa and his wife were walking back to the car after getting breakfast. Correa was in a good mood, excited to get into the editing bay and shape his episode into the perfect specimen. His phone buzzed and he fished it out of his pocket.

A news alert: Luke Perry, dead at age fifty-two.

He read the headline again, then read it aloud to his wife. The words tasted acrid in his mouth. He dropped to his knees on the sidewalk, still clutching his phone.

"I can't believe this," he said. He crumpled into himself on the concrete, one hand on his knee. His wife pulled him up for a long hug.

They did not have to say what the moment resembled. In 2016, driving home from his son's birthday party, Correa answered a phone call. It was devastating news: his father, at age sixty-three, had died from a heart attack in Brazil. No warning, no chance to say goodbye.

———

Production closed for two days. When Correa returned, he was in preproduction on another episode while the current one filmed, but Aguirre-Sacasa and line producer Connie Dolphin asked him to sub in for the current AD, who wasn't as known by the cast. They needed a familiar face, particularly Apa, who could not get through filming. "He just couldn't do it," Correa said. "The immediate aftermath was just so devastating." Correa tried to create a safe space for Apa, telling him that he could take as much time as needed to get ready for the scene.

"I've got your back," Correa said.

Aguirre-Sacasa came on the set and led a long moment of silence for Luke. The cast and crew worked their way through the episode, and the remaining ones of the season; Fred Andrews was "away on business" while Aguirre-Sacasa and the writers figured out the best way to honor Luke's death. Correa returned to directing for episode eighteen, "Jawbreaker," then he was promoted to a director/supervising producer role. His first duty in that new capacity would be directing the season four premiere, the in memoriam episode for Luke.

SHE IS FIVE MONTHS PREGNANT and turning over in her hands a malfunctioning chemotherapy cartridge. Her task was to slot it into the small iPhone-like machine that her mother stowed in a fanny pack cinched around her waist. A tube protruding from the device ferried medicine to a port inserted into her chest near her shoulder, hidden under a paisley nightgown. For some reason, the cartridge refused to slot into the machine. Margaret is afraid that if she keeps trying to jam it, it'll bust open or leak.

Her mother is lying on her bed, in a whorl of sheets. Her hair is now completely white; no longer the ash brown streaked with gray that Margaret used to pin into a soft mohawk when she was a child. Joanna assesses her with tired eyes.

"What do we do now?"

"I'll call the help line," Margaret answers with more confidence than she feels. There is a childish whim to drop the cartridge into a dumpster, punt the issue to her brother or someone else, but overwhelmingly, she longs to solve this problem.

A nurse on the help line walks her through a few minutes of punching codes, and the cartridge slides into place. To her mother, she rejoices. The old cheery front she knows how to assume from her teenage years.

But it is past midnight, and Margaret is flying out early tomorrow morning. Their brief visit, of watching Joan Crawford movies together and making her mom scrambled eggs, all she could eat, is over. Earlier in the evening, the assisted-living building had been alive right outside the front door; the nearby elevator chiming, friends and nurses bellowing their greetings. Now it's silent.

Her mother reaches her pale hand up to grab Margaret's. There is no more pretending between the two of them. James is close by, but he has children and can't be here all the time.

"I wish you could stay longer," Joanna says. Margaret wants to curl herself around her mother, to be her guardian. And yet, her life back in Los Angeles beckons. The baby inside of her.

"You're going to be okay, Mom," she says softly. She says it to comfort her mother, but also for herself, as a prayer. She only prays in the most dire of circumstances. She doesn't linger over what praying means to the impossible question of what she believes, she only hopes that someone is listening.

FORTY-NINE

JULY 2019, FOUR MONTHS after Luke's death. The cast and crew of *Riverdale*, led by director Gabriel Correa, were shooting the most emotionally difficult episode they'd ever make: "In Memoriam," the season four premiere, a stand-alone from the rest of the series. After mulling it over for months, Aguirre-Sacasa and the other writers gave Fred Andrews a hero's send-off. He died saving a stranger, played by Shannen Doherty, from a hit-and-run. Doherty's appearance fulfilled a longtime wish of Luke's; that his old friend be given a guest part in *Riverdale*. Luke's family also read the script and provided the photos that Fred's ex-wife, Mary, played by Molly Ringwald, sifts through toward the end.

In every way, the episode felt deeply considered, right down to choosing Correa, a trusted member of the *Riverdale* family, as its director. All the elements were in place to ensure a smooth shoot, but still, the reality was painful. The biggest challenge was that K. J. Apa didn't want to be there. He wanted to be anywhere but this place where Luke's absence was the sole focus of the day. The loss nudged its way into every frame, every line that mentioned Fred. There was a feeling, as Marisol Nichols recalls, that Luke might emerge from another room at any second now, donning someone's wig or performing some other silly stunt meant to shake off all the gloom.

"Please don't make me do another take," Apa said to Correa, more than once. Sometimes Correa could manage the request, knowing they'd gotten the coverage they needed, and sometimes he needed to push for more. As the shoot moved along, Apa's emotional exhaustion was evident.

In addition to exhaustion, and wanting to mourn in private, there was another issue nagging him: Apa wondered what the two-hundred-something crew members expected from him, both on and off camera. He felt like they were watching for his reaction. As Archie or himself, was he supposed to be crying all the time? Should he prove his love to his costar and TV father by rending out his dyed-red hair? What would be enough? He felt duty-bound to Luke, and at the same time, resentful of any expectations, real or self-imposed, for himself or his character.

Correa told him that people, including fictional ones, grieve in different ways. You can be a puddle of tears. Or angry and punch a wall. Or quiet with seemingly no reaction. It is nobody's business. There is no emotional roadmap. The only requirement is to be authentic to the moment, whatever that means right now.

Playfully, Correa produced an imaginary key and unlocked imaginary handcuffs around Apa's wrists.

"I am unshackling you," Correa said. "You're liberated from any pressure." The gesture helped Apa realize that there was no script to heed. He was free to follow what he felt in the moment, so long as it felt right. That was the only direction that mattered, for him and the rest of the cast.

———

For Correa, that search for the truth prompted him to make an important last-minute change. In the script, Archie drove his father's coffin past a sidewalk parade for Fred. People held signs saying, "We love you, Fred," and "We will never forget you." Originally the parade attendees were supposed to appear somber, but after Correa shot one take that way, he knew something wasn't right.

Instead, he directed the participants to react in different ways, including joy. Many are cheering for Fred as a show of support for Archie. Some are crying or frozen; some are looking on with a smile and tears in their eyes. Correa wanted to capture the whole range of human grief. Collectively, it was uplifting, and reflective of Fred.

"He was a force of good and joy," Correa says. "Everybody was there because Fred was the best of Riverdale."

——

Authenticity guided Nichols to express something for her character that was always hinted at but never spoken. As Hermione read Fred's obituary, written by Jughead, tears streamed down her face. She choked on sobs. Her reaction, as she sat in jail for conspiring to have Hiram killed, reached beyond an old friend or a former high-school sweetheart expressing sorrow.

"As far as I was always concerned, Fred was the love of her life," Nichols says. "And she made the wrong choice [picking Hiram], and she knew it." Hermione coming back to Riverdale at the start of the series, Nichols speculates, was a chance to start over and "to become the person she'd always wanted to be, and to do the right thing." Fred was a part of that plan, but once Hiram returned from prison and was back in control, "it was like she couldn't escape." Fred's death signaled another finality to Hermione: "The end of a possibility for a new life." Not only was she paying a steep price for her misdeeds by serving time, there was no longer the chance of redemptive love waiting for her. She was alone with her mistakes.

——

The field was a lush mid-summer green, dried in spots from the intensity of the sun. Clouds clung to the distant mountains, and then a sheath of blue sky. Correa picked that field and its simple farmland road as the place where Fred Andrews died, struck by a speeding car as he helped a stranger change her tire.

In a scene midway through the episode, Archie is there to retrieve his father's pickup truck and drive it home. As he sits in the cab, looking at Fred's things, a woman parks not too far behind him, with a bouquet of flowers. She places it in the grass, and the two start a conversation. Archie realizes this is the woman his father was helping, and the last person to see him before he was killed.

As the actors rehearsed and blocked the scene, Correa recalled that Doherty was already crying. Usually, blocking is a time when an actor will hold back on the emotions of the performance, saving it for the camera, but for Doherty, "she just couldn't. It was very real for her. And that set the tone." The other actors in the scene, the core four—Apa, Reinhart, Sprouse, and Camila Mendes—were overcome with tears as well. But they powered through the scene by leaning on each other. The scene ends with them all holding hands, with Doherty reciting the Lord's Prayer. The camera tilts up from the field to the sky, until the sun blots out the entire frame in white.

At the very start of filming the episode, Correa said a few words to honor Luke, but other than that, he didn't feel the need to make speeches. But after he called cut, and before the crew could swarm the set and rig the car for a night scene, Correa asked them all, cast and crew, to take a moment. This slowing down was the art of filmmaking that he and Luke always recognized, linking them as kindred spirits all those months ago. Here was the moment to protect and preserve, above all else. Time could go slack here. The cast and crew stood in silence, hugging each other, at the edge of the wild grass.

Correa said to them that the place was so perfect that it was a sign that Luke was here with them. Luke would've loved the rustic beauty of an open field and sunshine. There he was, somehow with them. The final light of the day bathed them all in gold.

HER DOCTOR SWINGS OPEN A *panel in the ceiling and three spot-lights turn on. The heat of the lights warm her lower body, pitched like a beetle on her back, legs hiked up in stirrups, and all her secret parts open to the room and its drafts and strange eyeballs. Such was the business of birth, this delivery, which had been deemed too complicated, what with her bilobed placenta and advanced maternal age, to try at home or any-where but a hospital.*

"All right, Margaret," says the doctor, "let's do this, the biggest push you can do. Now."

She bears down, for the ninetieth time in the last four hours. She'd pushed in all kinds of styles, as if in the Olympics for pushing. A showcase of gritting, squatting, groaning, laughing. With David encouraging her—"You're amazing!"—with the nurses cheering her on, with her midwife friend, Christian, rubbing her neck, and yet, despite all these pushes, her baby is somewhere in the canal. He's stuck in existential traffic. Not yet born, and no longer in the womb.

"Sweetheart," a nurse says, "this baby doesn't seem to know that he's being born. He's not helping you at all!"

"You've got more than that in you, Margaret. Try again!" Her mild-mannered doctor is playing the tough coach goading her to a win. Frankly, it pisses her off. Who is he, with his non-uterus, to tell her to push better? Like she hasn't been pushing for literal hours now? As if she is happy with a seven-pound baby stuck between her innards and the world?

She decides to scream, instead of the low groans Christian had taught her.

Blowing her lungs into it: "Get. The. Fuck. Out!" The room hushes. They all assume she is talking to the baby, and she was a little bit, but it was mostly to the doctor. To the situation.

"Well, that's one way to do it," the nurse says quietly. Awkward laughter

from some of them, including from Margaret. She's been in the hospital for three days already, because her water broke but labor wouldn't start until they pummeled her with Pitocin, which made her puke into a plastic pitcher. And then a doctor who ambled in at four a.m. to give her an epidural had jabbed her spine too many times, seemingly unable to find the right spot. An IV in her arm loosened from her vein. It went just under the surface of her skin and pumped so much fluid into her that her forearm blew up like a water balloon. The nurse gasped when Margaret gingerly lifted her bloated appendage and said, "Um, is it supposed to look like this?"

Her scream, as releasing as it was, wasn't effective. The baby hasn't heard her, or doesn't give a fuck, more likely. Christian says he's in military position, with his chin jutting out instead of tucked, which, to say the least, isn't conducive to birth.

Dr. D. badgers her into a few more pushes, and she tries, but she's wrung out. He summons this and that tool—a vacuum, a pair of tongs—but the baby won't budge. She feels like the statue of Kali, or a Sheela-na-gig, all frozen limbs and bared teeth above exaggerated vulva, frozen forever in the anguish of birth. At once reduced to her parts, and exalted for them, communing with all women and birthing mammals across the history of time and whatever blinked before time. Yet she longs to crawl back into the sanctity of her one self, with this all behind her.

"That's it. We need to get this baby out now," Dr. D. barks.

———

On a gurney, thundering down a dark hallway, her body writhing, bucking, completely out of her range of commands. Her back thumping over and over again on the cot, the contractions coming so hard and total at this point that somewhere, in the back of her mind, her teenaged self hangs out on a corner of grass, smoking a cigarette, and says, "Well, you're really in it now. Hang in there." Ah, this survivor girl who had seen some shit. She can be used for good. Yes, Margaret knows how to do this, this hanging in there.

———

Everyone is a voice, a bisected face between cap and a mask, or a set of gloved hands with forearms in sea-green scrubs. A new nurse appears out of stage left, seemingly with one task: to shave every bit of hair from her belly button down. Duty done, the nurse retreats past the operating lights and is never seen again. The anesthesiologist, Dr. M., comes in. The C-section can now begin.

"I have some good news for you," he says to her, dropping some potion into her IV. "Steve Bannon was fired today."

"Oh," she says. "That is good news." Then they proceed to lambaste Bannon while her waist, hips, her legs down to the toes, are numbed.

A few minutes of waiting. They can now begin. Dr. D. slices in. She can dully feel the scalpel across her torso, like a marker being drawn on her skin. Her leg twitches; she can still move it.

"Jesus," Dr. D. says, "she can still move her leg. Give her more!"

Dr. M. flies into adroit action and wham, her leg is dead.

Soft murmurs from Dr. D. now, letting her know that he is moving aside some organs, that the baby is going to be here any minute, that all the signs are looking good and—

His cry. Him.

He is being held just above her by one of the sets of gloves. He's yowling and splotchy red and already California tan. He stretches out his limbs, trying out his body.

"You're here," she says, "you're here. I was waiting for you!" The tears gush out of her, her hair dampening with them. "You're finally here. You're here." David is next to her, crying too, and they lean their foreheads together, their baby on her chest between them. Their little family.

The baby stares at her with imploring eyes. He doesn't seem surprised to be here, but he has questions. His world has been turned inside out. The dim outside is now the loud bright everything. He has questions, and they will need to be addressed. But it's okay for now because he knows her, his mother, her smell, her voice. He hangs on to her. With his mottled skin on hers, he slows his crying and then stops. He is satisfied, for now.

CHAPTER

FIFTY

CASTING DIRECTOR VICTORIA THOMAS had collaborated with Quentin Tarantino on *Django Unchained*, *The Hateful Eight*, and *Once Upon a Time . . . in Hollywood*, but her career was illustrious before their association. Her résumé included cult favorites (*Sid and Nancy*, *Repo Man*), several Tim Burton pictures (*Edward Scissorhands*, *Ed Wood*), and the kind of movies that live or die on casting, such as *Blonde*, which earned Ana de Armas an Oscar nomination for her role as Marilyn Monroe.

One of Tarantino's favorite games to play with Thomas and her vast mental repository of performers was Name That Actor. "He'll test me by throwing out the name of a supporting actor from some *Mannix* episodes," Thomas says, referencing the private investigator show that ran from 1967 to 1975. Considered one of the most violent of the era, it also delivered the first Emmy and Golden Globe Awards ever to a black actress, Gail Fisher, who rescued *Mannix* from dismal ratings when she joined in season two. "He'll float a name and then he'll just look at me and wait. And I'll say, 'I remember Stack Pierce,'" a character actor who appeared on a few episodes. "'I remember. Don't try to get that one past me.'"

In an effort to stump each other, "our dialogue naturally lends itself to supporting actors, character actors, and actors who didn't get the attention they may have deserved," Thomas says. She couldn't recall exactly when Luke's name first came up as a potential casting choice—she speculated it was for *Django*—but he'd long been on Tarantino's list. Before educating himself on film as a video store clerk, Tarantino, like so many American children, like Luke himself, was reared on TV. "He's not a snob about movie actors versus TV actors," Thomas says. "He's an appreciator of highbrow and lowbrow."

The initial meeting between Tarantino, Thomas, and Luke at her office was one of mutual respect and ease, Thomas says. Her associates, Bonnie Grisan and Jennifer Yoo, had already excitedly greeted Luke, object of their teen crushes. Yoo recalls that each time she saw Luke from that point forward, including at the wrap party more than a year later, he always looked directly into her eyes and "made you feel like you're the most important person in the room."

Thomas remembered that Luke was nervous but excited, and that Quentin, as is often his way, quickly disarmed him with a steady stream of chatter. He remembered certain roles of Luke's, including several *Criminal Minds* episodes where Luke recurred as a charismatic cult leader. Thomas and Tarantino were considering Luke for one of two parts in *Once Upon a Time . . . in Hollywood*, set in an altered 1969. He'd play either aloof movie star Steve McQueen, or Wayne Maunder, the real-life actor who played Scott Lancer on the short-lived CBS Western *Lancer*, a real show that Tarantino used as a guest star vehicle for his fictional 1950s TV actor Rick Dalton, played by Leonardo DiCaprio.

Tarantino and Thomas sat on the couch while Luke sat in a chair and read some sides.

"I always try to keep everything very easygoing," Thomas says of the atmosphere. "We want everyone to feel relaxed and as comfortable as possible."

It worked. Luke "seemed to settle in" to the role of Wayne Maunder, and the nesting-doll reality of being an actor inside a real but fictionalized Western TV show, inside of a contemporary movie set in an altered past.

In *Once Upon a Time*, past and present, reality and fiction all bump and collide to create a singular state, a kind of lucid dream where everything is crystalline and familiar but *off*. DiCaprio, playing an actor on the edge of being washed up, represents a dying breed in late-1960s Hollywood. He's the kind of chiseled man who was once sought after in the now-crumbling studio system, but he doesn't fit in with "the modern LA of the stoned sensibility . . . the fantasy-brothel where you can live the fantasy of your choice," as Pauline Kael wrote in her review of Robert Altman's *The Long Goodbye*.

The 1973 movie, she wrote, "is about people who live in L.A. because they like the style of life, which comes from the movies. It's not about people who work in movies, but about people whose lives have been shaped by them." Tarantino's picture taps into a similar spirit, but in *Once Upon a Time*, there's no separating the people of Los Angeles into industry folk and non—all are intrinsically wrapped up in moviemaking, and therefore the making of myth and cultural memory. A native Angeleno, Tarantino painstakingly re-created the Los Angeles of his youth, with original KJH broadcasts and an actual 1969 CoverGirl commercial featuring Susan Dey. He told *Esquire*, "I think of it like my memory piece. Alfonso [Cuarón] had *Roma* and Mexico City, 1970. I had LA and 1969. This is me. This is the year that formed me." The fabric of his memory can't be separated from the legends and lore of Hollywood, ruptured by the Manson family's nightmarish murderous rampage. Preying on celebrities and "regular" Angelenos alike, the Mansons fractured the hippie era, but also the sanctity of life in Los Angeles.

Our collective memory of Hollywood then and now informs the viewing. We know what's coming, whether it's Lucas Films's sci-fi franchise or the rom-com era being overtaken by endless Marvel and DC Comics properties, but Rick Dalton and Cliff Booth, his stunt double played by Brad Pitt, do not.

Luke represented a certain 1990s Hollywood, but could also feasibly plug in as another type from a bygone era. To Thomas, "Luke is one of those guys if he had been born twenty or thirty years earlier, he might've started in one of those Westerns shot on the backlot like Steve McQueen or like Robert Culp in *Trackdown*," she says, referencing Culp's breakout TV series that ran for two seasons in the late fifties. Casting Luke, Thomas says, added to that sense of a multiplicity of Hollywoods and realities.

For Tarantino, perhaps casting Luke was an irresistible way to secure the collective memory of Luke as more than a TV heartthrob from another era—similar to what he did for John Travolta and Pam Grier. "I think he got pigeon-holed," Thomas says, "during a time when you were either a TV actor or a movie actor. We both saw someone who was a good actor beyond the role that made him famous. Sometimes it takes someone like Quentin to let people know, hey, he's cool, he's good."

———

Casting director Vickie Thomas visited the *Once Upon a Time . . . in Hollywood* set when Luke was playing Maunder in the fictionalized version of *Lancer*. In the re-creation of the old Western street backlot at Universal, Luke was wearing a suit with tan leather details and a jaunty fedora with a cheetah-print band. It was the kind of getup too preening for any actual working cowboy, but just right for a showboating late-period Western. Scott Lancer was the "refined" Boston-educated half brother to Timothy Olyphant's gunslinger, Johnny Madrid Lancer (played in the original by actor James Stacy). In the primary scene of his character, Luke is acting with Leonardo DiCaprio, who's playing Rick Dalton acting as Caleb DeCoteau, the greasy, long-haired villain of *Lancer*'s pilot, holding a little girl (Julia Butters) hostage in a shadowy saloon. Caleb, or DiCaprio, masticating every morsel of his succulent dialogue, issued his demands to Scott.

"I'd say fifty thousand dollars would buy me a whole lotta chicken mole in Mexico."

"That's a lot of money," said Scott, tiptoeing around Caleb's temper.

Caleb demanded it be personally delivered by the patriarch, Murdoch Lancer, himself.

This set within a set was filled with the energy Thomas always saw on Tarantino's movies: a low-key excitement. A magnetism and purpose. On his sets, a frequent call-and-response occurs between director and crew. Tarantino, asking for another take, will say: "Let's do it one more time! Why?" The answer, cheered from every gaffer and actor: "Because we love making movies!"

But excitement and anxiety are frequent bedfellows. Was Luke nervous acting with DiCaprio? "I can't speak to any personal butterflies he might've been experiencing in his stomach, but he was there for a reason," Thomas says. "He could hold his own."

DiCaprio, for his part, was awed by Luke. On a November 2019 panel at the New Beverly Theater, DiCaprio said: "Honestly, as soon as I saw Luke on the set, I was brought back to my teenage past and felt starstruck. I remember being a young actor and he was television's James Dean figure, the guy that everyone was crazy about. It was honestly this feeling of anxiety before I got to talk with him. Even my friend who's named Vinnie who was on the set that day said: 'Holy shit, it's Luke Perry!'"

Eventually the two actors connected on the same level. "I got to finally sit down and talk with him, and man, he couldn't have been a gentler soul. He was so giving, and there was a purity and an honesty to him in talking about the industry and where his career was at and a gratefulness to be on that set working with Quentin. . . . It was a fantastic moment getting to spend the day with him and getting to know him."

Brad Pitt felt the same way. To *Esquire*: "It was this strange burst of excitement that I had, to be able to act with him. Man, he was so incredibly humble and amazing and absolutely committed. He couldn't have been a more friendly, wonderful guy to spend time with. I got to sit down and have some wonderful conversations with him."

All three of the actors lassoed success in Hollywood around the same time, though DiCaprio, an LA native who had been acting since age five, broke out at a younger age. Pitt was even briefly roommates with Jason Priestley, pre-*90210* days. Their lives were shadowing and intertwining all the while, finally intersecting the most meaningfully in *Once Upon a Time* (Pitt and DiCaprio were also in a Scorsese short film in 2015, *The Audition*).

About working with Luke, Tarantino said, "It was really fun. When we did one of his big horse scenes, Luke slides the horse to the front of the saloon and all the other riders fall in alongside him. I was like, 'Luke, do you want us to help you out? Do you want me to put a mark on the ground?' He was like, 'Quentin? You could take a dime and throw it in the dirt and I will land on that dime. The take you'll use is when everyone else gets it right.'"

Rory Karpf, a filmmaker who hired Luke to narrate some short documentaries around 2013, says Luke long had his eye on the future. "He told me, 'I'm going to make a big comeback when my kids are out of high school.'" *Once Upon a Time* was part of that plan. Rory and Luke met for dinner the night after one of his days on set. "It was the first time I'd ever seen Luke excited talking about a project. He was so into it." Part of what Luke responded to was the creatively rigorous atmosphere Tarantino upheld. "Luke saw a person who was in complete control of the set. And Quentin was doing things the way he thought they should be done. No cell phones, everybody sitting with each other," which appealed to Luke's egalitarian nature. "Luke hated the hierarchy of Hollywood. Anyone big-timing anyone else would get on his last nerve. At lunch, he loved that Leonardo DiCaprio was sitting with the grips."

When Karpf asked him what the best part was of working with Tarantino, he expected to hear about Tarantino's fearless writing or his deep film knowledge. Instead, Luke mentioned Tarantino's kindness. It wasn't the most common of compliments paid to a man often criticized for embracing on-screen gore and violence (and one incident behind the scenes as well; Tarantino apologized for a car accident that injured Uma Thurman on the set of *Kill Bill*). "Luke said he was the kindest director he ever worked with. He really made Luke feel like his contribution meant something," Karpf says. "He told him what a great job he was doing."

Three days before Luke's memorial, Tarantino cut together Luke's portion of the movie. When Karpf saw him at the ceremony, he mentioned how Luke felt. "Quentin was really touched by that. He said it meant a lot to him and that he tries to be that way," Karpf remembers. Tarantino dedicated the film to Luke's memory.

Luke, a TV star first, was existing once again in the small screen within the tight crop of genre. Albeit as some alternate version of himself, if he had been born twenty or thirty years earlier and taken the path Thomas had envisioned. But there was a sacred lifeline present, a redemptive exit sign lit in red: it was a film, preoccupied with remaking myths, made by one of the singular auteurs of our time. It was the last of Luke's personal Hollywoods.

AT THE MORGUE, SHE HAD lain her head on her mother's body, waiting for Joanna's hands to flutter to her hair, to soothe her. Joanna's skin was covered in delicate ice crystals. Her hands never came to her daughter's hair. They stayed still.

———

One of their last phone calls:

"I'm coming to see you, Mom."

"When?" Finally, the old light on in her mother's voice. The joyful anticipation.

"Thanksgiving." It was mid-October. By Thanksgiving, she could bring her baby with his first round of vaccinations on the plane. She'd be healed from her C-section.

"Oh."

"Can you hang on until then?" Margaret immediately regretted asking. She didn't want to acknowledge her own fear. It didn't seem dire yet, did it? Her mother had lost a lot of weight, was driving James crazy because most days she'd only consume milk, sometimes a plate of scrambled eggs, but the doctor kept saying, If she'll rally . . .

"I'll try," her mother said, still speaking with that voice, the one that had been vacant for months now.

———

When her mother didn't want to do something, she simply didn't. Her "no" was one crease on a silk pillowcase. There was no forcing her. There was no fight. No matter what the doctor said, or who was visiting when, she was done.

On October 30, the veil thinned and her mother slipped right through. Her womb already excised from her body, her digestive system in pieces. It happened as a sleep, a falling in and then, gone. James and his wife, Ingrid, at her side; her four other children driving and flying in from different parts of the country.

After the funeral, back at home, she tends to her baby. The days hum by, with him glugging milk from her breast, falling off into open-mouthed sleep. Next to him, she occupies a dozing awareness, grieving her mother. She has never felt closer to her, immersed in the work that absorbed and defined her, and she longs to pick up the phone and share it. Would motherhood have finally drawn them closer together?

It is only her and her brothers left. The next generation has now become the head generation. And though her brothers can recall more of her father than she can, they are all in the same position. The cords to both parents are now cut, and each one of them holds a frayed bit of it, with all the unanswered questions clamped forever shut in their mouths.

FIFTY-ONE

WHEN SANTINA MUHA WAS eight years old, growing up in working-class New Jersey, her friends down the block told her about the new drama for teens. They first tried to sell her on Jason Priestley, and she liked him well enough, but then Luke came on the screen.

"It was love at first sight. And then I was a Dylan girl forever. I had all the posters up on the wall, but he was the only one that got his own solo poster."

One of the stings of her childhood was that her mom wouldn't take her to the nearby Freehold Mall when Luke appeared there in the early nineties. Her mother, rightly, was afraid it would be a shitshow. Muha uses a wheelchair as the result of a childhood car accident. Her mom worried that her daughter, not even ten years old, would get knocked over.

"I never forgave her for that," Muha says, "until January 27, 2016."

Muha moved to Los Angeles in 2013 to pursue a career in comedy and entertainment and found success as a regular performer at UCB. She was also cast in a recurring role on *One Day at a Time* (and more guest spots on TV shows, including *Curb Your Enthusiasm*).

Everyone in Muha's life knew her feelings about Luke; her UCB biography mentioned her wish for her ultimate crush to attend a show. She had already met all the other main *90210* cast members at conferences or book signings, all except him. Then she hit a rough patch: Muha was hospitalized in fall of 2015, due to a serious infection. By January, she had been in a Chatsworth rehabilitation center for months, gaining back her strength. Seeing how much she needed a pick-me-up, one of her good friends, Dee Russo, sprang into action. Russo knew Luke's manager at the time, Steve Himber, and emailed him. Himber said he'd send Muha's contact info to Luke, but no promises. Russo assumed that her friend might get a signed headshot, at best.

A few weeks later, and Muha, freshly bathed with her hair in French braids and her glasses on instead of contacts, sat in her hospital bed, waiting for her friends to hand-deliver a burger from In-and-Out. She had just given them her order a minute ago—a Double-Double Animal Style with lightly toasted bun and fries—when someone knocked on the door. A nurse said, "Your visitor is here." Muha, confused because she'd just hung up with her friend, asked who it was.

"Luke," the nurse said.

"Luke who?" Muha asked. "I don't know any Lukes." In her head, she silently thought, *Luke Perry?* But of course, that wasn't possible.

"He's here, him and his dog," the nurse answered.

Oh, Muha thought, someone must've sent a therapy pup to cheer her up. Still, she quickly slicked on some lip gloss.

"Okay, let him in."

The door opened and first, his voice, "Excuse me, but are you Santina?"

"I start, like, Shazaming his face," Muha says, referencing the app that identifies the name of a song based on a few bars of music. "Okay, the chin, and there's the scar on the eyebrow, and—holy shit! That's really him!" It took time for her mind to leap over the years. "To me, Luke is eternally twenty-six or whatever, but here's a fifty-year-old man. Once I saw that scar, I knew."

He stepped out from behind the door and asked if he could close it. Then he approached and sat on the edge of the bed. He asked if he could hug Muha, who was "crying Spongebob Squarepants tears." In his flannel, he wrapped around her, "and I realize that I'm crying in Luke

Perry's arms ... and the flannel, it just smelled like *man*. Like hard-working handyman. He had paint on his jeans. That was big for me." The tears, she realized mid-swoon, had dampened his shirt.

"It's okay," Luke said. "It's just you and me." And Angel, his moon-eyed boxer mix whom Muha, despite being an extreme dog lover, could barely focus on.

Once Muha calmed herself, they talked as he sat in a chair next to her bed. He told her about being hospitalized with spinal meningitis soon after he moved to Los Angeles, how he questioned if he should go back to Ohio. He understood the ache of being sick and away from family. The tenor of the conversation was warm and open, but "you could tell he was reserved a little bit, guarded in terms of his private life." She could tell the guardedness was around his kids, and she made sure not to pry with questions. But after a while, the vibe shifted. Less fan and celebrity, and more "two people connecting, which was what I always wanted and what I always knew would happen, because I *knew* that we were connected."

Luke stayed for an hour, much longer than fan service required. After he left, he called her later that evening.

"I just wanted to say thank you so much for today," he said. "I've been thinking about it all day. It was such a great conversation, wasn't it?"

Muha, still glowing, replied, "Yes, it was great."

Then he said, "I'm so happy your mom didn't take you to the Free-hold Mall that day. That's not how we were supposed to meet. We were supposed to meet like this because now we know each other."

Reflecting on it years later, Muha says, "I don't know how he did it, but he surpassed him: Luke Perry is even better than Dylan McKay."

———

When it was announced in the news that he was hospitalized from a stroke, Muha was worried but convinced that the healthy, vibrant man who had visited her a few years ago was going to pull through. When he died a few days later, Muha heard the news as she was arriving to be a guest on a podcast. She sat in the parking lot, sobbing, and then after several deep breaths, she pulled herself together.

When she checked her phone after the podcast recording, there were more phone calls and texts from concerned friends than she received on her birthday, as if he was a member of her family. The tears immediately resumed.

She thought back to their conversation. A moment that now held new resonance: "He told me that he didn't want to be remembered as a teen heartthrob, though I don't think he used that word. He wanted to be remembered as a good person, he said." As all of the stories poured out about his kindness, Muha saw his wish coming true. Like the one from actor Colin Hanks who saw Luke in action on a packed plane. Hanks and his wife were coming back from Mexico. In the coach section with them were two quarreling kids at each other's throats. Crying, screaming, the whole works.

"If you're a parent, you understand," Hanks wrote on Instagram. "Sometimes there's nothing you can do. It was like this for close to two hours."

Then a savior appeared: "Ten minutes before landing, it starts to get real bad. Out of nowhere, a man comes from first class. Hat, beard, sunglasses, blowing up a balloon. He ties it off, hands it off like he's holding out a sword to a king."

Instantly, the kids calm down. Hanks doesn't realize that it's Luke until the two are standing next to each other at baggage claim. They've never met. Luke opens the conversation with some compliments about *Fargo*, which "blew my mind," Hanks said.

"I started singing his praises about how long I've admired him and also about the move with the balloon. 'That's a pro move! You can't teach that!' I say. He tells me he always flies with a couple of balloons for that reason, to give to screaming kids. Don't know if that's true, but [I] have no reason to believe it wasn't. Guy seemed like a true gent. Gone way too damn soon. Also, I gotta start traveling with some spare balloons," Hanks concluded.

Muha reads every last story over the next few weeks. They come from not only other actors or celebrities, but regular people such as Janet Grimes, the owner of Sisters, a diner in Dickson, Tennessee, that Luke frequented. He especially loved the cornbread.

"He acted like we were part of his family. He would always give you a hug," Grimes said. "I found him to be just a nice person. I enjoyed talking to him. He always knew you."

Reading all these stories, despite the loss, Muha "was so happy and warm inside, because that's what he wanted people to remember him for. I really don't remember seeing that many good deeds about another person coming out after death. Not like that." There was none of the backlash or reckoning that sometimes happens after a celebrity dies.

Muha and Luke took photographs that day in 2016, with Angel squeezed between them. One of the photos remains as the background image on her phone. "Nobody could've made me happier that day, walking into that room. To think about Luke Perry waking up in the morning and getting dressed to come see me. It's bigger than my brain can even comprehend."

FIFTY-TWO

MICHELLE CARR NEVER KNEW when her old friend Luke was going to pop back into Fredericktown. Her parents owned a farm and on a hot afternoon around 2008, as she was selling ears of corn and other produce at a farmstand on the side of the road, her cell phone vibrated in her pocket.

Unknown Caller. She answered.

"Hey, you look pretty cute out there in your tank top and jean shorts." She recognized his voice right away. Her high school's Biggest Flirt.

"What?"

"You must be selling a lot of corn."

"Luke, where are you?"

He had just driven by on his way to his parents' house. His two little kids were with him. He invited her to come by when she was done.

"Sure enough, when I arrived," Michelle says, "his mom had a place setting for me at the table." After dinner, they walked to the pond on his parents' property and taught Jack and Sophie how to fish.

"That's how he was," Michelle says. "If he showed up in town and he called and you were free, you got a chance to see him. He didn't come home a lot, but when he did, he kept it very private." His family did, too.

Another time, he called to tell her he was flying into Cleveland that night and wanted to know if she was free for dinner. Somewhere outside the city, "I ended up meeting him at this tiny little off-the-road restaurant that no one had ever heard of," she remembers. In a baseball cap and plain clothes, he was incognito to everyone but her. They sat for hours, playing songs on the jukebox until they closed the diner down.

Before Michelle's dad passed away in 2014, he had retired but still kept up a small produce business, mostly as a labor of love. Mr. Carr's pride and joy was his Apple Jack Moonshine.

While Michelle was at work, she got a call from her dad.

"What's up?" she asked. He didn't usually call at this time of day.

"Your friend Luke was just here."

"Luke Perry?"

"Well, isn't that the only Luke you know?"

"Yes, it is," she said. "But what do you mean he was just there?"

Her dad told her that Luke had just come by and for two hours, they had sat under the big tree on the front lawn talking about hunting, farming, old Fredericktown memories, everything under the sun. At one point, Mr. Carr broke out the Apple Jack Moonshine. All in all, it was a perfect afternoon that neither man had planned.

Slow had never left Luke's bones. Michelle remembered how they frittered away hours in junior high at the dry-cleaning business her parents owned back then. They would take turns hanging on to the rack, with the other one pressing the button, going around with all the pressed slacks and bagged dresses. A few months before he died, he texted her a video of a dry-cleaning rack on rotation and told her it always made him think of those times. When they were in high school, one of their friends got his driver's license before everyone else. They'd pile as many of them into that friend's van as could fit. Then they'd drive around for hours, listening to Led Zeppelin's "Going to California" and all the other songs that made the bitterly cold Ohio nights fly by in a haze.

———

In 2017, Michelle left Ohio for a position at the Charlotte, North Carolina, flagship store of Belk, a southern department store chain. The job was a step up in her career, and she was ready to try out a new town. By this time, Michelle had been divorced for several years; she was dating a bit, but nothing was clicking.

Luke told her about his friend Rory Karpf, a documentary filmmaker who Luke had collaborated with on a couple of projects. Karpf, a Charlotte resident, was fresh from his own divorce. Michelle thought Karpf sounded like a nice guy, but something held her back from calling. She was busy getting a handle on her new job. Then she had back surgery. Luke called her every day the week after, checking to make sure she had friends coming by, food on hand, medicine. Then he would nudge her as he did on nearly every one of their phone calls: "Shell, have you called Rory yet?"

———

When Rory Karpf was a senior in high school, he finally surrendered to the show he'd been hearing about since eighth grade. His crush liked *Beverly Hills, 90210*, so in order to get closer to her, he joined her Wednesday night watching parties, a double-header of *90210* and *Party of Five*. Rory was dropped into season five, which tracks Dylan's descent into active addiction. He promptly backtracked through all the seasons he'd missed.

"The show had a lot of depth," Rory says. "They were three-dimensional characters, which is rare for a show like that. And Luke brought so much humanity to his character." Rory also appreciated that Dylan still appeared as a full person, and not simply as a message delivery system for the War on Drugs. "He's addicted to drugs, but he's still interacting with people. He's not constantly on a bender."

As a budding filmmaker, Rory found inspiration in risky experiments such as "The Dreams of Dylan McKay," the episode where Dylan is in a coma after driving his Porsche off a cliff while high on heroin. As he lies twitching in his hospital bed, a doctor says the patient is in "a battle for the boy's soul." What follows are several nightmarish visions from Dylan's psyche. There's a suspiciously cheery Thanksgiving dinner at the Walshes, interrupted by serpents slithering around the turkey and a knock at the door from his dealer (played by Jon Gries). There's his erstwhile little sister, Erica, begging him to rescue her, and, in one of the series' several dream-state weddings, Valerie as his bride-to-be, who informs him in a deep distorted voice: "I am not Valerie. I am Brenda . . . and I want to be your wife." It's *90210* melodrama spiked by *Twin Peaks'* menacing mysticism. The unlikely combination wouldn't have worked without Luke's commitment to the conceit.

By the time Rory was in college, his fandom was on full display. For Halloween, he wore a Dylan mask as he trick-or-treated around Boston. He also hosted a party in his dorm room to watch Dylan's departure in season six, after the murder of his wife, Toni Marchette. He liked the whole show, but it was Dylan's character, and Luke's performance, that drew him in and kept him all the way through season ten. He also sought out the actor in other work, namely *Buffy the Vampire Slayer*, *8 Seconds*, and *Oz*.

After college, Rory worked as a special projects director for NAS-CAR. He had moved to Charlotte in 2004 to take the job. Seeing his chance to meet one of his heroes, he hired Luke to provide voice-over narration on a 2013 project about a NASCAR driver who served in World War II. Rory remembers that when a supervisor asked why Luke Perry of all people was narrating the project, he bluffed that Luke's father served in World War II, which was, as far as he knew, "total bullshit." Luke provided great narration, and the two hit it off well. By their second project, *The Play That Changed College Football*, this time with ESPN, they were exchanging ideas for documentaries. Luke told him he'd always wanted to capture Evel Knievel's story.

They ended up collaborating again on a 2014 ESPN short about

Marge Schott, the first woman to own and operate a Major League team, the Cincinnati Reds. This time, the connection was obvious; the native Ohioan was a lifelong Reds fan and remembered Schott's controversies well. To name but a few, she expressed admiration more than once for Hitler, and was also sued by a Reds executive who objected to her refusal to hire Black people. After that film, their friendship was cemented. Luke gave feedback to Rory on his script for *Grace Point*, a 2023 feature he directed starring John Owen Lowe as a young man who encounters some rough characters in a small town while on his way to a remote drug rehab.

"Luke would've been in it, if he hadn't passed away," Rory says.

When the Marge Schott documentary was done, a few ESPN anchors derided Rory's choice for narrator; it wasn't about Luke's actual work, just his name value at the moment. Rory was aware that his friend was in a career lull. Many of his movies at the time were straight-to-DVD projects or faith-based pictures that Luke didn't connect to whatsoever. Luke also seemed "curmudgeonly toward work in Hollywood," according to Rory. "It was very much a job for him at the time." His motivation, he told Rory, was mainly to stay close to LA so he could be home for his kids.

———

Occasionally Luke would field some of Rory's fan questions. Rory understood that Luke wasn't Dylan McKay, but he was still shocked when Luke casually mentioned he'd never been surfing. What about Dylan atop those waves? "He told me he was just really good at running into the water, and then running out of it," Rory recalls. Though *90210* had launched his career, Luke was far from sentimental about the output. As far as Rory could tell, Luke had never watched a single episode all the way through. When Rory expressed how annoyed he was at certain decisions the writers made with Dylan's character in season ten—why was he drinking again? Why bring his supposedly dead dad back to life?—Luke shrugged it all off, saying, "It's just a show, man. Don't think that hard about it." Rory never told him that he dressed as Dylan for Halloween.

———

A few years into their friendship, Rory went through a divorce. The loneliness of this new period in his life was excruciating at times. When Luke heard his friend was in town with no plans for Christmas—Rory's two young sons would be with his ex-wife—he invited him over.

Rory, dressed for a party, arrived at a house with no other guests in attendance and no food prepared. It was just Luke and his fiancée, Madison, packing for a trip to Bora Bora. They were leaving early the next morning. Luke offered to heat up some chili for him, but otherwise, no fuss was extended. Rory could see that it wasn't the best time for company, so he asked Luke why he was invited.

"I remember what that first year was like," Luke answered. "And I didn't want you to be alone."

———

On March 6, 2019, two days after Luke's death, Rory posted several pictures of Luke on Instagram, including one where he's holding Rory's two young sons with a big grin on his face. His lengthy, heartfelt tribute praised Luke as the most dedicated and loving father he'd ever seen.

In the comments, Michelle wrote, in part: "I'm not sure if my name sounds familiar to you, but Luke had been trying to get us to meet. . . . Every time we spoke, he asked me if I had connected with you. He really wanted us to meet, it was important to him. So I searched for you tonight and found you and wanted to reach out. I thought we could share in our grief of losing our amazing friend Luke."

———

On their first meeting a few days later, they each felt a connection, but they both privately doubted it. It was mere weeks after the death of their mutual good friend who wanted them to be together. Were they just responding to each other out of grief? Were they trying to make something beautiful spring out of obligation? The foundation of their conversations, at first, was Luke: Michelle shared how after his bulldog named Pig died, Luke texted her from the set of *Riverdale*, asking to see pictures of her two super-chonky English bulldogs, Bacon and Dozer. She told Rory that her favorite movie of Luke's was *8 Seconds*. The Lane Frost biopic resonated for Michelle because he was like "the Luke that I knew, just this sweet farm boy . . . whereas watching him play Dylan McKay, that was always a far stretch. It was definitely a character." Michelle saw him slip into something familiar again when he played Fred Andrews on *Riverdale*.

Over the course of a few more dates, Michelle and Rory's talks eventually opened up to other matters. Their kids, their dreams, their ideas about family. But they hadn't solidified anything when they attended Luke's memorial together at Skeet Ulrich's house. In fact, Rory had gotten them separate hotel rooms in LA for that night, not wanting to presume anything. At the memorial, a little blond boy ran up and scrutinized the two, then asked, "Are you guys boyfriend and girlfriend?"

They didn't know quite how to answer the question from Dashiell Priestley, Jason Priestley's nine-year-old son, but that night, the second hotel room sat empty. Though he remained as "a common denominator," Michelle says, "I think we realized that it wasn't just about the loss of Luke. We were really starting to fall for each other. It was just becoming about us."

A few months later, they watched *The Beat Beneath My Feet*, a 2014 movie set in London with Luke starring as a grunge rock god who went into hiding eight years ago. For most of the movie, Luke has a beard, but at the end, he is clean-shaven and playing guitar onstage with the neighbor kid he has befriended (played by Nicholas Galitzine, well known for *Red, White and Royal Blue* and *The Idea of You*). There's a moment when Luke gives Galitzine an encouraging nod. "He used to give *me* that kind of nod sometimes," Rory says. When he saw that gesture, innately Luke's, he cried for the first time about losing his friend.

"I still think about him every day," Rory says, holding back the tears that come easier to him now. "He genuinely was the best person I've ever known in my life. And I don't know why he was that way, he didn't have the easiest childhood." He was generous with his support over and over again. "He would call me from the set of *Riverdale*, send me texts and voice mails. He was just one of the most thoughtful people who was there for me."

Rory thinks often about a text he sent to Luke: "Just trying not to drown. I need to get past this divorce."

Luke responded: "You will. You're a born swimmer."

———

Rory proposed to Michelle in April 2020, and after waiting for the worst of the pandemic to settle down, they married on Christmas Day 2021, at a small impromptu ceremony at their house that Rory pulled together. He sheepishly admits that it wasn't perfect. Michelle was disappointed when he surprised her with a wedding dress that was too big. And she wasn't happy with the state of her hair that day. But her sister and niece got to work, and like the best couples know how to do, they rallied. The day turned into something sweet and tender. They read their vows with Dozer planted between them. The next summer, they celebrated in Nashville with a big party.

Their foundation has since expanded beyond Luke, the friend who brought them together. Instead, there is the bedrock of their own bond, the victories and struggles they share with each other regarding work or parenthood. But his memory is still with them, and grief draws them closer. Sometimes, in a quiet moment, Rory will turn to Michelle with a wistful expression. "I wish I could talk to Luke right now," Rory will say, and Michelle responds, "I know, I'd love to hear his voice again."

EPILOGUE

SUNDAY MORNING. THEY ARE HAVING a couple and their little boy over for a pancake brunch—Clay and Ali, and their five-year-old, Sam. The parents have never met, but Silas and Sam have been tussling in kindergarten, so the teacher suggested a family playdate to bond the boys.

David is whipping up his oatmeal pancakes. Margaret pours orange juice, washes berries, brews coffee. It's a little nerve-racking to have strangers come over for a meal, but also exciting, like a blind date.

The family arrives, and they are easy to talk to, friendly and warm. Ali, a tall therapist with a soft voice Margaret finds soothing, and Clay, a burly contractor with an Arkansas accent. After his childhood down south, he lived in Chicago, and they reminisce about their former lives there in the early aughts. The bars on every residential corner, fogged with American Spirit smoke.

Whatever friction the boys had, it falls away as they dive into Legos and toy cars. Still, she keeps one ear cocked. They set up a traffic jam, one of Silas's favorite activities. When you're five, traffic is exotic, all the toy cars harmoniously headed to the big city.

The adults engage in conversation. They ask what she is working on and she tells them.

"Oh, I have a story for you," Clay says with amusement. He proceeds to talk about a time, in the mid-aughts, at a red light in Valley

Village. He was sitting behind an old beat-up Kia minivan. The light turned green, and the car behind Clay started honking because the minivan hadn't moved. What Clay could see was that the minivan was waiting for an elderly man to cross the street. As the car behind Clay laid on the horn, the driver of the Kia sailed his hand out the window and flipped the bird, and then gestured to the old man. More honking, more middle finger, more angry pointing. Finally, the old man was safely across, and the Kia drove, but he kept brake-checking Clay in his black Jeep Wrangler.

Clay'd had enough; he drove up next to the Kia, with his window rolled down. Kia driver had his window down too, and he shouted: "Why were you honking, asshole? There was an old man crossing the street!"

Clay, embracing his full Arkansas, fired back: "It wasn't me, but I'll beat your ass, talking to me that way."

But then he stopped. He couldn't remember the actor's name, only the character.

He broke into a smile. "You're Dylan, right?"

Luke looked at him with total exasperation, answered with a flap of his hand, like "Get outta here," told Clay to fuck off, not with a lot of steam, more of a continuation of the "Get outta here," and zoomed off.

A few minutes later, they both pulled into the Whole Foods parking lot in Sherman Oaks, where Luke gave him the stink eye before entering the store. And that was their last interaction.

Clay doesn't hold a grudge. "I just couldn't believe he was driving that old Kia," he says.

This tracks with what she knows about Luke, including that exact car. At one point, he only had lawn furniture in his home; what's the point of getting nice furniture wet with water from the pool? The man was into wearing hard-core normcore outfits—fanny packs, cargoes, rumpled shirts—before normcore had a name. For someone who'd once been ob-jectified, he was unconcerned with outward appearances, which she finds endearing.

And, of course, he staunchly defended the elderly man. Forever a champion of life's underdogs and invisible ones.

———

The stories kept coming like this, from random corners of her LA existence. Always a degree or two removed. Her online mom's group becomes a fount of connections—the niece of his old neighbor, a producer who recorded him for a SYFY channel radio play, an actor friend who knew Mark Espinoza. Another acquaintance, an art installer, had hung art in his house. Oops, actually, that was Jason Priestley (and this confusion of identities happened more than once).

How was it possible that she had never met him, had never interviewed him, after all these years living and writing about pop culture in LA? Of course, it was possible not to, but it made less and less sense as she immersed herself in his life, especially his cinematic one. Dylan McKay trying to ready himself for his father's funeral, a moment that always made her weep because he tries to blink back his tears, like she did. At any moment, it seemed like he would call. "So I've heard you're working on a biography? I don't know how I feel about that . . ." She had been told by several in his circle that he would've been stunned at the outpouring after his death. That he wasn't a biography guy, for all kinds of reasons (including privacy, especially regarding his kids, and humility), so while still shining a light into his life, she tried to leave certain corners respectfully dark.

Some of his connections wanted to talk, and some didn't. All members of his immediate family declined to participate, which then made it hard to get cooperation from the 90210 actors. Certain people had very strong protective feelings. One well-known actor and documentarian even accused Margaret of being a "creepy" profiteer, before eventually apologizing. Some worried she would confuse him with his most famous character—that fear seemed to be borrowed from his own. Others were excited to share. Each reaction was a portal into the myriad ways we

handle grief. We can become sentinels, set up in front of churches to pro-
tect the treasures inside. Don't you dare ransack this sacred place. Or we
can invite the stranger in. Many entrusted her with their gold. To those
who did, she is grateful for that openhearted faith.

The point was always to attempt some kind of art, in duality. To see
what happened when two histories collided, dovetailed, and refracted
across nearly thirty years. To contemplate the gaping distances and emo-
tional close ranges. He was very guarded about his private life, so she
would offer up her own. More than a traditional biography, she hopes
that he would've responded to a work that rose up out of his life to create
a whole secondary existence.

———

A moment that revolved in her consciousness: After writing about Dr. F.,
she realized that she had not googled him in a while. She tended to do that
once a year or so, to make sure he was still alive. He was getting on. After
she'd moved to Los Angeles, she had kept in touch. On visits to Chicago,
she'd drop by his office for sessions she could now afford to pay for. She had
written him a few gratitude notes over the years. Still, they eventually fell
out of touch, and more time had lapsed than she'd meant. So she'd googled
him, and there it was. He had died of heart failure and prostate cancer at
age eighty-four. She had to double-check his date of death several times:
March 4, 2019. The same as Luke's.

If only she had reached out at least one more time. She hadn't thanked
him enough, from this vantage point, deeper into her adulthood with her
pains lessened because of him. In researching and writing about Luke over
the last year, she'd found herself in awe of his ability to cultivate com-
munity, to frequently reach out to those he loved, especially if he knew
someone was having a hard time. She, on the other hand, had a habit of
disappearing, especially when she was busy and overwhelmed. She hadn't
always tended to her friendships and connections in a way that repre-

sented her actual love and feelings. Between having a child and the pandemic, so many people had drifted away.

She called friends she'd fallen out of touch with, and some she just wanted to talk to more. The rule was to call, not to text, and preferably out of the blue. The element of surprise was part of the magic—too many surprises in adult life are not the good kind.

On breaks from her computer, often while walking with the sun shining on her skin, she spoke to the people she loved. The world was closer than she knew, filled with loved ones who had missed her voice too. They were scattered back throughout time. It made her fall in love again, with possibility as much as people.

———

She hates telling anyone what to do, but she'll risk being prescriptive because it's worth it. After you close this book, pick a person and reach out to them. Maybe you're struggling or they're struggling, or you've let too much time slip by. Call them and invite in nostalgia. Talk with your old friend about what you used to do together: the too-much beer, or the regular restaurant that's gone now, or the TV star you both pined for.

ACKNOWLEDGMENTS

MY GRATITUDE TO MY editor Sean Manning for his path-lighting and encouragement; to my agent Erin Hosier, for soothing my panic at key moments; and to Yvette Grant and everyone at Simon & Schuster who made this book better.

Immense thanks to all those in Luke's life who spoke with me. I will never forget that trust. Particularly to Chuck Rosin, David Sheinkopf, and Rory Karpf. I'm also grateful to the inspiring fan communities, and especially Pete Ferriero, who provided me with great leads and the kinds of details that only a Dylan McKay scholar would know.

I'm thankful for the people in my life, past and present, who are a part of this book. I am indebted to my family, especially my brothers and my uncle Gene, for reading and rooting for my work. Also to the Earle family for their kind and tangible support, Sasha Earle and Andy Hall especially. To the Earles and Wapplers, a part of my heart is always in Michigan or following you wherever you are.

I benefitted from fruitful conversations with many friends and colleagues, most of all Taffy Brodesser-Akner, Caroline Williams, Joanne Kim, Shari Geitzenauer, Jade Chang, Amanda Yates Garcia, Gesa Buttner Dias, Rodolfo Reis Dias, Anthony Miller, Elina Shatkin, Grace Krilanovich, Jason Moran, Kate Wolf, Maggie Butler, Molly Culhane, and Katie Norby.

I am a working parent, a balance that wouldn't be possible without help. Maria Ross, thank you for caring for my son with love. And to the cousins crew for helping to keep Silas company when I needed it most: Marta Cross, Rachel Elder, and Tessa Pelias.

My most profound gratitude to my husband, David Earle, for reading, editing, thinking, calming, and caretaking for Silas and me. Great news: we can watch regular TV again.

My mother and father are with me always. Dr. F., thank you for changing my life.

And finally, my beloved son, Silas. I'm so glad you love books. Let's read them all together.

NOTES

What follows are a couple of notes on how to read the following blend of traditional sourcing and a more modern take on using sources, original interviews, YouTube deep dives, etc. to dramatically recreate certain scenes from Luke Perry's life. For original interviews, I have cited the first quote from each interview only; the following quotes in the chapter from the interviewee are also taken from the original interview, unless noted otherwise. Also, to avoid a tangle of ibids, I have only repeated a source in the same chapter when using it for a direct quote or a significant detail; otherwise, it is safe to assume these sources were used extensively in each chapter. At the end, there's a more general bibliography.

PROLOGUE

xiii *The experience of motherhood:* Marina Warner, Introduction, in *Down Below* by Leonora Carrington (New York: New York Review Books, 2017).
xiv *Luke Perry is dead:* Lynn Elber, "Luke Perry, heartthrob on '90210,' dies at 52 after stroke," Associated Press, March 4, 2019.

CHAPTER 1

3 *He needed time to cross:* "Luke Perry: In His Own Words," *Us Weekly TV*, spring 2019, https://www.youtube.com/watch?v=9wNEKkhmQnU.
4 *Luke Perry focused on Dianne Young:* "Casting Season 1 with Dianne Young," *Beverly Hills 90210 Show*, Oct. 12, 2002. https://podcasts.apple .com/us/podcast/beverly-hills-90210-show/id1510639221.
5 *"Not only did I not think":* Author interview with Charles Rosin, Dec. 14, 2022.

CHAPTER 2

7 *On Oct 11, 1966, Coy Luther Perry III was born:* Lynn Elber, "Luke Perry, heartthrob on '90210,' dies at 52 after stroke," Associated Press, March 4, 2019.

7   *picture of fellow Ohio native Paul Newman:* Kevin Sessums, "Wild About Perry," *Vanity Fair*, July 1992.

7   *one of his favorite shows:* Oliver Jones, "Luke Perry's Great Escape," *Us Weekly*, Feb. 5, 2001.

7   *Luke debuted in his first play:* Luiane Lee, " 'Guy in the box' gets heroic role: Luke Perry used to pretend to be an American hero and now he plays one," *The Province*, Feb. 25, 1994.

8   *Around age twelve, he and his family:* Author interview with Michelle Carr, Nov. 10, 2022.

8   *Luke was also a decent left-handed:* Luke Perry, MTV's *FANatic*, November 1998. https://www.youtube.com/watch?v=cRBEFJSKFKo.

8   *His parents divorced:* Ibid.

8   *"I always felt that I should have been able to protect her":* Ibid.

8   *Luke's true father figure:* Obituary of Thomas Stevenson Bennett, Snyder Funeral Homes, https://www.snyderfuneralhomes.com/obituaries/Thomas -Stevenson-Bennett?obId=22965387.

9   *The guy who would be voted Biggest Flirt:* Jeannie Park, "Down and Out (Not!) in Beverly Hills," *People*, Nov. 4, 1991.

9   *pulling pranks:* Luke Perry, interview, *Late Night with David Letterman*, May 5, 1992. https://www.youtube.com/watch?v=k3KEJcPKjsI&t=78s

10 *For several months, he shared:* Author interview with David Sheinkopf, March 15, 2023.

10 *commercials, like one for Mars bar:* Luke Perry Mars Bar commercial, 1988, https://www.youtube.com/watch?v=O6stcgu4j7s.

10 *"It's funny, I never envisioned myself going out to Hollywood":* Ibid.

CHAPTER 3

13 *Aaron Spelling moved his office:* David A. Keeps, "When Aaron Spelling Ruled Television: An Oral History of Entertainment's Prolific, Populist Producer," *Hollywood Reporter*, Sept. 18, 2015.

13 *Spelling's butler:* Author interview with Darren Star, Feb. 1, 2023.

13 *He called his boss Mr. Spelling:* Author interview with Tony Shepherd, Dec. 12, 2022.

14 *a recent UCLA grad:* "Darren Star on Creating 'Beverly Hills, 90210,' " Television Academy Foundation, Oct. 6, 2015, https://interviews.television academy.com/interviews/darren-star.

14 *Star lifted elements:* Ibid.

15 *a Canadian actor cast at the eleventh hour:* "Darren Star on Casting 'Beverly Hills, 90210,' " Television Academy Foundation, Oct. 6, 2015. https://www .youtube.com/watch?v=fGRC1kc9Qss&t=112s

15 *Luke put his grubby sneaker:* "Casting Season 1 with Dianne Young," *Beverly Hills 90210 Show*, Oct. 12, 2002.

CHAPTER 4

19 *"It was awful"*: Author interview with Tony Shepherd, Dec. 12, 2022.
20 *"I don't remember it being a flub"*: Author interview with Charles Rosin, Dec. 14, 2022.
20 *"They were never as convinced"*: Author interview with Darren Star, Feb. 1, 2023.
20 *The first ten checks*: Luke Perry panel at Dragon Con, Atlanta, Georgia, Sept. 5, 2010.

CHAPTER 5

23 *"I just walked out of a roomful of fools"*: "Luke Perry Talks Getting Rejected 256 Times Before First Gig," Sway's Universe (website), Jan. 24, 2013. https://www.youtube.com/watch?v=A9i8jcPyleU.
24 *"He was my sweet little cowboy"*: Author interview with Julie Resnick, March 22, 2023.

CHAPTER 6

27 *A little bubble of viewership*: Author interview with Charles Rosin, Dec. 14, 2022.

CHAPTER 7

32 *"Mad, bad, and dangerous"*: Antonia Fraser, *Lady Caroline Lamb* (New York: Simon & Schuster, 2023).

CHAPTER 8

39 *"I just remember this one scene"*: Author interview with Darren Star, Feb. 1, 2023.
39 *"in craphole Valley restaurant/bars"*: Jason Priestley, *Jason Priestley: A Memoir* (New York: HarperOne, 2014).
40 *"We got real famous real fast"*: Panel with Jason Priestley and Luke Perry, Fan Expo 2013, https://www.youtube.com/watch?v=Swrgh5cI_Ew&t=433s.

CHAPTER 9

43 *Affiliates in the south*: Author interview with Charles Rosin, Dec. 14, 2022.
43 *a conversation about teen sex*: Roberta Wax, "Teensomething," *Emmy* 13, no. 5 (Oct. 1991).

44 *"I never wanted the show to be moralizing"*: Author interview with Darren Star, Feb. 1, 2023.

CHAPTER 10

45 *When James Dean died*: "James Dean," *We Didn't Start the Fire: The History Podcast*, Nov. 14, 2021.
45 *"I'm not James Dean"*: Luke Perry, interview by Maria Shriver, *Today*, 1992.

CHAPTER 11

49 *"Hair was very important"*: David A. Keeps, "When Aaron Spelling Ruled Television: An Oral History of Entertainment's Prolific, Populist Producer," *Hollywood Reporter*, Sept. 18, 2015.
49 *two American traditions*: Author interview with Charles Rosin, Dec. 14, 2022.
50 *"I'll never forget sitting by the pool"*: Author interview with Darren Star, Feb. 1, 2023.

CHAPTER 12

53 *"I can roll"*: Author interview with David Sheinkopf, March 15, 2023.
53 *Sheinkopf's agent*: David Sheinkopf, *Village Idiot: A Manhattan Memoir* (New Jersey: Full Court Press, 2022).
54 *shot in thirty-six days*: Stephen Garrett, "A Conversation with Jordan Alan of 'Kiss And Tell', the Improv Director," *IndieWire*, Oct. 22, 1997.
54 *Luke wrote it off as a disaster*: Carla Hall, "Teen Heartthrobs: The Beat Goes On," *Washington Post*, Oct. 3, 1991.
54 *a soulful connection*: Rose Dommu, "Remembering Luke Perry's Friendship with Trans Icon Alexis Arquette," *Out*, March 5, 2019, https://www.out.com /celebs/2019/3/05/remembering-luke-perrys-friendship-trans-icon-alexis -arquette.
54 *transition to female*: Alexis Heigl, "How Alexis Arquette's 'Fiercely Defensive' Family Stood by Her on Her Transition Journey and Beyond," *People*, Sept. 13, 2016.
54 *particularly David and Patricia*: "Why Luke Perry is 'like family' to David Arquette," *Jess Cagle Podcast*, July 7, 2020.

CHAPTER 13

61 *George Clooney had one too*: Justine Hankins, "Farewell Max, the pig who came between George and his women," *Guardian*, Dec. 6, 2006.

61 *her pet pig Wilbur:* Samantha Highfill, "Molly Ringwald reveals she's returning for more Riverdale," *Entertainment Weekly*, Jan. 25, 2019.

61 *"It was beautiful":* Sessums, "Wild About Perry."

61 *"I don't keep him":* Carla Hall, "Teen Heartthrobs: The Beat Goes On."

62 *"Oh god, yeah":* Author interview with David Sheinkopf, March 15, 2023.

62 *"Well, Irma walked over":* Leslie Jordan, "Did I just call Luke Perry's house a pig sty?," Facebook video, March 15, 2022.

62 *"Luke's house":* Jay Martel, "Scenes from the Cast Struggle in Beverly Hills," *Rolling Stone*, Feb. 20, 1992.

62 *the bad boy of television's:* Scott Glover, "Tarzana: '90210' Star Gets to Keep His Pet Pigs," *Los Angeles Times*, July 17, 1993.

CHAPTER 14

63 *By 1992:* Sessums, "Wild About Perry."

63 *The next year:* K. Fitzgerald, "TV's hottest number? Teen fans plus *90210* add up to 60 licensing deals," *Advertising Age*, June 1, 1992.

63 *By the spring of 1995:* E. Graham McKinley, *Beverly Hills, 90210: Television, Gender, and Identity* (Pennsylvania: University of Pennsylvania Press, 1997).

CHAPTER 15

67 *"Play it, Davey Shein":* Author interview with David Sheinkopf, March 15, 2023.

67 *The upstairs VIP area:* Betty Goodwin, "So Long, Valentino, Hello, Sean," *Los Angeles Times*, Feb. 16, 1992.

CHAPTER 16

76 *"We got squished":* Barbara Serrano, "Bellevue Mob Scene Over Teen Heartthrob—Five Hurt In Crush To See TV Actor," *Seattle Times*, May 10, 1991.

76 *"We knew how to get him out":* Author interview with Julie Resnick, March 22, 2023.

76 *"All I saw was my car's":* "See Luke Perry Being the Coolest Celeb of All Time in Vintage Interview with Jason Priestley," *ET Canada* interview, *Perez Hilton*. Accessed Nov. 2, 2023. https://perezhilton.com/luke-perry-jason-priestley-90210-interview-video/.

77 *"It's scary":* "Luke Perry on Becoming America's Heartthrob: 'It's Scary,'" *Inside Edition*, Aug. 20, 2019, YouTube video, https://www.youtube.com/watch?v=rEVwF7II5GI.

CHAPTER 17

81   *"I got hit in the back"*: Berta Delgado and Liz Doup, "Melee at the mall, 20 injured during surge for heartthrob," *Sun Sentinel*, Aug. 11, 1991.

81   *"I had no idea"*: "Fans hurt in crush to meet TV heartthrob," Associated Press, Aug. 11, 1990.

82   *"Feel my pulse"*: Lisa Schwarzbaum, "Beverly Hills, 90210, TV's Hottest Number," *Entertainment Weekly*, Sept. 6, 1991.

82   *"I felt weird the first time"*: Luke Perry, interview by Maria Shriver, *Today*, 1992.

CHAPTER 18

83   *"Shannen would come to the set"*: Author interview with Charles Rosin, Dec. 14, 2022.

84   *"They continued to kiss and kiss"*: Author interview with Larry Mollin, Dec. 14, 2022.

84   *"There was a time"*: Lisa Schwarzbaum, "Luke Who's Talking," *Entertainment Weekly*, March 11, 1994.

84   *"we had some problems but"*: Panel with Jason Priestley and Luke Perry, Fan Expo 2013, https://www.youtube.com/watch?v=Swrgh5cI_Ew&t=173s.

CHAPTER 19

87   *"If it wasn't for Luke Perry"*: Author interview with Fran Rubel Kuzui, Jan. 31, 2023.

89   *Deep into* Buffy's *six-week shoot:* Joe Rhodes, "Movies: On Location: Eeeeyew . . . Gross. Where's My Wooden Stake?: 'Buffy the Vampire Slayer' turns the table on teen horror films, with a heroic damsel, a hunk in distress and, says the director, some serious issues that go for the jugular," *Los Angeles Times*, May 31, 1992.

CHAPTER 20

95   *"If you don't come"*: Author interview with Julie Resnick, March 22, 2023.

96   *"There are a lot of pent-up frustrations"*: Sessums, "Wild About Perry."

98   *"He made us, the writers"*: Author interview with Charles Rosin, Dec. 14, 2022.

CHAPTER 21

105   *the annual Spelling Christmas eve party:* Tori Spelling, *sTORI Telling* (New York: Simon Spotlight, 2008).

CHAPTER 22

111 *two auditions that day in 1993*: Author interview with Mark Espinoza, April 20, 2023.

CHAPTER 23

117 *"I would ride every morning"*: Ingrid Sischy, "Elizabeth Taylor: Chapter Two," *Interview*, March 23, 2011.

117 *charismatic bull-rider Lane Frost*: Ted Harbin, "The spirit of Lane Frost lives on in bull riding," *Oklahoman*, Jan. 31, 2002.

117 *deeply moved to play Frost*: "News 8's George Pennacchio interviews Luke Perry about film '8 Seconds' in 1994," CBS 8 San Diego, 1994, https://www.youtube.com/watch?v=0-i5Ccr-9DI.

117 *Luke fought hard*: Diane Goldner, "A 1994 interview with Luke Perry, promoting '8 Seconds' from Manhattan," *AM New York*, Feb. 25, 1994, https://www.amny.com/entertainment/luke-perry-interview-1-28120764/.

118 *less-potent position*: Philip Wuntch, "Perry wouldn't be thrown off his dream of '8 Seconds,'" *Las Vegas Review-Journal*, Feb. 28, 1994.

118 *a niche topic*: "Luke Perry '8 Seconds' 1994—Bobbie Wygant Archive," The Bobbie Wygant Archive, 1994, YouTube video, https://www.youtube.com/watch?v=dPzYxuWs6Fw.

118 *pitching studio after studio*: "'8 Seconds' Took Forever for Luke Perry," *St. Louis Post-Dispatch*, Feb. 23, 1994.

118 *"incredible work ethic"*: Rissa Shaw, "Bull rider who trained Perry for '8 Seconds' says actor had lasting impact on rodeo world," KWTX, March 4, 2019.

119 *"Luke Perry's the only reason"*: Tuff Hederman, interview by Jack Ingram, *The Jackin' Around Show*, Feb. 11, 2021.

119 *"He was so conscientious"*: Jimmie Tramel, "Lane Frost's mother shares her appreciation for Luke Perry," Associated Press, March 16, 2019.

119 *none of the actors involved*: John Petrakis, "'8 Seconds' offers a long and bumpy ride," *Chicago Tribune*, Feb. 25, 1994.

119 *lukewarm reception*: Joe Brown, "Luke-Warm '8 Seconds,'" *Washington Post*, Feb. 25, 1994.

119 *screenwriter Monte Merrick*: Maria Sandoval, "Buzzer Sounds for Perry's '8 Seconds' to Glory," *Santa Fe New Mexican*, March 4, 1994.

120 *riled up at the sentimental fare*: "Activists protest rodeo movie," Associated Press, Feb. 27, 1994.

120 *"Before 8 Seconds, those small rodeos"*: Thomas Mooney, "How Luke Perry's Rodeo Movie '8 Seconds' Illuminated Life Outside the 90210," *Rolling Stone*, March 4, 2019.

CHAPTER 24

123 *when Luke first read the script*: Author interview with Charles Rosin, Dec. 14, 2022.
124 *"Luke had a tendency"*: "Child Is Father to the Man," *Beverly Hills 90210 Show*, Jan. 7, 2021.
124 *"This is Emmy-worthy acting"*: Jennie Garth, "Feeling for Dylan," *9021OMG*, podcast, July 11, 2022.

CHAPTER 25

129 *"He wants to make movies"*: Tom Jicha, "Perry, Locklear not leaving—yet," *Sun Sentinel*, July 1995.
130 *"We just decided from the get-go"*: Author interview with Rebecca Gayheart, March 23, 2023.
131 *a 1997 sci-fi movie*: Nathan Rabin, "Control Nathan Rabin 4.0 #175 Invasion (1997)," Nathan Rabin's Happy Place (website), Feb. 16, 2021, https://www.nathanrabin.com/happy-place/2021/2/16/control-nathan-rabin-40-175-invasion-1997.
131 *a farm near Van Lear*: Chris Gadd, "Dickson Co. remembers star resident Luke Perry," March 13, 2019.
131 *a devastating event*: Eric Todisco, "Rebecca Gayheart says she 'didn't want to live' after killing 9-year-old boy in car accident," *People*, May 21, 2019.
132 *"didn't want to live"*: Rebecca Gayheart, "Rebecca Gayheart Dane Is the Only One with a Painful Secret, Episode 6," in *The Only One in the Room*, podcast, May 21, 2019.

CHAPTER 26

137 *"It was perfect"*: Author interview with John McNaughton, April 21, 2023.
140 *"Not only does Judd"*: Michael Wilmington, "A Wild 'Life': Ashley Judd's stunning performance makes a good crime drama even better," *Chicago Tribune*, Oct. 25, 1996.
140 *one of the visual architects*: Eric Rudolph, "The Man Behind the Curtain of HBO's Oz," *American Cinematographer*, Sept. 1997.

CHAPTER 27

143 *"It offers such extraordinary visions"*: Roger Ebert, "The Fifth Element movie review," *Chicago Sun-Times*, May 9, 1997.
143 *an eight-day shoot*: Luke Perry panel at Dragon Con, Atlanta, Georgia, Sept. 5, 2010. https://www.youtube.com/watch?v=tbueXPo9hz4&t=5s.

CHAPTER 28

150 *"They always want to know"*: "Remembering Luke Perry," *The Morning Show*, March 5, 2019, https://www.facebook.com /watch/?v=2366136700065431.

151 *"none of us would be here"*: Lisa Respers France, "Luke Perry's kind words for Shannen Doherty," CNN, Nov. 14, 2016.

CHAPTER 29

155 *"Elephants come home to die"*: Tom Jicha, "Heartthrob returns; Perry rejoins *90210*, takes up where he left off three years ago," *Sun Sentinel*, Nov. 18, 1998.

155 *"Not unlike a young Orson Welles"*: Virginia Vejnoska, "Bad boy's back in town: Luke Perry returns to '90210,'" *Atlanta Constitution*, Nov. 18, 1998.

155 *"I like knowing where I'm going"*: Luke Perry, MTV's *FANatic*, Nov. 1998.

156 *"Taking care of the actors"*: Author interview with Charles Rosin, Dec. 14, 2022.

156 *He died in January 2001*: "Paul Waigner; Emmy-Winning Producer," obituary, *Los Angeles Times*, Jan. 27, 2001.

156 *"Apathy coupled with whatever"*: Paul Brownfield, "Class Dismissed!" *Los Angeles Times*, May 17, 2000.

157 *"Never say never"*: Oliver Jones, "Luke Perry's Great Escape."

CHAPTER 30

161 *the first show to be released*: Alan Sepinwall, *The Revolution Was Televised: The Cops, Crooks, Slingers and Slayers Who Changed TV Drama Forever* (self-published, 2012).

161 *under pressure*: Author interview with Tom Fontana, Jan. 31, 2023.

162 *a prison explosion*: Alfred Blumstein and Allen J. Beck, "Population Growth in U.S. Prisons, 1980-1996," *Crime and Justice*, Volume 26 (1999): pp. 17-61.

162 *"a national emergency"*: Jones, "Luke Perry's Great Escape."

CHAPTER 31

167 *"I always said that Oz"*: Author interview with Tom Fontana, Jan. 31, 2023.

168 *"As much as he appreciated"*: Author interview with Dean Winters, Feb. 28, 2023.

170   *"Oh yeah, I got to do"*: Damian Holbrook, " 'Riverdale' Star Luke Perry Takes Us on a Trip Through His TV Past: 'I Know What Dylan McKay Did For Me,' " *TV Insider*, March 2, 2017, https://www.tvinsider.com/125913 /luke-perry-riverdale-90210-jeremiah/.

CHAPTER 32

173   *"The first day we met"*: Author interview with Sean Dugan, Feb. 22, 2023.
173   *legends in the Oz universe*: Bruce Fretts, "Matt Dillon falls into 'Oz,' " *Entertainment Weekly*, July 9, 1999.

CHAPTER 33

177   *"it was like when"*: Author interview with Dean Winters, Feb. 28, 2023.

CHAPTER 34

181   *"In hindsight, I wish"*: Author interview with Darren Star, Feb. 1, 2023.

CHAPTER 35

183   *"But Luke didn't care"*: Author interview with Chris Barish, March 6, 2023.
183   *cofounded the restaurant chain*: Kate Storey, "The Rise and Fall of Planet Hollywood," *Esquire*, June 9, 2021.
185   *The cowboy traditional*: Tom McNamara, "The American Songbag: I Ride an Old Paint," aired Aug. 25, 2012, on PBS.
185   *The narrator rides his paint*: "Old Paint: About the Song," Ballad of America, https://balladofamerica.org/old-paint/.
185   *"The song came to them"*: Carl Sandburg, *The American Songbag* (New York: Harcourt, Brace & Company, 1927).
185   *"It's an old cowboy song"*: Michelle Manning Barish, Instagram, post from March 4, 2019.

CHAPTER 36

189   *muscled up to Luke*: Author interview with Sean Dugan, Feb. 22, 2023.
190   *"Hey, are you OK?"*: Author interview with Dean Winters, Feb. 28, 2023.

CHAPTER 37

193   *chunks of plaster*: Sandra Laville, "Chandelier brings the house down," *Guardian*, May 17, 2004.

193 *"He was obviously quite concerned"*: Danielle Demetriou, "When Harry met Sally, the ceiling fell in . . . literally," *Independent*, May 17, 2004.

193 *fifteen people required treatment:* Alex Marshall, "Ceilings in London Theaters Keep Falling Down," *New York Times* (international edition), Nov. 27, 2019.

194 *the reviews were:* Rhoda Koenig, "When Harry Met Sally, Theatre Royal, Haymarket, London," *Independent*, Feb. 28, 2004.

194 *less than impressive:* Matt Wolf, " 'Harry' proves to be a stage mismatch," *Variety* 394, no. 3 (March 2004).

194 *eviscerating:* Kate Copstick, "When Harry Met Sally: Why did they need to meet again?" *Scotsman*, Feb. 24, 2004.

CHAPTER 38

195 *The machines crowding the hospital bed:* "Jason Priestley's Close Call," ABC News, Jan. 30, 2003, https://abcnews.go.com/2020/story?id=123675&page=1.

195 *"Jay, Jay, it's Luke":* Jason Priestley, interview by Barbara Walters, *20/20*, January 2003.

196 *Priestley, his throat sore: Jason Priestley: A Memoir.*

196 *"So we had rain towers":* Jason Priestley, interview by Ian Hansomansing, "Reinventing Jason Priestley: Life After 90210 and his latest project," *CBC News: The National*, Jan. 8, 2023.

CHAPTER 39

199 *The year is 2021:* Chauncey Mabe, " 'Jeremiah,' premiering Sunday night on Showtime," Knight Ridder Tribune News Service, March 1, 2002.

199 *"It felt like":* Author interview with Malcolm-Jamal Warner, March 24, 2023.

200 *"I'm too old for this [stuff]":* Terry Morrow, "Perry delves into dark world of sci-fi in 'Jeremiah,' " *Knoxville News-Sentinel*, March 1, 2002.

201 *increasing tension:* John J. Joex, "Sci Fi TV Genre Gems: Jeremiah (2002)," CancelledSciFi.com, Jan. 2, 2021. https://www.cancelledscifi.com/2021/01/02/sci-fi-tv-genre-gems-jeremiah-2002/.

202 *Sigh-Fi:* John Levesque, "New Showtime Series Is More Sigh-Fi than Sci-Fi," *Seattle Post-Intelligencer*, March 1, 2002.

202 *a loyal following:* Press release, "SEAN ASTIN SPEAKS OUT; 'Jeremiah' Star Amazed at Fan Uproar Over TV Show," Worlds of JMS (website), Nov. 8, 2003, https://www.worldsofjms.com/jeremiah/uproar.htm.

202 *"I would've loved to continue on Jeremiah":* Luke Perry panel at Dragon Con, Atlanta, Georgia, Sept. 5, 2010. https://www.youtube.com/watch?v=tbueXPo9hz4&t=5s.

CHAPTER 40

209 *his 2022 memoir:* David Milch, *Life's Work: A Memoir* (New York: Random House, 2022).

210 *"There's only one person I've worked with":* Author interview with John McNaughton, April 21, 2023.

210 *"The greatest writer on television, hands down":* Luke Perry panel at Dragon Con, Atlanta, Georgia, Sept. 5, 2010. https://www.youtube.com /watch?v=jxPPxeOCxj0&t=60s.

CHAPTER 41

213 *"I don't do politics":* "Luke Perry on Sherrod Brown," C-SPAN, Oct. 10, 2006, https://www.c-span.org/video/?c4784154/user-clip-luke-perry -sherrod-brown.

213 *"About a week and a half before [my father] died, he got a call from Luke Perry":* Ben Peters, "His father delivered Luke Perry. Now Sherrod Brown is mourning him," *Roll Call,* March 4, 2019.

213 *"Luke did events across Ohio":* Michael O'Neil, X (formerly Twitter), post on March 4, 2019, https://x.com/abefromanohio/status/1102637712543268866 ?s=20.

214 *"The number one question with [the] new show 90210":* "Luke Perry Bizarre Interview: Touts Barack no 90210," WGN News, Sept. 23, 2008, https:// www.youtube.com/watch?v=u1udI3Kn_aQ&t=24s.

215 *"He got infuriated by someone":* David Iserson, X (formerly Twitter), post on March 4, 2019, https://x.com/davidiserson/status/1102637377892233216 ?s=20.

CHAPTER 42

219 *"If I'm being honest":* Author interview with Ari Bagley, May 2, 2023.

219 *former Mormon missionary:* Benjamin Gourley, IMDb, https://www.imdb .com/name/nm1377076/.

CHAPTER 43

222 *he could scream at:* "Luke Perry," interview with World Screen, YouTube, Nov. 18, 2010, https://www.youtube.com/watch?v=IajjmnXYgEE.

223 *he dreamed up Goodnight:* Nancy Mills, "Luke Perry presides over 'Goodnight': His fellow '90210' hunk Priestley directs TV movie," *USA Today,* Jan. 26, 2011.

223 *interviews promoting the film: "The Justin Bieber of 1991":* "See Luke Perry

Being the Coolest Celeb of All Time in Vintage Interview with Jason Priestley," *ET Canada* interview, Perez Hilton, 2013, https://perezhilton .com/luke-perry-jason-priestley-90210-interview-video/.

CHAPTER 44

227 *"The actor and novice skateboarder"*: Paul Hodgins, "Former star on '90210' insists he's still alive," *Orange County Register*, Oct. 29, 2011.

227 *"He's very much alive"*: Lew Irwin, "Luke Perry's Death Claims Are a Hoax," Contactmusic.com, Oct. 29, 2011.

227 *celebrity demises:* Nur Ibraham, "Why Are Online Death Hoaxes so Popular?," Snopes.com, Sept. 22, 2022.

228 *"100% fabricated"*: Natalia Finn, "9021-Oh-No-They-Didn't! Luke Perry Survives Latest Celeb Death Hoax," *E! Online*, Oct. 28, 2011.

228 *"I'm feeling pretty old tonight"*: The Late Show with Stephen Colbert, Season 2, Episode 29. Oct 21, 2016. https://www.facebook.com/watch /?v=966613193483432.

CHAPTER 45

233 *"I was enamored by him, in a way"*: Author interview with David Rapaport, Feb. 14, 2023.

234 *"I didn't really want to read the script"*: "Luke Perry: New Archie Series 'Riverdale' Is Like '90210' on Steroids," *Today*, Jan. 20, 2017.

236 *"I like playing the dad"*: Jean Bentley, "Luke Perry on 'Riverdale,' '90210' Similarities and Whether Fred Andrews Takes After Jim Walsh," *Hollywood Reporter*, Jan. 26, 2017.

236 *"Luke Perry's forehead"*: Rebecca Onion, "Luke Perry's Riverdale Role Made Him a Sex Symbol All Over Again," *Slate*, March 4, 2019.

CHAPTER 46

241 *"He saw the bigger picture of it"*: Author interview with David Rapaport, Feb. 14, 2023.

242 *"If I had a cold"*: K. J. Apa, interview, *The Tonight Show Starring Jimmy Fallon*, April 27, 2019, https://www.youtube.com/watch?v=Pg6wXYA75uA.

242 *"Concentrate on the work"*: K. J. Apa and Luke Perry, interview, *Today*, Oct. 8, 2018, https://www.youtube.com/watch?v=dZUO09MTxe4.

242 *"He's one of the best people"*: K. J. Apa, interview, *The View*, March 9, 2020, https://www.youtube.com/watch?v=Ej7oBX252Y4.

242 *"He was somebody who I could look"*: "Luke Perry's Birthday Tribute," *Beverly Hills 90210 Show*, Oct. 12, 2020.

CHAPTER 47

245 *"He was extremely generous"*: Author interview with Marisol Nichols, Feb. 3, 2023.

CHAPTER 48

253 *"Luke, nothing would make me happier"*: Author interview with Gabriel Correa, June 6, 2023.

CHAPTER 49

259 *Luke's family also read the script:* Claudia Harmata, " 'Riverdale' Cast Recalls Making 'Difficult' Luke Perry Tribute Episode: 'His Spirit Is Still with Us,' " *People*, Oct. 6, 2019.
259 *"Please don't make me"*: Author interview with Gabriel Correa, June 6, 2023.
261 *"As far as I was always concerned"*: Author interview with Marisol Nichols, Feb. 3, 2023.

CHAPTER 50

267 *"He'll test me by throwing out"*: Author interview with Vickie Thomas, May 3, 2023.
267 *the first Emmy and Golden Globes Awards*: Seth Abramovitch, "Hollywood Flashback: 'Mannix' star Gail Fisher Made Emmys History in 1970," *Hollywood Reporter*, June 19, 2022.
268 *"Made you feel like"*: Jennifer Yoo, statement via email, May 5, 2023.
269 *"The modern LA of the stoned sensibility"*: Pauline Kael, *Reeling* (New York: Little Brown, 1976).
269 *original KJH broadcasts:* Tara Bitran, "How 'Once Upon a Time in Hollywood' Secured Clip Clearances to Re-create 1969," *Hollywood Reporter*, Jan. 31, 2020.
269 *"I think of it like my memory piece"*: Michael Hainey, "Quentin Tarantino, Brad Pitt, and Leonardo DiCaprio Take You Inside 'Once Upon a Time . . . In Hollywood,' " *Esquire*, May 21, 2019.
271 *"Let's do it one more time"*: Author interview with Vickie Thomas, May 3, 2023.
271 *"Honestly, as soon as I saw Luke"*: Chris Willman, "Once Upon an Epic Panel at the New Beverly: Tarantino, DiCaprio, Pitt and Robbie Reunite to Talk 'Hollywood,' " *Variety*, Nov. 3, 2019.
271 "It was this strange burst of excitement": Hainey, "Quentin Tarantino, Brad Pitt, and Leonardo DiCaprio Take You Inside 'Once Upon a Time . . . In Hollywood.' "

272 *"It was really fun"*: Clark Collis, "Quentin Tarantino remembers working with the late Luke Perry on *Once Upon a Time in Hollywood*," *Entertainment Weekly*, July 23, 2019.

272 *"He told me, 'I'm going to'"*: Author interview with Rory Karpf, Oct. 28, 2022.

CHAPTER 51

277 *"It was love at first sight"*: Author interview with Santina Muha, Jan. 11, 2023.

280 *"If you're a parent, you understand"*: Robyn Merrett, "Colin Hanks Shares Sweet Story About the Touching Way the Late Luke Perry Helped a Packed Plane," *People*, March 5, 2019.

281 *"He acted like we were a part of his family"*: Chris Gadd, "Dickson Co. remembers star resident Luke Perry." *Tennessean*, March 13, 2019.

CHAPTER 52

283 *"Hey, you look pretty cute out there"*: Author interview with Michelle Carr, Nov. 10, 2022.

285 *"The show had a lot of depth"*: Author interview with Rory Karpf, Oct. 28, 2022.

EPILOGUE

293 *"Oh, I have a story"*: Author interview with Clay Reed, Oct. 5, 2023.

BIBLIOGRAPHY

The following materials were helpful in providing biography, background, color, and depth. It's not exhaustive, but it gives a good sense of the rabbit holes I've enjoyed for the past year.

Armstrong, Jennifer Keishin. "I thought I was a Brandon girl. But Luke Perry helped me realize that all I ever wanted was a Dylan McKay." *Washington Post*, March 6, 2019.

"Beverly Hills 90210 Producer Talks College Years, Slams New 90210." Teen DramaWhore.com, Jan. 17, 2010. https://teendramawhore.com/2010/01/17 /beverly-hills-90210-producer-talks-college-years-slams-new-90210/.

Bricker, Tierney. "Trashed Dressing Rooms, Co-Star Couplings, Fist Fights and Firings: Secrets of the Original Beverly Hills, 90210 Revealed." *E! Online*, Aug. 7, 2019.

Brodesser-Akner, Taffy. "The Lives They Lived: Luke Perry." *New York Times*, Dec. 23, 2019.

Correa, Gabriel. Interview by Pete LePage, Justin Tyler, and Alex Zalben. *Comic Book Club*, podcast, Oct. 13, 2022. https://comicbookclublive.com /2022/10/13/riverdale-after-dark-gabriel-correa-interview/.

Darke, Chris. "Normal Life," *Sight and Sound*, March 1997.

Donnelly, Joe. "Why Luke Perry's death is so personal for many forgotten Gen Xers." *Los Angeles Times*, March 6, 2019.

Fry, Naomi. "Luke Perry Knew What He Meant to So Many." *New Yorker*, March 5, 2019.

Garcia, Gabriela. "Remembering Beverly Hills, 90210's Only Latino Lead, a Character Who Deserved Much More," *Remezcla*, Oct. 25, 2018.

Garth, Jennie, with Emily Heckman. *Deep Thoughts from a Hollywood Blonde*. New York: NAL, 2014.

Gaughan, Liam. "Now Is the Right Time to Recognize 1992's 'Buffy the Vampire Slayer' as a Camp Classic." *Collider*, July 1, 2022.

Gliato, Tom. "The Luke of Love." *People*, Dec. 6, 1993. https://people.com/archive/the-luke-of-love-vol-40-no-23/.

Greene, Ray. "Reviews: Buffy the Vampire Slayer." *Boxoffice* 128, no. 10 (September 1992).

Hemphill, Jim. "Revisiting Luke Perry's Great Unheralded Performance in 'Normal Life,'" Talkhouse (website), March 6, 2019, https://www.talkhouse.com/revisiting-luke-perrys-great-unheralded-performance-in-normal-life/.

Hochman, Steve. "Movies; Whatever," *Los Angeles Times*, March 8, 1998.

Holden, Stephen. "Film Review: A Femme Fatale Who's A Little Loony," *New York Times*, Nov. 1, 1996.

Jung, Alex E. "How Riverdale Found Its (Hot) Archie Andrews." *Vulture*, Feb. 15, 2017.

Kickham, Dylan. "12 things you never knew about Beverly Hills, 90210." *Entertainment Weekly*, Sept. 29, 2023. https://ew.com/article/2015/10/04/beverly-hills-90210-things-you-never-knew/.

Kreizman, Maris. "Luke Perry Was the First Bad Boy I Loved." *New York Times*, March 5, 2019.

Lagatta, Eric. "Ohioan Luke Perry remembered as a kind soul who never forgot where he came from." *Columbus Dispatch*, March 6, 2019.

Lyons, Casey. "The Mushrooms That Ate Luke Perry." *Orion*, Sept 2, 2022. https://orionmagazine.org/article/luke-perry-mushroom-shroud-90210-riverdale/.

Maslin, Janet. "Review/Film; She's Hunting Vampires, and on a School Night." *New York Times*, July 31, 1992.

Mitovich, Matt. "I Couldn't Do 90210 Without Aaron Spelling." *TV Guide*, July 3, 2008. https://www.tvguide.com/news/yellowstone-season-5-part-2-returns-when-ending-teaser-everything-else-to-know/.

Nahas, Aili. "David Arquette Opens Up About His 'Gracious' Friend Luke Perry: 'He Became Part of My Family,'" *People*, Aug. 13, 2020.

Parker, Ryan "Alec Guinness Warned James Dean About His Car One Week Before Deadly Crash," *Hollywood Reporter*, July 11, 2017.

Perman, Stacy, Meg James, and Ryan Faughnder. "Fox oral history: Inside the legendary studio at the end of its run." *Los Angeles Times*, March 8, 2019. https://www.latimes.com/business/hollywood/la-et-disney-fox-fox-oral-history-20190308-htmlstory.html.

Perry, Luke. Interview by Arsenio Hall. *The Arsenio Hall Show*, May 15, 1992.

Perry, Luke. Interview by Take2MarkTV, 1994, YouTube video, https://www.youtube.com/watch?v=wvpUvhDqkd0&t=8s

Piepenbring, Dan. "Luke Perry's Startling Vulnerability in the 'Beverly Hills, 90210' Episode 'The Dreams of Dylan McKay.'" *New Yorker*, March 8, 2019.

Priestley, Jason, and Luke Perry. Interview by Billy Bush. *The Billy Bush Show*, Jan. 21, 2021. https://www.youtube.com/watch?v=UjhwYqPtMrw.

"Quentin Tarantino on How He Directs Actors on Set." AFI Movie Club, Feb. 7, 2022, YouTube video. https://www.youtube.com/watch?v=dfllQYnrCVs

Redic, Geoffrey. "Luke Perry's hometown of Fredericktown remembers a 'good kid' who made it big." ABC News at 6, March 4, 2019.

Reinstein, Mara. "The 90 Most Important Moments of Beverly Hills, 90210." *The Ringer*, Aug. 7, 2019. https://www.theringer.com/tv/2019/8/7/20757684 /90210-beverly-hills-best-moments.

"Remembering the 'Buffy the Vampire Slayer' Movie and Joss Whedon's First Superhero." *Y! Entertainment*, May 5, 2015. https://www.yahoo.com /entertainment/joss-whedon-buffy-the-vampire-slayer-118217991342 .html?guccounter=1.

Robinson, Tasha. "Joss Whedon." *AV Club*, Sept. 5, 2001.

Rockler, Naomi. "From Magic Bullets to Shooting Blanks: Reality, Criticism and Beverly Hills, 90210." *Western Journal of Communication*, Vol 63; Iss 1, (Winter 1999): 72–94.

Several episodes of the podcast, *Beverly Hills 90210 Show*. https://podcasts.apple .com/us/podcast/beverly-hills-90210-show/id1510639221.

Tuggle, Zach. "Luke Perry kept strong connections to Central Ohio." *Mansfield News Journal*, March 4, 2019.

Villarreal, Yvonne. "An Appreciation: The best bad boy; Why Luke Perry's Dylan still has a hold on me." *Los Angeles Times*, March 5, 2019.

Winter, Lisa. "Death by Nostalgia, 1688." *The Scientist* 1, no. 1 (February 2022).

Yang, Ziyan, Tim Wildschut et al. "Patterns of brain activity associated with nostalgia: a social-cognitive neuroscience perspective." *Social Cognitive and Affective Neuroscience* 17, no. 12, (December 2022).